Current Trends in Preparatory Proceedings

Laura Ervo • Anna Nylund
Editors

Current Trends in Preparatory Proceedings

A Comparative Study of Nordic and Former Communist Countries

Springer

Editors
Laura Ervo
School of Law, Psychology and Social Work
University of Örebro
Örebro, Sweden

Anna Nylund
Faculty of Law
University of Tromsø
Tromsø, Norway

ISBN 978-3-319-29323-3 ISBN 978-3-319-29325-7 (eBook)
DOI 10.1007/978-3-319-29325-7

Library of Congress Control Number: 2016935069

Printed on acid-free paper

This Springer imprint is published by Springer Nature
The registered company is Springer International Publishing AG Switzerland

Preface

The project Current Trends in Preparatory Procedures—Comparative Studies in Nordic and Former Communist Countries were founded by the NOS-HS (Joint Committee for Nordic Research Councils for Humanities and the Social Sciences) in 2014–2016. The project was based on workshops where the book was prepared by the project members. The kick-off seminar was in Örebro organised by Laura Ervo. Anna Nylund arranged the mid-seminar in Tromsø. The final seminar will be organised in Budapest in late 2016 by Adél Köblös as soon as the book is published. This anthology is the fruit of the project.

The anthology covers the preparatory stage in civil procedure and is mainly focused on the non-mandatory cases from a comparative perspective between the Nordic and the former communist countries. One of the greatest challenges for today's civil procedural law all over the world is effectiveness and speediness. In order to achieve this objective, legislators tend to introduce new legal institutions and carry out overall reforms affecting even the structure and role of the judiciary and the course of civil litigation. One of the ways legal disputes can be adjudicated within a reasonable time and soundly is to emphasise the role of the preparatory phase of the proceeding and make the parties more active in solving their dispute. Legislators also tend to ease the workload of the courts by directing the parties to choose alternative ways of dispute resolution. This study aims to throw light on two different but special streamlines of European development in this field, one of which is the Nordic trend. Here, Finland, Denmark, Norway and Sweden are studied. The other is the development in the Baltic and other former communist countries that joined the European Union in 2004. That group consists of Poland, Slovenia, the Czech Republic, Slovakia, Estonia, Latvia, Lithuania and Hungary. The reasons for the latter choice were to choose countries that have a longer experience with western legal culture and to avoid a fragmented structure. It was impossible to study all former communist countries. Even though the original roots of all chosen countries were close to each other (i.e. adopting the continental system), after World War II the development of these procedural regimes took different directions, while now the studied countries face similar problems again. The study attempts to show similar ways of thinking, bearing in mind, nevertheless, that the previous directions of development of civil procedural laws may result in different solutions.

The project was planned mainly by the principal applicant Professor, Dr. Laura Ervo (the University of Örebro, Sweden, and Adjunct Professor/Docent at the Universities of Helsinki, Eastern Finland, and Turku, Finland). Professor, Dr. Anna Nylund (the University of Tromsø, Norway), Associate Professor, Dr. Lin Adrian (the University of Copenhagen, Denmark) and Professor, Dr., LL. M. Jakob Juul-Sandberg (the University of Southern Denmark) were enthusiastic enough to join in the project as co-applicants. The other project members were Professor, Dr. Aleš Galič (the University of Ljubljana, Slovenia), Associate Professor, Dr. Vigita Vėbraitė (the University of Vilnius, Lithuania), Associate Professor, Dr. Anna Piszcz (the University of Bialystok, Poland) and Legal Counsel, Dr. Adél Köblös (the Constitutional Court of the Republic of Hungary). All project members have put excellent effort into the workshops and project anthology. Therefore, we want to thank you all very warmly for your wonderful co-operation during these project years.

Professor, Dr. Alan Uzelac (the University of Zagreb, Croatia) and Adjunct Professor (docent), Dr. Kaijus Ervasti (the University of Helsinki, Finland) have peer reviewed the texts and come with their deep expertise and detailed feedback that has been very valuable for the project publication. The peer review process has been double blind, but it is time to open the curtains and say thank you for your wonderful work and appreciated expertise.

Satu Svahn, who holds a juris doctor degree from Brooklyn Law School and a master's degree in urban planning from New York University and who is a member of the New York State Bar Association, has worked hard and in a surprisingly rapid way in order to check the English language of the whole manuscript. Her expertise and effective way to work and co-operate is incomparable.

Our multi-expert, Professor, Dr. Anna Nylund who is one of the editors has even effectively fixed the index and other technical unifying. All authors are grateful for your technical skills! We also are grateful for your clever thinking and wide expertise as to the contents and sharp eyes—even for formal mistakes. Thank you for your purposeful but kind, patient and motivated way to co-operate.

The project publication has been published by Springer, and we are very grateful for this possibility to make results known in English and outside the Nordic and former communist countries. It is rather difficult to find an English material on both studied groups of countries, and it is unique to find a comparative analysis made between them. We hope that this volume could be of help for foreign readers and cover this lack from its side. Executive Editor Dr. iur. Brigitte Reschke and other colleagues at Springer have been both effective and professional and made it much easier for us to come out with our final product, thanks to these wonderful characteristics.

It is time to finish the pleasant project and fruitful co-operation with this book, but we do hope the discussion will continue and cause new possibilities for further researches, projects and co-operation.

Örebro, Sweden Laura Ervo
Tromsø, Norway Anna Nylund
November 2015

Contents

Chapter 1
Introduction to the Preparatory Stage of Civil Proceedings

Anna Nylund

Abstract The main hearing model used in civil proceedings may enhance the efficiency of civil litigation. The preparatory stage is a key ingredient in the model, enabling case management, clarification of issues and concentration of the case to the disputed questions. It may also facilitate judicial settlement efforts and early disposal of cases. In recent decades, the main hearing model has been implemented in several European countries that utilise common law, Nordic law, Germanic civil law and Romanic civil law. Moreover, international model principles of civil procedure are based on the model. The core assumptions of the preparatory proceedings are adapted to the local legal culture and tradition. Many of the former communist countries, by contrast, still have a piecemeal type of civil proceedings. The pleadings stage is followed by several short hearings where the evidence and arguments are collected. This introductory chapter introduces the reader to the assumptions and concepts behind preparatory proceedings and their role in the main hearing model. Other structures of civil proceedings are discussed briefly. The connection between promotion of amicable solutions through court-connected mediation and judicial settlement efforts and preliminary proceedings is also studied.

1.1 Introduction to This Book

The quest for swift, cheap and fair civil proceedings is ubiquitous in a time of austerity and increased focus on efficiency. The cost and duration of litigation must be proportional to the aim of seeking a materially correct result. Across jurisdictions, legislators have introduced alternatives to full-scale litigation, reforming the structure and principles of court proceedings to provide for cheaper, swifter civil proceedings leading to correct results. Pre-trial, or preparatory, proceedings have

A. Nylund (✉)
Faculty of Law, University of Tromsø – The Arctic University of Norway, 9037 Tromsø, Norway
e-mail: anna.nylund@uit.no

L. Ervo, A. Nylund (eds.), *Current Trends in Preparatory Proceedings*,
DOI 10.1007/978-3-319-29325-7_1

been introduced, or reinforced, to provide for both efficient proceedings and a sound basis for a correct judgment. Amicable solutions, through judicial settlement efforts and court-connected mediation, have been another vehicle to achieve sound results in a timely and economic manner. These reforms have an impact on the course of civil proceedings and on the role of the judiciary.

The research in this book explores preparatory proceedings as a tool to promote efficiency and correct judgments in civil proceedings in first courts. We have chosen to use the terms *preparatory proceedings and preparatory stage* instead of pre-trial proceedings. First, the word pre-trial often reflects the practices of American-type of civil proceedings, where the pre-trial phase consists of discovery and a culturally specific type of judicial case management. The role of the judge in the US civil proceedings is far more passive than in its European counterparts. Second, the idea of a trial is also culturally and historically tied to civil litigation in common law jurisdictions.[1] Third, the ALI/UNIDROIT Principles of Transnational Civil Procedure, principle 9, have also chosen not to use the term pre-trial proceedings. There, the interim phase is used to describe the preparatory stage and final phase (or final hearing) to describe the main hearing stage. For the purpose of this book, the term preparatory proceedings or preparatory stage seems to be the most appropriate, as it underlines the main objective of the stage: the preparation for concentrated main hearing, where the parties present their claims, arguments and evidence directly to the court.[2]

The articles in this book explore if, and the form and extent of which, preparatory proceedings have been implemented in the Nordic[3] and former communist countries. This study includes eight former communist countries: the Czech Republic, Estonia, Hungary, Latvia, Lithuania, Poland, Slovakia and Slovenia. These countries joined the European Union in 2004. The Nordic countries have a main hearing structure of civil proceedings, where the preparatory stage is vital. Most former communist countries have a *piecemeal* structure of civil proceedings, with no preparatory stage, or a very limited one. Both the Nordic countries and the former communist countries often receive little attention in comparative studies.

By including both countries having a main hearing model and countries that do not have it, a comparison can be done on several levels. The countries can be studied and compared individually, highlighting the special traits of each country or studying how the same problem has been solved in different ways or how the same solution leads to different outcomes. The countries can also be compared within the respective group to study similarities and differences within each group. By comparing the two groups, the main hearing model can be studied as an "ideal type", on

---

[1] See Andrews (2003), pp. 33–36, Friedenthal et al. (2005), pp. 2–3 and Marcus et al. (2009), pp. 1–2.

[2] Stürner (2005), p. 225 also uses the term preparatory. See also Murray and Stürner (2004), p. 191 ff.

[3] The term Nordic and the term Scandinavia refer to the same five countries: Denmark, Finland, Iceland, Norway and Sweden. Nordic is more precise, but in this book, Nordic and Scandinavian are used interchangeably. Iceland is not part of this study.

a more general level. We can understand which factors lead to successful implementation of the main hearing model, and which will hamper the implementation of the model. The study will also shed light on the piecemeal structure of civil proceedings.

Different aspects of preparatory proceedings are explored, *inter alia* the following: Does the introduction of preparatory proceedings, as they are defined in the main hearing model of civil proceedings, provide for swifter and less costly civil litigation? Do preparatory proceedings enhance the quality of justice, and if so, how and why? How is the preparatory stage regulated? How does the regulation affect the course and results of the proceedings? Do the same problems arise in different countries in spite of different structures and principles of civil proceedings? Do different solutions to the same problem lead to the same or different results?

The functioning of the preparatory proceedings—and civil proceedings, in general—depend on a number of factors, including the history of and earlier forms of civil litigation, the legal culture, mentality and society at large.[4] The Nordic countries have had three-stage civil proceedings with a brief written or oral preparatory stage for decades, with the exception of Finland. The former communist civil proceedings did not have a "proper" preparatory stage. Today, the former communist countries are not a coherent group.

The principle of party autonomy, the role of settlements and judicial discretion are embedded in the Nordic legal culture. During the communist era, these ideas were seen as "bourgeois individualism".[5] The research in this book sheds light on how historical and cultural contingencies are reflected in the structure, regulation and role of preparatory proceedings. An important question is if preparatory proceedings fit some legal cultures like a glove, while they are at odds with others. Thus, this book has a legal cultural aspect in addition to a more "technical" aspect.

Settlement is an increasingly popular means to achieve early and relatively inexpensive disposal of cases. Different mechanisms of encouraging settlement have been introduced in most European countries. A duty to pre-action negotiations, judicial settlement efforts, court-connected mediation and out-of-court mediation are some of the most common tools. In some countries, court-connected mediation is the result of Europeanisation of civil procedure, in others it was introduced to provide an alternative road to justice.

Judicial settlement efforts and court-connected mediation are connected to preparatory proceedings. Both are often conducted during the preparatory stage and both have largely the same goals as preliminary proceedings; in other words, to provide for early dispute resolution. They can also contribute to clarification of the case or partial resolution of the case. As the preparatory stage and promotion of settlement are intertwined, this study includes a discussion on judicial settlement efforts and court-connected mediation. Important questions are *inter alia* the following: To what extent is judicial settlement efforts and court-connected

[4] Ervo (2014, 2015).

[5] See Chap. 5.

mediation used? What is the role of them in the preparatory proceedings? To what extent and in which ways do legislation and policies favour settlements? How is court-connected mediation regulated? Who can serve as a court-connected mediator? What are the incentives to participate in court-connected mediation? How has the legal culture reacted to judicial settlement efforts and court-connected mediation?

In this introductory chapter, the concept of preparatory proceedings is introduced. In Sect. 1.2, the structure of civil proceedings in different European traditions of civil proceedings is examined. In Sect. 1.3, the main hearing model of civil proceedings is studied closer. The goals and structure of the main hearing model in general and the preparatory stage in particular are covered. The main hearing model is based on assumptions on the role and function of civil proceedings, civil courts and judges. These assumptions are investigated in Sect. 1.4. In Sect. 1.5, the role of judicial settlement efforts and court-connected mediation in preparatory proceedings is discussed. The relationship between amicable settlement and the preparatory stage are also studied. Section 1.6 contains an introduction to the structure of the book.

1.2 Introduction to the Structure of Civil Proceedings

Taxonomies of European civil procedure systems are generally based on the divide between civil law and common law. The civil law group is further divided into a Germanic group, a French group and an Italian-Canonical group.[6] In addition, some authors have identified a former communist (or socialist) group. The continuing existence of the former communist group has been debated, as the civil procedure systems have been reformed and developed in different directions.[7] Finally, the Nordic, or Scandinavian, countries form a distinct group beyond the civil law/common law divide.

Each of these groups has traditionally had different structure of civil proceedings. In *common law* countries, the first stage consisting of written pleadings is followed the pre-trial stage where evidence is collected, documented and disclosed. The claims, argumentation and evidence are presented to the court during the trial. The role of the judge has traditionally been passive.

In the *Germanic* group, there have been two models, the German and the Austrian. According to the German civil procedure code from 1877, civil proceedings started with the pleadings stage. An oral second stage and a third stage of collection of evidence and clarification followed. In the final stage, the parties presented the evidence to the court, which decided the case. The structure of the

[6] See Damaška (1986), Cappelletti and Garth (1987), pp. 8–10, Stürner (2002, 2005), Amrani-Mekki (2010).

[7] Stürner (2002), Uzelac (2010), Galič (2015).

Austrian civil procedure, was, and still is, slightly different. The pleadings stage is followed by an oral preparatory stage. The parties present their claims, arguments and evidence during the final stage often consisting of several hearings.

The proceedings the French and the Italian-Canonical group, the *Romanic group,* have had a similar structure. The first stage of civil proceedings is the pleadings stage. The second stage is fact-finding, where evidence is presented to the instructing judge. In the final stage, the court hears the case without taking evidence. Especially the second stage often consists of a number of hearings. The distinction between the stage where evidence is taken and the stage where the merits of the case are discussed is important.[8]

The (former) *communist model*, was based on civil law traditions with socialist ideas merged into the understanding of the role of courts and goals of civil procedure. The pleadings stage is followed the hearing stage consisting ideally of one unitary hearing (single hearing model). However, in practice, the hearing was often held in a piecemeal manner with many hearings, often lasting less than an hour each. The model has survived the fundamental societal changes and is still in use.[9] This procedural model was identified by Damaška as the "*piecemeal* trial".[10]

In piecemeal hearings, there is no comprehensive, compulsory preparatory stage and no concentrated main hearing. After the pleadings stage, or sometimes already after the statement of claim has been filed, the case proceeds to the hearing stage. At the short hearings, one of the parties presents arguments in writing. The opposing party usually asks the court to adjourn the hearing in order to get an opportunity to consider and prepare the next steps. The evidence is also presented in a fragmented manner, only one or a few persons are heard at a single hearing. Written evidence may be presented at any hearing. New arguments and evidence may be introduced until the judge closes the hearings stage and decides the case is ripe for decision. Written preparation may be allowed, but it is not mandatory, nor is if commonly used.

In the *Nordic* group, the structure of civil proceedings was influenced by the Austrian model. The pleadings stage was followed by a brief preparatory stage. The proceedings culminated in the main hearing. In Finland, the structure of civil proceedings followed the old Swedish model until 1993. The pleadings stage was followed by the final stage consisting of several short hearings.

In recent decades, the *main hearing model* of civil procedure has become popular. The model was originally introduced in Germany in 1976 (*Vereinfachungsnovelle).* In the 1987 reform of Swedish civil procedure, some of the German ideas were adopted and the role of the preparatory hearings strengthened.[11] In the English reform of civil procedure in 1998, the main hearing model was refined and

[8] Varano (1997), Stürner (2005), pp. 223–225 and 237–239, Hazard et al. (2001), pp. 773–778.

[9] Uzelac (2010), Chaps. 5, 7 and 8.

[10] Damaška (1986), pp. 50–51.

[11] See SOU 1982: 86 Sveriges Offentliga Utredningar. Översyn av Rättegångsbalken 1. Processen i tingsrätt Del B. Motiv m.m. Delbetänkande av rättegångsutredningen, pp. 82–85.

implemented in a common law context.[12] Both the English and German rules have been an inspiration for reforms of the structure of civil proceedings in numerous countries representing different groups of civil procedure.[13] The models have thus contributed to the tendency of convergence between civil law and common law.[14]

In the main hearing model, civil proceedings consist of *three parts*: the pleadings stage, preparatory stage and a single concentrated main hearing, where all claims, grounds for the claims, evidence and legal arguments are presented directly to the judge or panel deciding the case. The key element of the main hearing model is the preparatory stage, the role of which is to ensure early disposal of cases, timely hearings, and a single concentrated hearing where the parties present their claims, arguments and evidence directly to the court deciding the case. The model is considered to enhance efficiency and promote substantially correct results. It requires changes in the role and functioning of the court, among others, requiring case management, clarification of legal and factual issues, and judicial settlement efforts. As the model emphasises concentrations of proceedings, it could also be considered the "concentrated model".

The basic traits or the "ideal type" of the main hearing model is clear. Yet, when the model is adopted and implemented by different national systems, some of the features change to a certain extent. The regulation and practices of civil proceedings are shaped by the ideology, structure and tradition of the underlying civil justice system and court culture.[15]

The texts in this book study how the main hearing model is adapted, understood and practiced in the Nordic and former communist countries. In countries that do not have the main hearing model, the question of why the main hearing model has not been implemented and the resistance towards the model will be discussed.

1.3 The Main Hearing Model and Preparatory Proceedings

The main hearing model of civil procedure consists of three stages. The first stage is the (1) *pleadings stage,* where the parties initiate the court process and present their claims, defences and the main arguments and evidence. During (2) the *preparatory stage,* the single main hearing is prepared. The judge is involved in case management to ensure timely disposition of the case. During the final stage, (3) the *main hearing,* the court hears the case in one single, concentrated hearing.

[12] Woolf (1996), p. 59 ff.

[13] The Spanish civil procedure is based on the model Díez-Picazo Giménez (2005) and Stürner (2005), pp. 224–225.

[14] Stürner (2002), Amrani-Mekki (2010), Cadiet (2010), Chase and Walker (2010), Damaška (2010), Glenn (2010), Taruffo (2010).

[15] (Prütting (2002), pp. 319–321 and Trocker and Varano (2005).

The main hearing model is becoming increasingly popular. In addition to many countries adopting the model, it is used as the foundational framework of the ALI/UNIDROIT Principles of Transnational Civil Procedure (PTCP).[16] It is also used in the project on European rules on civil procedure under the auspices of the European Law Institute (ELI).[17]

The main hearing model of civil procedure culminates in a single, concentrated, oral main hearing. A concentrated main hearing serves both the purpose of efficiency and the purpose of making main procedural principles effective.[18] By concentrating the presentation of claims, legal and factual arguments and evidence to a single hearing (which might be carried out over several consecutive days), the court achieves the best basis for its decision. The process is oral and adversarial. The main hearing model is considered efficient since the parties, the lawyers and the judge only need to prepare for the main hearing once, and do not need to use time to recall what happened at earlier hearing(s).[19] The pleadings stage and especially the preparatory stage are important tools to ensure a concentrated main hearing.

The *pleadings stage* (initial stage) is when the proceedings are initiated. The pleadings stage is short; it consists only of filing the statement of claim, service of it and the statement of defence. During the pleadings phase, the parties present their claims, defences and other contentions in writing. The aim is to identify the case and give the court an opportunity to strike out cases in which it lacks jurisdiction, in which one of the parties lacks legal standing, or in which any other requirements are not met.[20]

The purpose of the *preparatory stage* is, as mentioned, to prepare the main hearing. The sense of preparation is not a technical one, i.e. deciding on time management and other technical issues. On the contrary, according to the main hearing model, preparatory proceedings allow clarification of applicable law, the facts and evidence available. *Clarification* requires active case management and contact with the parties. Oral preparatory meetings may be held in addition to or in lieu of written preparation.[21] Successful preparatory proceedings in a main hearing-model of civil procedure require an active *case management*. The role of the judge is not to passively oversee collection of evidence, nor to actively engage in collecting and taking evidence. Instead, the judge helps parties to clarify what the most important legal and factual issues are, correct misunderstandings and to sort out the relevant evidence available. Active case management is the key to a successful preparatory stage.

[16] Principle 9.

[17] See Stürner (2005), pp. 223–225.

[18] See Kramer (2014), p. 4 and 11.

[19] Kramer (2014), p. 9.

[20] Kramer (2014), pp. 7–8.

[21] Andrews (2013), pp. 198–203 and Zuckerman (2005), p. 149.

During the preparatory stage the dispute itself, the questions of fact and law are often transformed. It becomes clear what the case actually is about. The aim of the preparatory stage is also to crystallise the case, let the case evolve and transform, and boil it down to the core questions. Clarification of relevant questions of fact, law and evidence (*Richterliche Aufklärungspflicht* in German) may lead to parties dropping claims or amending them. Parties may also drop evidence as a fact has become irrelevant or undisputed, or the opposing party has provided persuasive evidence for his or her case. The main hearing is shorter and more to the point, limited to relevant legal arguments, facts and evidence. Thus, the court gets a better basis for its decision. In short, proceedings become more efficient.[22] The principle of concentration, thus, has a two-fold meaning: the main hearing is concentrated, and the legal and factual arguments are concentrated to the relevant ones during the preparatory stage.

Attempts to crystallise the case, or to boil it down to its core, may reveal *common ground*.[23] Consequently, the entire case or part of it may be disposed of due to dropped claims or settlement. In addition, judicial settlement efforts and court-connected mediation are efficient means of disposing cases before the main hearing (see below Sect. 1.5).

The final stage is the *main hearing,* which is conducted during a single day or several consecutive days. During the main hearing, the parties present their claims, grounds for the claims, evidence and the legal arguments for their case directly in front of the judge or panel of judges deciding the case. Only the material presented in the main hearing is taken into account when the case is decided. The hearing is based on the principles of *concentration and immediacy*. The duration and the structure of the hearing vary between the systems: in some systems presentation of the case, claims and arguments is the most important part; in other systems, the presentations of the parties are brief. However, the basic structure and the principal idea is the same in all systems.

1.4 Assumptions of the Main Hearing Model of Civil Procedure

The main hearing model used in civil procedure is based on certain assumptions on enhancing procedural efficiency. The model is also implicitly based on ideas about the goals of civil justice, the role of the parties and of the judge and the role of courts of first instance. These ideas are intertwined. Despite differences between different legal systems many similarities can be found in countries that utilise the main hearing model.

---

[22] See Kramer (2014), pp. 8–9.

[23] Andrews (2013), pp. 197–202.

Civil procedure has dual goals: *to resolve individual disputes and to implement societal goals and policies*. The functions can be identified as the private function and the public function, respectively.[24] Each civil procedure system balances between the two functions, and each system can be placed somewhere on the continuum of the two extremes. Within the private function, there is a tension between the role of courts as problem-solvers, trying to find the best solution to the (underlying) problem of the parties, and the role of courts as providers of efficient jurisdiction.[25] Active case management, judicial settlement efforts and court-connected mediation enable courts to provide problem-solving. The introduction of the main hearing model usually strengthens the private function of courts and especially the problem-solving function.

Party disposition and party initiative are important principles, as the parties must initiate the proceedings, present the evidence and arguments. In the main hearing model, the preparatory stage requires an active judge who is involved in *case management and clarification of the case*, and, thus, in developing the case. However, the role of the judge is not inquisitorial. The parties are responsible for presenting relevant arguments and evidence. Although the court decides what the law is (*jura novit curia),* the parties are obliged to present arguments and facts relevant to the applicable legal rules. The judge is bound both by the claims and factual background of the case. Additionally, the arguments and evidence offered ties the hand of the judge, to some extent.

The judge has to balance between actively working for clarification by helping the parties to sort out less relevant arguments and facts (and introducing more relevant ones), and refraining from dictating the course of the proceeding, see PTCP principles 10, 14, 21 and 22. This role is clearly different from the traditional passive role of judges in common law and the traditional active, inquisitorial role of judges in civil law jurisdictions.[26]

The role of *preclusion* of new claims, arguments and evidence is central in the main hearing model. By having a clear time limit, the claims and the factual basis for the case can be "fixed" before the main hearing. The parties and the court will know which pieces of evidence will be presented and which persons will be heard during the main hearing. To allow for clarification and identification of main issues, the limit is usually set at the end of the preparatory stage. New legal arguments may be introduced as long as the other elements remain the same. This is a consequence of the principle of *iura novit curia*. Rules of preclusion compel the parties to prepare the case in a timely manner and allow the parties to prepare for the main hearing. However, if the rules on preclusion are too strict, the parties may be tempted to frontload the case with all possible claims, facts and evidence. Finding the essence of the case will be more difficult. The same problem arises if the time

[24] Galič (2014).

[25] Uzelac (2014), pp. 5–19 and 25–26 and Ervo (2013).

[26] Hazard et al. (2001), pp. 773 and 777–778. Case management has been debated and criticised in the United States, see *e.g.* Marcus (1993) and Gensler (2010).

limit for preclusion is early, by applying the principle of eventuality. On the other hand, too flexible rules on preclusion or a lenient application of the rules on preclusion may water down preclusion and ultimately result in a less concentrated main hearing.

The goal of civil justice is to *balance a substantially correct result with efficient proceedings and proportionate use of resources*. Zuckerman notes that the English Civil Procedure Rules of 1998 have a three-fold aim: to render correct judgements by proportionate use of the resources and within a reasonable time. Expediency is accomplished by setting deadlines and planning the conduct and timetable of the court proceedings. By involving the parties in forming the plans, the court can consider the views of the parties. The parties know the facts and the case, and therefore often have a better opportunity to estimate *inter alia* how much time they will use on hearing a specific witness. The balance between proportionate use of court and party resources, and correct results is achieved by case management, where the main hearing is concentrated to the most relevant questions of fact and law, and where less relevant evidence is dropped.[27]

To achieve a proportionate use of resources, the proceedings must be tailored to each case. To tailor a case, a court must take into account the factual and legal complexity of the case, importance of the case to the parties and society, and the quality of the work of counsel. The proceedings must be *flexible*. To gain flexibility, the judge must have *discretion* to shape the proceedings.[28] Although discretion is a key to efficient proceedings, there is a danger that "the judges will exercise their powers in a capricious, inconsistent and unpredictable way".[29] Judicial discretion is a prerequisite for efficient case management and clarification of issues. Hence, the legal system must view judicial discretion as primarily a virtue, not a vice, in order to accomplish the goals set out in preparatory proceedings.

Tailoring the proceedings to the particular case also implies *cooperation between the parties and the court*. It is neither the parties alone, nor the judge alone, who decide on the course and timing of the proceedings. The judge makes decision having discussed the matter with the parties. The judge can amend the plan for the preparatory proceedings having discussed the issue with the parties. The parties are expected to be loyal to the plan since they have been involved in making it. Although the judge should have a flexible and open approach, too much leniency towards the wishes of the parties has a pernicious influence on achieving efficient proceedings. The judge has the last word on the course of proceedings and time limits must be enforced for the proceedings to be efficient.

Another goal of the main hearing model, and the case management function, is to *do away with the problem of the court of first instance being "a rehearsal"* for the second round at the court of second instance. Often the case has evolved and transformed throughout the process in the first instance. Cases have been reheard in

[27] Zuckerman (2013), pp. 128–130. See also Uzelac (2014), pp. 19–23.

[28] Andrews (2003), pp. 333–361.

[29] Andrews (2003), p. 343.

the appellate court, because the parties have not been able to sort out the case before the early stages in the appellate court.[30] By focusing on clarification during the preparatory hearing and by including (stricter) rules on preclusion of new evidence and amendment of pleadings, the first instance should be the "real" trial, the "real" hearing. Instead of re-examining the case, the appellate courts should focus on contested parts of the judgement.

1.5 The Role of Judicial Settlement Efforts and Court-Connected Mediation in Preparatory Proceedings

Early disposal of cases and clarification are important goals of the preparatory stage. Settlements are often a by-product, and sometimes even a goal, of clarification. The judge helps the parties to discover common ground and can point out the costs and a possible settlement range. Case management gives the judge an active role in shaping the proceedings and in communicating with the parties during the preparatory proceedings. The duty to promote clarification and to manage actively the case makes judicial settlement a natural part of preparatory proceedings. Settlements are also a method to dispose of cases early in the proceedings. Hence, judicial settlement efforts and preparatory proceedings are often interconnected.

The global Alternative Dispute Resolution (ADR) movement has promoted settlement through judicial settlement efforts, negotiation and mediation as ways to reduce costs related to resolving legal disputes and to provide the parties with better dispute resolution procedures and better results. Court systems in many western countries have adopted mediation schemes. The parties are encouraged to try mediation—or another form of ADR procedure—before going to court or during the preparatory stage. Increasingly, courts offer court-connected mediation.[31]

Judges have two basic tools for promoting settlements: judicial settlement efforts and court-connected mediation. Both have become an integral part of many national civil procedure systems, and an important part of the preparatory proceedings. Despite having the same goal of promoting settlement, there are significant differences between the judicial settlement efforts and mediation.

Judicial settlement efforts refer in this book to any effort of a judge to promote settlement within the court proceedings. The judge promotes settlement in the role of a judge, "in robe", and decides the case if the parties do not settle. The judge may do more than just suggest the parties negotiate to settle the case, but the role as a judge puts limits on the efforts, *inter alia* suggesting solutions. The activity of the judge and the concrete actions are limited by the requirements of impartiality,

---

[30] Hazard et al. (2001), p. 774 and 778.

[31] See principle 24 of the ALI/UNIDROIT Principles of Transnational Civil Procedure (2004). For a history on the development of mediation, see Menkel-Meadow (2001).

adversarial trials and procedural fairness. Successful judicial settlement efforts usually result in a court settlement, which is binding upon the parties as a judgement.

Court-connected mediation[32] refers to voluntary settlement activities conducted by one or more neutral third parties who assist the parties in reaching their own solution in a pending court case. The court is engaged in the mediation—an engagement that can range from minimally providing a controlled list of mediators to which the parties can be referred to a full in-house service. The service is to some extent regulated by law, decrees, ethical guidelines, court rules or similar instruments. Mediation can take place at any point in time after the case is filed and before the final ruling.[33]

Mediation can also be organised outside the court proceedings, *out-of-court mediation*. The parties may initiate mediation before or instead of going to court either due to a mediation clause in a contract, as an *ad hoc* agreement or because they are by law obliged to try to find an amicable solution before going to court. The contract to mediate does not always hinder initiation of court proceedings, thus out-of-court can run parallel to regular court proceedings or can be initiated by parties when the case is already pending. The court may also suggest that the parties try mediation and stay the proceedings for a certain period of time to give the parties time to mediate. A settlement in out-of-court mediation is binding as a contract between the parties, unless there is a separate process to make it enforceable and binding as a judgment.

1.6 The Contents of This Book

The second part of this volume focuses on the preparatory stage in the Nordic countries. In the second chapter, the East-Scandinavian countries of Finland and Sweden are discussed and contrasted. Sweden has a strong tradition of preparatory proceedings. In contrast, Finland had archaic proceedings until 1993, when the structure and form of civil proceedings underwent a radical reform. The role of the different pace of modernisation is discussed. In Chap. 3, the flexible and pragmatic Norwegian rules on preparatory proceedings are examined. Norway and Denmark constitute West-Scandinavian civil procedure systems, where civil proceedings have a more common-law-type adversarial and oral character. At the end of Chap. 3 Norway and Finland—who have surprisingly different civil procedure systems—are contrasted. In Chap. 4, the Danish system, which is historically and culturally closely affiliated with the Norwegian system, is discussed.

[32] Court-connected mediation is also referred to as court-annexed mediation, in-court mediation, and court-conducted mediation.

[33] For more details on the definitions, see Chap. 9.

The third part of this volume focuses on former communist countries. In Chap. 5, the rules on preparatory proceedings in Slovenia, the Czech Republic and Slovakia are examined. As part of Yugoslavia, Slovenia was able to keep its windows open to the West and Western legal ideas. One interesting topic is if Slovenia is still today different than some other former communist countries or if the mind-set of the communist regime overshadows current civil procedure thinking and practices. Chapter 6 consist of a comparison of the Baltic countries Estonia, Latvia and Lithuania. They have all been through rapid and thorough reforms of civil proceedings with an intention to implement the main hearing model. Chapter 7 casts light on Polish civil proceedings and the impact of the frequent reforms. In Chap. 8, the recurrent reforms of Hungarian civil procedure are discussed in light of the former rules, which were model after Austrian civil procedure.

In the fourth part, conclusions answering the questions posed will be drawn. Chapter 9 discusses the role of judicial settlement efforts and court-connected mediation in the countries studied. While it is not a comprehensive comparative analysis offering details about the countries in this study, it is a more general analysis of variations in the use of and attitudes to mediation as a tool for resolving legal disputes. By giving examples from selected jurisdictions, the reasons for and consequences of differences are discussed. The tenth, and final, chapter disseminates the role of the main hearing model and preparatory proceedings in Nordic and former communist countries. It tries to answer research questions and identify and assess similarities and differences between countries and across European legal cultures.

References

ALI/UNIDROIT (2004) Principles of Transnational Civil Procedure (2004). Uniform Law Rev. 9(4):758–808

Amrani-Mekki S (2010) The future of the categories, The categories of the *Futur*. In: Walker J, Chase OG (eds) Common law. Civil law and the future of categories. LexisNexis, Markham, pp 247–266

Andrews N (2003) English civil procedure. Fundamentals of the new system. Oxford University Press, Oxford

Andrews N (2013) Andrews on civil processes, vol I Civil Proceedings. Intersentia, Cambridge

Cadiet L (2010) Avenir des catégories, catégories de l'avenir: perspectives. In: Walker J, Chase OG (eds) Common law. Civil law and the future of categories. LexisNexis, Markham, pp 635–656

Cappelletti M, Garth BG (1987) Introduction – policies, trends and ideas in civil procedure. In: Cappelletti M (ed) International encyclopedia of comparative law, vol XVI civil procedure. Mohr Siebeck, Tübingen

Chase OG, Walker J (2010) Introduction. In: Walker J, Chase OG (eds) Common law, civil law and the future of categories. LexisNexis, Markham, pp li–lxviii

Damaška MR (1986) The faces of justice and state authority. Yale University Press, New Haven

Damaška M (2010) The common law / civil law divide: residual truth of a misleading distinction. In: Walker J, Chase OG (eds) Common law. Civil law and the future of categories. LexisNexis, Markham, pp 3–22

Díez-Picazo Giménez I (2005) The principal innovations of Spain's recent civil procedure reforms. In: Trocker N, Varano V (eds) The reforms of civil procedure in comparative perspective. G. Giappichelli Editore, Torino, pp 33–66
Ervo L (2013) Changing civil proceedings - court service or state economy. In: Nekrošius V (ed) Recent trends in economy and efficiency of civil procedure. Vilnius University Press, Vilnius, pp 51–71
Ervo L (2014) Nordic court culture in progress: historical and futuristic perspectives. In: Ervo L, Nylund A (eds) The future of civil litigation. Access to court and court-annexed mediation in the Nordic countries. Springer, Cham, pp 383–408
Ervo L (2015) Comparative analysis between East-Scandinavian countries. Scandinavian Stud Law 61:135–152
Friedenthal JH, Kane MK, Miller AR (2005) Civil procedure, 4th edn. West, St. Paul
Galič A (2014) Does a decision of the supreme court denying leave to appeal need to contain reasons? In: Adolphsen J, Goebel J, Haas U, Hess B, Kolmann S, Würdinger M (eds) Festschrift für Peter Gottwald zum 70. Geburtstag. C.H. Beck, München, pp 159–173
Galič A (2015) The aversion to judicial discretion in civil procedure in post-communist countries: can the influence of EU law change it? In: Bobek M (ed) Central European Judges under the European influence: the transformative power of the EU revisited. Hart, Oxford, pp 99–124
Gensler SS (2010) Judicial case management: caught in the crossfire. Duke Law J 60:669–744
Glenn HP (2010) A western legal tradition? In: Walker J, Chase OG (eds) Common law. Civil law and the future of categories. LexisNexis, Markham, pp 601–620
Hazard GC, Taruffo M, Stürner R, Gidi A (2001) Introduction to the principles and rules of transnational civil procedure. NY Univ J Int Law Politics 33:769–784
Kramer XE (2014) The structure of civil proceedings and why it matters: exploratory observations on future ELI-UNIDROIT European rules of civil procedure. Uniform Law Rev 12 (2):218–238
Marcus RL (1993) Of babies and bathwater: the prospects for procedural progress. Brooklyn Law Rev 59:761–825
Marcus RL, Redish MH, Sherman EF, Pfander JE (2009) Civil procedure. A modern approach, 5th edn. West, St. Paul
Menkel-Meadow C (2001) Introduction. In: Menkel-Meadow C (ed) Mediation. Theory, policy and practice. Ashgate, Dartmouth, pp xiii–xxxviii
Murray PL, Stürner R (2004) German civil justice. Carolina Academic Press, Durham
Prütting H (2002) Die Strukturen des Zivilprozesses unter Reformdruck und europäische Konvergenz? In: Gottwald P, Roth H (eds) Festschrift für Ekkehard Schumann zum 70. Geburtstag. Mohr Siebeck, Tübingen, pp 309–325
Stürner R (2002) Zur Struktur des europäischen Zivilprozesses. In: Roth H, Gottwald P (eds) Festschrift für Ekkehard Schumann zum 70. Geburtstag. Mohr Siebeck, Tübingen, pp 491–505
Stürner R (2005) The principles of transnational civil procedure. An introduction to their basic conceptions. Rabels Zeitschrift für Ausländisches und Internationales Privatrecht 69:201–254
Taruffo M (2010) Some remarks about procedural models. In: Walker J, Chase OG (eds) Common law. Civil law and the future of categories . LexisNexis, Markham, pp 621–628
Trocker N, Varano V (2005) Concluding remarks. In: Trocker N, Varano V (eds) The reforms of civil procedure in comparative perspective. G. Giappichelli Editore, Torino, pp 243–267
Uzelac A (2010) The survival of the third tradition? Supreme Court Law Rev 49:377–396
Uzelac A (2014) Goals of civil justice and civil procedure in the contemporary world. Global developments – towards harmonization (and back). In: Uzelac A (ed) Goals of civil justice and civil procedure in contemporary judicial systems. Springer, Cham, pp 3–31
Varano V (1997) Civil procedure reform in Italy. Am J Comp Law 45:657–674
Woolf BH (1996) Access to justice: final report to the Lord Chancellor on the civil justice system in England and Wales. HIMSO, London

Zuckerman AAS (2005) Court control and party compliance - the quests for effective litigation management. In: Trocker N, Varano V (eds) The reforms of civil procedure in comparative perspective. G. Giappichelli Editore, Torino, pp 143–161
Zuckerman AAS (2013) The revised CPR 3.9: a coded message demanding articulation. Civ Justice Q 32(2):123–138

Part I
Preparatory Proceedings in Nordic Countries

Chapter 2
Swedish-Finnish Preparatory Proceedings: Filtering and Process Techniques

Laura Ervo

Abstract This chapter covers the preparatory stage in civil litigation in Sweden and Finland. The main attention is devoted to the historical development and recent reforms in civil proceedings that have affected in both countries the forms of preparatory proceedings. It is typical in both countries that at first civil proceedings were oral, immediate and concentrated in the very pure way where practical needs let to fairly quick modifications. The current situation is more flexible and could even be described as a hybrid between written and oral forms. Effectiveness and the wide use of modern technologies are common goals as well, especially in Sweden, whereas court-connected mediation is a current topic in Finland. In both countries, civil proceedings are clearly focused on preparatory proceedings and the main hearing. The main function of preparatory proceedings is to work as a filter between these two stages. As soon as the case matures for decision making, the court has wide possibilities to finish the proceedings and make a binding decision. Only the most complicated or disputed cases that include oral testimony continue to the main hearing.

2.1 The Main Features and Background

In this chapter, preparatory proceedings of two East-Scandinavian[1] countries, namely Finland and Sweden, are compared. The reason behind this comparison is firstly in the common history of the named countries, until the year 1809 Finland

[1] Geographically, Finland is usually not included into the Scandinavian countries. The geographical concept Fennoscandia is not suitable either because it includes a part of Russia. Culturally and sociologically Finland, however, belongs into the same group of the Nordic countries and, in this sense, the term East-Scandinavian is sometimes used. "Eastnordic" would be more correct but not well-established as a term. Therefore, Finland and Sweden are referred to with the term "East-Scandinavian".

L. Ervo (✉)
Örebro University, School of Law, Psychology and Social Work, S-701 82 Örebro, Sweden
e-mail: laura.ervo@oru.se

L. Ervo, A. Nylund (eds.), *Current Trends in Preparatory Proceedings*,
DOI 10.1007/978-3-319-29325-7_2

was namely a part of Sweden. After that Finland became an autonomous part of Russian empire and even during that autonomous period Swedish laws were still valid in Finland. When Finland got its independence 1917 the Swedish heritage was still important and a good start for the legislative work in the independent state. After that the deep co-operation between the Nordic legislators continued until Sweden and Finland joined into the European Union in 1995. From that on, European legislative co-operation has partly replaced this Nordic co-operation, but still, Sweden is often a good example for the Finnish legislator when it comes to procedural reforms.[2]

The other reason for this comparison is that in the field of procedural law the wide and deep reforms have been typical in the both named countries during the recent 25 years. In 1993, the new Finnish legislation entered into force to harmonise the system of general lower courts and to reform the civil procedure based on earlier Swedish reforms. In 1997, a corresponding reform of the criminal procedure was carried out, and, in 1998, appellate procedure at the courts of appeal was modernised in order to bring it into line with the procedural reform in the lower courts.[3] The Finnish reform of 1993 was, however, too fundamental and there were many problems caused by too strict rules,[4] which were made more flexible in the re-reform 2003. The reason for strict rules in 1993 was the legal culture and the tradition to implement statutes. The legislator wanted to make sure that the system will be changed even in the practice and not only to be law in books. Still, the tool caused other problems and was needed to be softened.[5]

In Sweden, the so-called more modern process have been a big reform since 2008. The main aim of the reform was to create a new type of procedure in the general courts that fulfil the demand of an efficient and purposive procedure, however, without risking the fair trial.[6] One big issue in the reform was the wide use of modern technologies. For example, it is now possible for all trial parties to participate through video conference.[7]

Both in Finland and Sweden, the preparatory proceedings are based on the written preparation and an oral hearing. It is typical in the East-Scandinavian countries that the preparatory stage is used as a filtering system and as soon as the case is ready to be solved the decision can be made to avoid the unnecessary further proceedings. Therefore the main function of the East-Scandinavian preparatory stage is to make the case ripe for the decision-making. There are wide possibilities in the both countries to solve the case already at the written stage if there is no need for an oral hearing at the preparatory stage or the main hearing. In

[2] Ervo (2014), pp. 386–390, Ervo (2015), pp. 137–138.

[3] Leppänen (1998), p. 427.

[4] Lesknen (2002), pp. 630–631.

[5] On current Finnish problems see Chap. 3 in this book.

[6] Prop. 2004/05:131.

[7] See Chapter 5 § 10 (SCJP).

addition, the possibilities to solve the case during the oral hearing without a main hearing are wide.

Still, the court communications and the principle of orality have an absolute value in the reformed East-Scandinavian proceedings and the most recent trends to extend the early decision-making at the written stage without any oral connection between the court and parties have been criticised. The expansion towards the written procedure and quick decision-making seems to rather be based on the problems in the State economy than changes in the way of thinking.

The other main common denominator in the preparatory stage in Sweden and Finland is the aim to promote settling the case by friendly settlements during the preparatory level by judicial settlement efforts (both in Finland and Sweden) or court-connected mediation (especially in Finland). That is why, communication (mainly orality) and parties' involvement (especially in the form of party autonomy) plays a significant role in the East-Scandinavian preparatory proceedings.

2.2 Reforms

2.2.1 The Recent History in Finland: Full of Procedural Reforms

Finnish procedural law has undergone major changes since 1990s. In 1993, legislation entered into force to harmonise the system of general lower courts and to reform the civil procedure. In 1997, a corresponding reform of the criminal procedure was carried out, and, in 1998, appellate procedure at the courts of appeal was modernised in order to bring it into line with the procedural reform at lower courts.[8] After these main reforms, there have been many smaller re-reforms concerning both civil and criminal procedures as well as the proceedings at appeal courts. The reason for these new reforms is that the original reforms have not been successful in all points of view and there have been a need for repairing the new procedural system. Because the reforms have been of a fundamental nature, even for the preparatory stage, it is necessary first to shed light on the reform concerning the civil proceedings in order to understand the current preparatory proceedings in Finland.

The reforms of 1993 have divided the hearing of civil cases into a preliminary stage and a main hearing. Prior to these reforms, the main problem was the lack of preparation that litigants and lawyers perpetrated in the courts. That time the Finnish proceedings were typically according to the piecemeal style. Frequently neither the facts at issue nor the disputed points of law were known to anyone before the first court hearing. This, of course, was the cause of many adjournments. There tended to be many sessions before the court could render its

[8] Leppänen (1998), p. 427.

judgment and it was also possible that the membership of the court might change in the meantime. Clearly, this was neither very rational nor any sort of guarantee of a fair judicial hearing. In Finland, prior to these reforms, no equivalent preparatory process took place in ordinary civil cases. Only the labour court[9] had used a special preparatory stage since 1970s.[10]

In the old styled procedure, written statements in pleadings were allowed. The procedure was only partly oral and otherwise based on the records. The parties used written statements even in the court sessions in order to explain their claims, grounds and judicial arguments. The written statement was given to the court and to the opposing party in the session. The opposing party and the court did not know the contents of the statement beforehand, because of the fact that the opposing party normally asked for adjournment in order to research the statement and to answer to it. The adjournments were, therefore, common and in the next session the opposing party answered with the new written statement again and the same circle continued and led to new adjournment.[11]

It was even allowed and quite usual in practice that the composition of the court changed during the proceedings because it consisted of so many sessions. It was quite lawful that in the next session there were new members behind the table of judges. The new members researched the case by the earlier records and therefore the old procedure was not based on the principles of orality, immediacy and concentration. It was even quite possible, lawful and usual that the members, who had accepted the evidence, did not decide the case, but new members did it basing their evaluation of evidence on the records. So, the problems were the lack of concentration, immediacy and orality as well as delays in the proceedings.[12]

The key purpose of the reform was to improve legal certainty. It was considered that oral, direct and concerted proceedings would enhance legal certainty. It was further emphasised that the decision should be arrived at without delay and that the proceedings should not cause excessive costs.[13]

In 1993, the old civil procedure was replaced by an oral, immediate and concentrated procedure. In order to achieve this, it was necessary to divide the

---

[9] The Labour Court is one of the Finnish special courts, and it hears and tries the legal disputes arising out of collective agreements or collective civil servants' agreements or out of the Collective Agreements Act or the Act on Collective Civil-Servant Agreements. A prerequisite for a matter to fall within the competence of the Labour Court is that the specific question involves the competence, validity, contents or extent of a collective agreement or the correct interpretation of a clause in such an agreement. In addition, cases in which it is questioned whether a course of action is in accordance with the collective agreements or Acts mentioned above fall within the competence of the Labour Court. The Labour Court also imposes the sanctions for a breach of these agreements and Acts. More information on the Labour Court in English is available on the web: http://www.tyotuomioistuin.fi/en/index.html, visited 2015-09-04.

[10] Ervo (1995), p. 58.

[11] Lappalainen (2002), pp. 6–8, Sippo and Välimaa (2003), pp. 1–4.

[12] Lappalainen (2002), pp. 6–7, Sippo and Välimaa (2003), pp. 3–4.

[13] Ervasti (2004), p. 507.

procedure into two stages: the preparatory proceedings and the main hearing.[14] Since 1993, the preparatory stage has had a very important role in the Finnish civil proceedings.

The model for this reform was found mostly in the civil procedure in the other Nordic countries, *especially Sweden*. According to *Leppänen*, the structure of the Finnish civil procedure departed with this reform from the civil procedure in Germany and Austria, with which it has traditionally had a close affinity.[15] On the other hand, particularly Austria has been named as a model in the Government Bill for the whole reform.[16]

The reform of 1993 was intended to increase the chances of litigants obtaining a correct, well-founded, judicial decision whilst simultaneously streaming the procedures involved. The lower courts were being equipped to deal with intricate cases more thoroughly than before and with straightforward cases more quickly than earlier. The underlying values were due process of law on the one hand and the rational disbursement of resources on the other.[17]

The reformed procedural system can be described as a "filter" or "strainer" system. The principal aim of the system was to make it possible to decide the cases immediately when they are clear and ready for deciding. Only complex or unclear cases will have to go through the whole system. This is how the judicial power of the state hopes to dispense its resources in a rational way.[18] The preparatory stage has, of course, very important role among this "filter" system. However, this ideal was soon proved to be unsuccessful because the proceedings became too upfront. Both judges and attorneys were too careful and invested too much time and effort in preparatory stage, which made the preparatory stage very heavy and the main hearing remained as a torso.

The reformed system requires the whole case to be prepared well beforehand. Under the old system it was possible to lawyers to prepare cases piecemeal, as the proceedings evolved, and to eke out the preparatory work over a substantial period of time. The new powers of the courts compel litigants and their lawyers to be far more conscientious when they are preparing their cases for trial.[19] For instance, the threat of the preclusion compels the parties and their representatives to prepare the whole case already in the beginning of the case because if the legal fact[20] or the

[14] Leppänen (1998), p. 427.

[15] Leppänen (1998), p. 427.

[16] HE (1990:15).

[17] Ervo (1995), p. 56.

[18] Ervo (1995), p. 60.

[19] Ervo (1995), p. 61.

[20] The term "legal fact" refers to the fact that is immediately relevant to the outcome and is needed to be successful in court. In the other words, parties have to claim and proof the existence of these facts to win the case, for instance, that the debt exists and is due for payment. Parties' and lawyers' arguments are based on legal facts.

piece of evidence has precluded, there is no possibility to reveal to it later.[21] This is, of course, very effective in one way, but on the other hand, it can also make the proceedings expensive and slow when the parties have to take all possible conditions into consideration even beforehand.

The reforms were intended to bring about a situation where there is no possibility of adjourning the case, and where everything will be decided in one session. It was no longer permitted to ledge or to read from written statements at the hearings,[22] and the proceedings are required to be completely oral.[23]

The key aspect is immediacy, which is enhanced by concentration. The judgment may be based only on material introduced at the main hearing. The judges may not be changed in the course of the main hearing. Also, the main hearing may not be adjourned without imperative reasons and, even then, adjournment is permissible only for a short period.[24]

In order to achieve these aims of orality, immediacy and concentration in the procedure there were strict rules in the Finnish Code of Judicial Procedure (FCJP) and these main principles were accepted although without exceptions. Because the procedural culture before the reform had been very different from these main aims, strict regulation was needed in order to achieve these aims in practice. However, as said before, the rules were found soon too strict and there was again a need for reform.[25]

The reformed civil procedure did not resolve all procedural problems in Finland. Even some new problems arose. Empirical studies reveal that legal expenses had increased and that civil procedure took somewhat longer than was the case earlier. This was due to a number of reasons, and the new procedure is not the only reason,[26] but it was and is responsible for this kind of development as a one "player" on the field of jurisdiction.

A primary problem related to the civil preparatory proceedings was that in practice the preparatory stage had not acquired a sufficient profile of its own, as a stage separate from the main hearing and one serving the main hearing. The unnecessary burden has been put on the preparatory proceedings by the practice of the parties to plead their cases at that stage as if it was the main hearing. A contributing factor appeared to be an unduly strict application of the preclusion rule.[27]

The strictness of preclusion is ultimately determined by the threshold of an acceptable excuse. *Leppänen* said in his research already in 1998 that for the truth goal and the fairness of civil procedure, the threshold should be relatively low. Too

---

[21] Chapter 6, Section 9 (FCJP).

[22] Chapter 5, Section 15c, Paragraph 3 and Chapter 6, Section 3 (FCJP).

[23] Ervo (1995), pp. 56–57.

[24] Chapter 6 Sections 1, 10, 11, Chapter 24 Section 2 (FCJP), Leppänen (1998), p. 428.

[25] Lappalainen (2002), pp. 15–18, Sippo and Välimaa (2003), pp. 4–8.

[26] Leppänen (1998), p. 437, Lesknen 2002, pp. 632, 638–641.

[27] Lappalainen (2002), pp. 15–17, Leppänen (1998), p. 437, Sippo and Välimaa (2003), p. 6.

high a threshold would also have the disadvantage of burdening the preparatory stage, as the parties would have to take the precaution of finding and stating all the potential circumstances and evidence at that stage. On the other hand, for the effectiveness of the preventive threat of preclusion the threshold must not be placed too low.[28] *Leppänen's* prognosis came into truth with the amendments in 2003 and the standard of proof concerning the existence of the excuse was lowered. However, the amendment covers only the possibility to add the new pieces of evidence. It will not cover the legal facts, where the preclusion rule is still quite strict.

To sum up the main problem after the reform in 1993 was that the preparatory stage became too massive. In practice, the preparatory stage had not acquired a serving profile that is *preparation for the main hearing* but the parties advocated in a full manner already during the preparation. They pleaded their cases at that stage in the manner of the trial. In the main hearing they usually repeated the same grounds and legal arguments, which was not the idea of the preparation, of course. The main reason for this was the fear of the preclusion.

2.2.2 The More Modern Proceedings: The Swedish Revolution of Process Techniques

The current Swedish Code of Judicial Procedure dates from 1948. The Swedish Code of Judicial Procedure is founded on a number of fundamental principles of procedural law, which are all intended to guarantee the best possible preconditions for the free examination of evidence. Also, in Sweden, like in Finland, the principles of orality, immediateness and concentration are basic procedural principles. The principle of orality implies that a case must be decided after an oral hearing. A party to the hearing may not read from deposed texts. The principle of immediateness means that the judgment can be based only on what has occurred during the main hearing. The principle of concentration means that the case must be so well prepared that it can be concluded as an entity at a single main hearing. No lengthy delays in the main hearing are allowed.[29]

Also, in Sweden, like later in Finland, when put into practice, it proved with the passage of time that the radical application under the Swedish Code of Judicial Procedure (SCJP) of the above principles led in some cases, to difficulties. It has even asked if the current SCJP still is the same code or if the latest reforms have changed the named fundamental principles so much that the spirit of the code is no longer based on the same aims as in 1948.[30]

One of the reasons for this was that a number of proceedings had reached a size and scope that could hardly have been foreseen in 1948. In a major reform of the

---

[28] Leppänen (1998), p. 436.

[29] Ekelöf et al. (2011), pp. 11–13, Lindell (2012), pp. 118–120, 290.

[30] Ekeberg (2013), p. 175.

Swedish Code of Judicial Procedure in 1987, amendments were therefore implemented that provided the possibility for some divergence from the above mentioned principles when warranted in view of the circumstances of each particular case. The principle of orality is since the reform of 1987 based on the idea of functionality. The court should choose between written or oral preparation taking into consideration the practical needs to maximise the easiest way of communication and understanding of the case and claims of parties. In principle, it is even allowed to have written preparation only but in literature it is said that totally written preparation should not be used even in technically complicated cases because the parties can easily write over each other. Therefore, oral exchange of views is recommendable in all cases even if the orality should no longer be the absolute principle but, for instance, technically complicated parts of the case can be presented in a written way to make the understanding easier.[31] The main point in the preparation is to maximise the communication, understanding and clearing the case. For instance, the main principle still is that a party to the preparatory hearing may not read from deposed texts because of the principle of orality. After 1987, there has, however, been an exception to this rule and nowadays the reading from the text is allowed, if it helps to understand the question.[32] So, the principle of orality is no longer an end in itself but it can be modified by reasonable proceedings.

In 2008, a rather substantial reform, the so-called more modern process (EMR) entered into force. The main aim of the reform was to create an efficient and purposive procedure in the general courts. The reform became famous thanks to the extensive use of modern technology by hearings. Through new rules it is now possible to let everyone in a trial participate through video conference.[33] The video conference system was first tested during the years 2000–2006 in some courts. The principles and qualifications were almost the same as for using the phone.[34] The experiences during testing were mostly positive and that is why the system became permanent with the EMR reform.[35] In 2016, the legislator took the next step and made the novelties of EMR even stricter and wider by so-called EMR II reform.[36] Already since 1988 it has been possible the use the phone in the cases, (1) when it is reasonable or (2) if the costs or other inconveniences would be too high in comparison to the interest of the case.[37] The using the phone is now very usual in Swedish courts and the experiences has been mostly positive. Some negative sides have been reported like the technical problems and that the opinion of the parties

[31] Prop. 1986/87:89, p. 1, Lindell (2012), p. 43, 290.

[32] Chapter 42, Section 13 (SCJP), Lindell (2012), p. 290.

[33] Chapter 5, Section 10 (SCJP).

[34] Lindell (2003), p. 261.

[35] Bylander (2005), p. 126.

[36] Lagrådsremiss En modernare rättegång II, 13 maj 2015.

[37] Chapter 42, Section 10 (SCJP).

has a significant role in considering if it is reasonable to use the phone hearing or not.[38]

Alongside the use of the technology, the other tool to make the proceedings quick and effective is summaries and schedules. The district courts must, namely issue time tables and summarise the parties' positions in the case. The parties are to a great extent responsible to help the court in these respects.[39] The duty to make a summary has become stricter in 2016 when the next step in the more modern process (EMR II) entered into force. Earlier it was a duty of a court to write a summary if it was probable that the summary made the procedure more effective. From 2016 on, the court has a duty to write a summary in co-operation with parties if there is no reasons according to which the summary were unnecessary.[40]

By the new legislation, the legislator wanted also to clarify that the point of weight in the judiciary should be in the district courts. As a result, the audio visual records from the district court are replayed at the main hearing in the court of appeal and in the most cases the persons are not questioned again in the court of appeal. This implies that the court of appeal will try the case on the same material as was tried by the district court. Therefore the role of appeal is more to control than to try the case.[41]

The most distinctive to the Swedish modern proceedings is the wide use of modern technologies, which has its positive sides but also drawbacks.[42] The recent reforms have also been criticised because the participation in the proceedings becomes more or less indirect as soon as the participation happens via technical links[43] even if according to the legislator's surveys the experiences have mostly been positive.[44]

The other main feature is flexibility, which recently has become more and more typical for the Swedish civil proceedings and the procedural form is mainly up to the single case and the ways to handle it in a reasonable and functional way. The Code of 1948 has lived with the times and got adapted to modern needs. The

[38] Bylander (2005), p. 125.

[39] Chapter 42, Sections 6 and 16 (SCJP), Ekeberg 2013, p. 172.

[40] Chapter 42, Section 16 (SCJP 2016), Lagrådsremiss En modernare rättegång II, 13 maj 2015.

[41] Ervo and Dahlqvist (2014), pp. 260–263, Prop. 2004/05:131, En modernare rättegång – reformering av processen i allmän domstol, p. 1.

[42] The wide use of modern technology can have even psychological effects. On the one hand, according to empirical studies, people who had been heard via video link had been found less trustworthy compared with people who were heard in person in the court. On the other hand, the possibility to avoid personal appearance has caused less stress among victims and by that mean resulted to the better outcome what the quality of the narrative is concerned. Landström et al. (2012), p. 197.

[43] Bylander (2004), p. 63.

[44] SOU 2012:93, del 1, SOU 2012:93, del 2. See also Léven and Wersäll (2011), pp. 30–31 where the authors (who are judges at the court of appeal) see the EMR reform as positive one despite of the fact that the reform was highly criticised before it entered into the force and still is especially among advocates.

proceedings are no longer cases "here and now" like in 1948 and which still is the case in many criminal cases, but they are more complexed. Therefore, flexibility in forms is needed and the fundamental principles of orality, immediateness and concentration can no longer be followed fully, but it is necessary to adapt them to the other needs.[45] Still, it can be asked if this flexibility has caused some chaos and in which content the fundamental principles still are valid. Especially, since EMR II "everything goes" and there seems to be not that much left of orality, concentration and immediateness in the Swedish civil proceedings.

2.3 Forms and Functions

2.3.1 Functions

As already explained above, the most important function for the preparatory proceedings also in the East-Scandinavian countries is to make possible a concentrated main hearing. That is the so-called concentration function. Normally, without an adequate preparation it would be impossible to conduct a trial without adjournments. Therefore, in cases which reach the main hearing, the preparatory proceedings serves the main hearing. To the end that the concentration of the main hearing becomes possible, the "object" of the civil procedure—that is, the claims of the parties and the grounds for them need to be established as well as the evidence specified in the preparatory stage.[46] Especially in Sweden, the legislator has recently stressed the efficiency of the preparation and put much effort in making the preparatory stage even more efficient than before. The concrete tools for that are the above mentioned flexibility, summaries and schedules and, furthermore, the strict rules on parties' duties and sanctions if they neglect to fulfil them.[47]

However, preparatory proceedings have even other functions. One is the resolution function. It means that as soon as the case is ready to be decided, that should happen and only the most contentious cases should go through the whole proceedings. The aim in that is to save resources and to allocate them to hard cases. Undisputed cases and cases which become clear should be resolved and decided quickly and economically. As soon as the further proceedings become superfluous, the case should be decided and the procedure should be finished.[48]

The judge should also actively focus on judicial settlement efforts between the parties during the preparatory stage, which is the so-called settlement function. The law places the judge under a specific obligation to focus on judicial settlement efforts at the preliminary stage both in Sweden and Finland. An oral preliminary

[45] Ekeberg (2013), p. 175.

[46] Lappalainen (2003), p. 773, Leppänen (1998), p. 428.

[47] Lindell (2012), pp. 291–292. See in details Sect. 2.4 in this article.

[48] Lappalainen (2003), p. 773, Leppänen (1998), p. 428.

session affords the judge a good opportunity to conduct the proceedings actively and to contribute to settling the case. In carrying out duties related to the preparatory proceedings the judge must, on the other hand, also ensure that the procedure remains fair and expeditious.[49] There has been a wide discussion in the legal literature on the limits of the judicial settlement efforts.[50] Some are of opinion that it risks the impartiality of a judge.[51]

2.3.2 *Forms: Over and Back Again*

2.3.2.1 Swedish Efficiency

One characteristic feature of the East-Scandinavian procedure in civil cases is the distinction between preparatory proceedings and the main hearing. As already explained above, both the Finnish and Swedish legislators have recently stressed the significance of the preparation and much effort has been put to intensify that stage. The main reason behind this policy is the need to be effective to save public resources especially now when states struggle in economic crisis even in the North Europe.

The purpose of the preparatory proceedings is to bring the case to such a state of readiness that it can be decided upon in an unbroken sequence at the oral main hearing. Therefore, the aim is to ensure that the facts relied upon by each of the parties are made sufficiently clear to permit the other party to determine if and to what extent it is necessary for him or her to adduce evidence in support of the case. The purpose is further to clarify the legal grounds relied upon and the nature of relief sought.[52]

When a claimant wishes to have an issue considered, a written statement of claim has to be submitted to the court and the case will begin with it. In the statement of claim, the claimant must state the claim and the grounds that are wished to invoke in support of the claim. The claimant must further submit the written evidence that is intended to be produced. In addition, it has to be stated what he or she intends to prove with each item of evidence. With the "grounds" it is not meant the background of the case, but the circumstances that are judicially relevant. Correspondingly, "what he intends to be prove" in the means the detailed list on the themes of evidence (the theme of evidence is an assertion on some legal fact)[53] and on the pieces of the evidence.[54]

---

[49] Leppänen (1998), p. 428.

[50] Ervo (2011), pp. 340–344.

[51] Ervo (2011), pp. 343–344, HE (78/2000), p. 47.

[52] Lundblad (1990), p. 149.

[53] Lappalainen (2003), p. 778.

[54] Fitger (1993), p. 243, Chapter 5, Section 2 (FCJP), Chapter 42 Sections 1–2 (SCJP).

If there is some formal impediment or if the statement of claim fails to fulfil certain requirements, the district court may reject the claimant's claim.[55] If exceptionally, it was to be apparent from the statement of claim that the claimant's petition is obviously groundless; the Court is empowered to reject it out of hand. Otherwise, the district court serves the statement of claim on the defendant.[56]

This preparatory scrutiny is usually rather superficial. Thus, for instance, the rule that the evidence should be set out in the application is not strictly applied. The reason is that usually questions of evidence can be assessed only when the defendant has stated his case indicating what facts are in dispute. However, if the court should find that the statement of claim fails to reach the minimum standard it will order the claimant to make necessary supplements, failing which the statement of claim will be dismissed.[57]

When serving statement of claim, the court decides whether the preparatory proceedings are to begin in writing or orally. It is relatively common that the defendant is ordered to respond in writing and this is also the main rule according to statue. The statement of defence must contain the views of the defendant vis–àvis the claims the claimant and the grounds on which the views are based. The contents of the statement of defence should mirror the claimant's statement of claim.[58] Normally, the response is forwarded to the claimant for a further statement of views, following which a time for a meeting is appointed.[59]

At the oral preparatory hearing the parties are entitled to supplement and elaborate upon their positions. They are also entitled to request clarifications from the other party. The task of the judge at this stage is, by questioning the parties, to attempt to remedy any instances of obscurity or incompleteness that occur in the submissions of the parties, so-called substantive procedural guidance.[60] During the preparation the parties have to reveal all the legal facts and the pieces of evidence with the threat of preclusion. According to the Chapter 42, Section 22 (SCJP), it is named only the pieces of evidence that is facts. However, the same rule will cover also legal facts.[61] The rule of preclusion in the Chapter 43, Section 10 (SCJP) is not as strict as the rule of preclusion still is in Finnish legislation. According to the Swedish law, the court may consider if the legal fact or the piece of evidence is precluded or not. The requirements are that the party wants to make harm to his or her opposite party with this kind of method or if he or she has in every case neglected procedural duties grossly way with this manner. However, it is possible in non-mandatory civil cases to use the stricter preclusion rule—identical to the

[55] Capter 42, Sections 3, 4. (SCJP)

[56] Chapter 42, Section 5 (SCJP).

[57] Chapter 42, Section 2–3 (SCJP), Lundblad (1990), p. 150.

[58] Lundblad (1990), p. 150.

[59] Chapter 42, Section 6 (SCJP).

[60] Chapter 42, Sections 8–10 (SCJP).

[61] Lindell (2003), p. 260.

Finnish one—already during the preparation if the party neglects his or her duties.[62]

The requirements for using the rule of preclusion then are that the party will make his/her position substantively better with the late revealing of legal fact or presenting the piece of evidence. The gross negligence is estimated on the basis of the concerned parties' own capacity to act in proceedings.[63]

Generally, the judge should also attempt to bring about judicial settlement efforts between the parties. How active the substantive procedural guidance and how energetic the moves towards judicial settlement efforts should be is a much-debated question,[64] but the reforms of recent years have largely aimed at strengthening these elements in the preparatory proceedings.[65]

It is not unusual that the preparatory proceedings then revert to being held in writing. In that event, the parties are to indicate the oral evidence they intend to produce. It is also possible for them to submit further supplementary matter. Thereafter, a time for the main hearing in the case is scheduled.[66]

It should be emphasised that the judge has large discretionary powers to choose between written or oral preparatory proceedings. The above description is, thus, but one of many possible variations. By way of example, it might be mentioned that the preparatory proceedings could be entirely in writing and that two or more preparatory hearings are held.[67] The purpose of the preparatory proceedings is to prepare the case for the main hearing. The court should, therefore, consider and chose the way of preparation that serves this purpose best.[68]

However, normally the statement of defence is written and, after that, the oral preparatory hearing is organised. After the preparatory hearing, the preparatory stage should be finished. According to the government's bill, there should not normally be more than one oral preparatory hearing. In practice it is, however, usual that there is more than one oral preparatory hearing in more complicated cases. If the party has no attorney or other representative, it may be easier to prepare the case in oral hearing straight away. The court should also consider the costs when weighing the suitable way of preparation. If the value of the interest in the case is

[62] Chapter 42, Section 15 (SCJP).

[63] Fitger (1993), p. 257.

[64] There has been a wide discussion both in Sweden and Finland, how wide the substantive procedural guidance can be. See for instance Lappalainen (2003), p. 806. In Sweden, the substantive procedural guidance has become more active during the latest 10–30 years. If the party takes part in procedure without the help of a lawyer, the guidance can compensate the lack to some extent. Brolin et al. (1997), p. 78 and Fitger (1993), p. 247, compare with Brolin et al. (1997), p. 79, where they personally recommend that the lack of an attorney would not to be a reason for more effective substantive procedural guidance. The substantive procedural guidance has also seen as one of the most important tools to make the proceedings effective. Brolin et al. (1997), p. 78.

[65] Chapter 42, Section 17 (SCJP).

[66] Chapter 42, Section 9 (SCJP).

[67] Chapter 42, Section 9 (SCJP).

[68] Arg. Lundblad (1990), p. 150.

not very high, the presumption is that the court will prefer the written preparation. According to the Swedish Code of Judicial Procedure, even the preparation as a whole can be written. This is, however, not a reasonable way to prepare the case because in the oral hearing the communication happens directly and the clarifying of the case is easier, as already argued earlier.[69]

It is a duty of the court to make a written summary of the case during the preparation if the summary can be seen as a benefit for the case.[70] During the preparatory stage, the court makes also the schedule that will help both parties and the court to make their own timetables and to prepare the case well in time. In large and complicated cases, the court may even use the list on current questions and themes clarified in the case. The list helps to structure the case.[71] The meaning of the schedule has been made more important with the amendment of Chapter 42, Section 6 (SCJP). According to the new rule, the parties have to control that they can act in planned time. If the schedule is too strict or otherwise unsuitable, they have to inform the court that they cannot follow it.

Should the parties agree the case may also be decided on its documentary merits. The case can also be determined on the documents if the main hearing is not needed having regard to the investigation in the case nor requested by any of the parties.[72] The main principle is, however, that there should be the main hearing. The main hearing is always needed if oral testimony is presented. It is namely impossible during the preparatory stage to take the oral testimony. Even in the cases, where the decision is based on the documentary merits, it is recommended to have the main hearing. In a hearing, the parties can communicate better and it gives better possibilities for advocacy. Oral proceedings can also be quicker.[73]

2.3.2.2 Finland: New Rules, Old Tricks

In Finland, a preliminary hearing is presided over by one of the legally trained members of the District Court. The civil preparatory proceedings are divided into two phases. The first phase is in writing and consists of a statement of claim, the statement of defendant and other later written statements, if any from the parties.[74]

The statement of claim must identify the nature of the claimant's claim and set out its detailed factual nature. It must also reveal the forms and origins of the evidence on which he proposes to rely and must set out what that evidence is alleged to establish. This statement will not be a substitute for ordinary evidence because the use of written testimony will not be allowed but parties and witnesses

[69] Lindell (2003), p. 259.
[70] Chapter 42, Section 16 (SCJP).
[71] Lindell (2003), p. 269.
[72] Chapter 42, Section 18 (SCJP).
[73] Brolin et al. (1997), pp. 141–142.
[74] Leppänen (1998), p. 428.

are heard orally in the main hearing. However, since 2003, written evidence, such as documents, may nowadays be used and evaluated even at the preparatory stage and there is no need to organise the main hearing in all cases if there are no oral pieces of evidence. A contested case may, namely, be decided solely on the basis of written preparation, if the nature of the case is such that a decision on it does not require conduct of the main hearing and none of the parties oppose the case being decided in the written preparations.[75] But despite of this possibility, the claimant is always required to enclose proofs of evidence from him or her and the witnesses he or she proposes to call.[76]

If the statement of claim is allowed, the defendant will be invited to respond to it within a given time limit.[77] It is a duty of the court to send the statement of claim by post. The defendant should then sign the statement of claim and return it to the court. This procedure tends to usually work. If the defendant does not sign and return the statement of claim, it may have to be served by bailiffs.[78] The defendant will have to reveal his or her own evidence in the same way as the claimants had to do in the statement of claim.[79] Normally, the statement of defence should be in writing, but in some situations the court may summon the defendant to answer directly in the oral preparatory hearing.[80]

The court can nowadays exhort a party to deliver a written statement to the court before a preparatory hearing normally only once. The courts, namely, tried to keep the old written traditions—which were not that concentrated either—alive despite of the reform in 1993, which was based on the orality and concentration. The tool for that was the possibility to exhort a party to deliver a written statement to the court before a preparatory hearing, if it deems this necessary.[81] This possibility was very often used and many times in the same case until even this rule was reformed again in 2003 and from that on max only one statement is usually allowed.[82] So, the old habits came and continued at the preparatory stage instead of the main hearing, where they were strictly forbidden in the Finnish Code. All this made the proceedings slow and expensive.[83] Therefore, current Section 15a in Chapter 5 (FCJP) is stricter than the earlier Section 15, Paragraph 2 was. The rule has always also been that the written statement should cover some special questions, which the court should point at. Free correspondence is not allowed.[84]

---

[75] Chapter 5, Section 27 a (FCJP).

[76] Chapter 5, Section 1 (FCJP) and Ervo (1995), pp. 58–59.

[77] Chapter 5, Section 9 (FCJP).

[78] Chapter 11 (FCJP).

[79] Ervo (1995), p. 59.

[80] Chapter 5, Section 9 (FCJP).

[81] Chapter 5, Section 15, Paragraph 2 (FCJP).

[82] Chapter 5, Section 15a (FCJP).

[83] Lappalainen (2002), p. 16.

[84] Lappalainen (2003), p. 789.

Also, judges were afraid of the prohibition to adjourn the cases in the name of concentration. Therefore, they used the preparatory stage in order to secure the concentration of the main proceedings. There were very many preparatory hearings and adjournments between these sessions, which was not strictly enough forbidden in the Finnish Code although it was not the ratio of the law.[85] That way the court could secure the "concentration" in the main hearing, when it was only the dwindled procedure in which the evidence was taken and otherwise the parties only repeated their preparatory arguments. The actual advocacy had happened already during the preparation, which was not necessarily concentrated but could consist of adjournments and many sessions like in the old style of proceedings.[86] What took the biscuit were extended preparatory sessions for just before the main hearing to avoid the threat of preclusion and to (formally) follow the strict rules on concentration. *Summa summarum*, the reform and its aims led to its travesty in practice. The re-reform in 2003 tried to solve the problems mentioned above.

Because of the preclusion in a case amenable to settlement a party shall not in the main hearing invoke a legal fact that he or she has not invoked in the preparation, unless he establishes a probability that he or she has had a valid reason for not doing so.[87] Oral evidence is not introduced until the main hearing, but the preliminaries to the presentation of evidence are made in the preparatory stage as explained earlier. The preliminaries serve the purpose of making it possible to introduce evidence in a concentrated manner at the main hearing. Concentration at the main hearing requires that the evidence is specified in advance in order to spare the trial from unforeseen legal facts. Therefore, the parties must inform the court of all the evidence that they wish to present as well as what facts they intend to prove with each piece of evidence (the so-called themes of evidence). Correspondingly, in the preparatory stage, the judge must actively clarify the legal facts and pieces of evidence to be introduced at the main hearing and their related themes. As soon as the preparatory stage is concluded a party may no longer without an acceptable excuse introduce evidence or reveal to new legal facts in so-called non-mandatory civil cases (where settlement is permissible) that he or she did not specify at the preparatory stage.[88] Because the rule of preclusion was found too strict and therefore unreasonable the standard of proof concerning the excuse lowered since the re-reform in 2003. This amendment covers, however, only the pieces of evidence and not the legal facts that still will preclude quite easily.[89] It is also possible to introduce new pieces of evidence even without the acceptable excuse if

[85] The case has to be extraordinary large and complicated if the more than one oral sessions during preparatory proceedings are needed. Lappalainen (2003), p. 791.

[86] Lappalainen (2002), p. 16.

[87] Chapter 6, Section 9 (FCJP).

[88] Leppänen (1998), p. 429.

[89] Earlier the standard of proof was in Chapter 6, Section 9 (FCJP) "probable cause" and since 2003 the new piece of evidence has been allowed according to the same Section if the court "may assume" that he or she had an acceptable excuse.

the opposing party will give the permission for that.[90] This amendment with two different standards of proof has sometimes seen problematic.[91]

As explained above, from 2003 on it has been even allowed to decide the case during preparation on the basis of documentary merits. However, this possibility should not be used too often. The idea is to make it possible to decide even a disputed matter after a written preparation without an oral preparatory hearing and a main hearing. The requirements are that the parties will give their consents to this kind of decision and in the light of the nature of the case there is no use to organise the main hearing.[92] The merits cannot be based on the oral testimony in such situations. To take oral evidence is only allowed in the oral main hearing.[93] This amendment in 2003 was a rather fundamental one, because the strict rule of the reform in 1993 was that the disputed matter has to be decided in the main hearing always.

In the case, the contested case is decided at the written preparatory stage, where there will be no oral preparation at all. The meaning is not to use oral preparations for legal argumentation but, whenever it is needed, there should be even a main hearing in the case. Still, if the case matures during the oral hearing it is possible to organise a main hearing straight away and to have it immediately after the oral preparation. Then the case can be decided after this type of immediate main hearing. Section 27a in Chapter 5 (FCJP) allows the decision making at the written preparatory proceedings only when this type of oral argumentation and discussion is not needed. Even if there is no oral testimony, the main hearing can be necessary to discuss and argue. Especially, if one party is without legal counsel, it might be easier to present the case orally. Section 27a provides some flexibility to make a decision even in contested cases already at the preparatory stage but it does not give any possibility to avoid the main hearing, whenever such is needed.[94]

The second phase after written preparation is conducted orally in the form of a preliminary hearing. A single professional judge is responsible for the civil preparatory proceedings.[95] From 2003 on it has also been possible to step over the oral hearing if it seems to be unnecessary. In such situations, the next phase will be the main hearing.[96] Otherwise, the preliminary hearing begins with a review of the written submissions from the parties and ends with a settlement of the case, or with the judgment or with the default judgment, or with the decision to proceed to the main hearing.[97]

---

[90] Chapter 6, Section 9, paragraph 2 (FCJP).

[91] Lappalainen (2003), p. 801.

[92] Lappalainen (2003), pp. 812–817.

[93] Chapter 5, Section 27a (FCJP), Lappalainen (2002), pp. 103–106, Lappalainen 2003, p. 774, Sippo and Välimaa (2003), pp. 157–182.

[94] HE (32/2001), pp. 56–58.

[95] Lappalainen (2002), p. 36, Lappalainen (2003), p. 790, Leppänen (1998), p. 428.

[96] Chapter 5, Section 15b (FCJP).

[97] Sippo and Välimaa (2003), pp. 182–185.

It is one of the main objectives of the preliminary hearing to bring about favourable legal facts for the parties to reach a compromise and to settle their dispute. It is possible that the judge may be able to make a proposal for friendly settlement.[98] It is a duty of the court to make a written or oral summary of the case during the preparation. The role of this summary became even more important with the re-reform of 2003.[99] The form and the need, as well as a suitable time for summing up the case, depend on the current circumstances.[100] If the case will be decided at the written preparatory stage, the summary must be written.[101]

Since 2003, the oral preparation can be organised even by phone or by some other suitable technique. The requirements are that it will be reasonable in the light of the functions of the preparation and if there are not many and no large questions to clarify.[102] Even the session where the phone or other technique is used is public, which means that the general audience may be at present and the audience have to have the possibility to hear all the discussions.[103] From 2003, in the court have to make during the preparation also the timetable of the case and even otherwise inform the parties of the progress of the case.[104]

The procedures in mandatory civil cases differ a little from the ordinary proceedings in the non-mandatory cases. The main difference is that the rule of preclusion does not cover the mandatory civil cases. In addition, there are some differences in cases of specific types of claim.[105] However, there are not actually tailored preparatory stages to specific types of claim, but the form is usually at least mainly the same.

There are only a few precedents of the Supreme Court that concern the preparatory stage. Only five cases were found (the Supreme Court precedents) from the database called Finlex (http://www.finlex.fi), where the preparation constitutes its very core.[106] The one concerns the problems in minutes and the burden of proving the allegation.[107] The other concerns the possibility to make a final decision at the preparatory stage.[108] The third covers sanctions in the preparatory stage.[109] Even

[98] Chapter 5, Sections 15c, 20, 21 and 26 (FCJP), Ervo (1995), p. 59.

[99] Lappalainen (2003), p. 808.

[100] Chapter 5, Section 24 (FCJP), Lappalainen (2003), p. 809.

[101] HE (32/2001), p. 58.

[102] Chapter 5, Section 15d (FCJP).

[103] HE (32/2001), p. 44 and Lappalainen (2003), p. 792.

[104] Chapter 5, Section 18 (FCJP).

[105] See for instance Chapter 5, Section 14 (FCJP), which covers provisions on negotiable promissory notes.

[106] Sought by the index term "civil case" that brought 35 cases. Only five concerned the preparatory stage, visited 2015-09-07.

[107] KKO 1997:90.

[108] KKO 1997:25.

[109] KKO 2011:104.

the two other cases concern sanctions[110] and if it was possible to solve the case without an oral main hearing at the written preparatory proceedings only.[111] A few precedents do, however, not mean that there were no problems in the preparatory stage, but the problems are different sort and not applicable for appealing.

2.4 The Procedural Sanctions as Tools for Efficiency

2.4.1 The Judgement by Default

In the preparatory proceedings, decision is usually permissible only on formal grounds.[112] Otherwise, a case can be dismissed; a judgment by default may be given against a party who is passive; or a judgment may be given in accordance with the acknowledgement of a party.[113]

If the defendant is passive and does not give any reply to the court, the court can still decide the case. In Finland, according to Chapter 5 Section 13 (FCJP), the case must be decided without continuing the preparation if, in a case amenable to settlement, a defendant who has been exhorted to respond in writing, (1) has not delivered the required response before the deadline or (2) has not presented grounds for contesting in his response or has referred only to grounds that are manifestly irrelevant to the decision on the case. In this event, the action will be upheld by a judgment by default. In so far as the claimant has abandoned the action or it is manifestly without a basis, the action will be dismissed by a judgment.

In such cases, the decision-making takes place in the antechamber of the court. The decision is then a default judgment by which the defendant loses the case and the claims of the claimant are accepted. This kind default judgment is possible in cases in which the defendant fails to provide a reply within the time allowed. This is also possible in cases in which the reply fails to present the grounds on which the debtor contests the application, or if he or she refers only to such grounds that clearly have no relevance to the decision of the case.[114]

The default judgment is possible even when the party neglects to send the written statement in time or which the court has requested, and the opposing party is asking the decision by default. The default judgment will be also possible in the

[110] KKO 2000:22.

[111] KKO 2012:38.

[112] As explained earlier, since 2003, in Finland even contentious cases can be resolved in the written preparation if there is no oral testimony and if the parties so agree. However, it is always the court that makes the decision on the fact if the case is suitable to be decided during the preparatory stage after the oral hearing or based on the written preparation but anyways without the main hearing.

[113] Chapter 5, Section 27a (FCJP), Lappalainen (2003), pp. 773–774 and Leppänen (1998), p. 428.

[114] Chapter 5, Sections 13 and 14 (FCJP) and Ervo (2001), p. 123.

non-mandatory cases if the party who has been invited personally to the oral session not appear and the opposing party is asking the decision by default.[115]

In Sweden, the situation is very similar. If a defendant fails to file a statement of defence, or if the parties fail to attend a hearing, a judgment in default may be issued.[116] With the EMR reform the rules became stricter.[117] The parties' responsibility to co-operate in an active way is nowadays very much stressed by the Swedish legislator to keep the procedure effective. Therefore, the arsenal of procedural sanctions was broadened at the same time.

2.4.2 *Preclusion*

The rule of preclusion has already been introduced above. The main sanction for negligence in reporting legal facts or evidence is the preclusion of further evidence or legal facts. In accordance with law, preclusion is directly connected with the conclusion of the preparatory proceedings, a moment where the evidence or the legal facts will "freeze".[118]

The parties to the case are not allowed to refer to new evidence or to allege any new legal facts that were not relied upon at the preparatory hearing. This is a governing principle of the reforms. The courts are empowered to operate a rule of "preclusion" (similar to the English system of striking out pleadings or refusing to give leave to a party to amend existing pleadings). A party who wishes to change the grounds of the claim at the main hearing will have to have exceptional reasons for asking to do this. The aim, of course, is to eliminate surprises at the main hearing.[119]

During the preparatory stage, the parties are usually free to produce new evidence. However, if a party is already guilty of omission, in a non-mandatory civil case the judge may during the preparatory stage urge the party to fulfil the obligation under threat of preclusion within a fixed time limit. After the limit, the party is no longer allowed to produce new evidence without an acceptable excuse.[120] If the judge uses this tool of case management, the decision of the time limit has to be written and naturally the party has to be informed of the new deadline. This is an effective tool to intensify the preparation in the situations where parties or their counsels are not hard-working, co-operative or professionally talented lawyers. However, using this tool may also lead to situations where the case will not become properly prepared and investigated because of too early

---

[115] Chapter 12, Section 10 (FCJP).

[116] Chapter 42, Sections 11–12 and Chapter 44, Sections 2, 7b, 7c, 8, 9 and 10 (SCJP).

[117] Bylander (2007), p. 518.

[118] Leppänen (1998), p. 435, Lindell (2012), p. 291.

[119] Ervo (1995), p. 60, Lappalainen (2003), p. 800, Lindell (2012), p. 291.

[120] Chapter 5, Section 22 (FCJP), Chapter 42 Section 22 (SCJP), Leppänen (1998), p. 435.

preclusion rule. Still, the question is how much of this preparatory and especially investigative work belongs into the court and which part is the duty of the parties and their counsels. One specific problem in the Finnish procedure is according to Nylund that the work is not rationally dealt between Finnish judges and lawyers compared with Norway.[121]

Summa summarum, the meaning of preclusion is preventive. The rule of preclusion forces the parties to state their evidence at the preparatory stage. With a growing risk of incorrect judgment, application of preclusion in an individual case is not without problems. In this sense, the legislator has emphasised the general functionality of the civil procedure over the correctness of solution in individual cases.[122]

2.4.3 Litigation Costs and Cost Sanctions

In the East-Scandinavian countries, a case cannot be resolved against a passive party merely on the formal ground that the party has neglected to duly report her or his evidence or legal facts to the court in the preparatory stage. The only procedural tool is to use preclusion as explained above and the threat of legal costs is the other preventive instrument in the legislation for such situations. Therefore, "the sanction" which may follow is the payment of expenses. One party may be obliged to pay the portion of the litigation costs of the other party that he or she has brought about through wilful negligence or carelessness whether or not those costs would otherwise be for him/her to pay. In exceptional cases, the counsel of a party may be required to pay the expenses personally, if he/she has neglected his/her duty as counsel.[123] The rule covers situations of all other kind where the party has neglected some of his/her procedural duties and is therefore guilty for the delay of proceedings or some other harm to the opposing party. The threat of payment of expenses covers then those situations where the fact or the piece of evidence is not yet precluded but the negligence of a party or counsel causes extra work or waste of time. According to the main rule, the party who loses the case shall be liable for all reasonable legal costs incurred by the necessary measures of the opposing party.[124] The same rule covers the preparatory stage.

In Sweden, the winning party is normally entitled to the reimbursement of litigation expenses by the losing party. The possibility of allowing each party to defray his/her own costs is limited. If a party is considered having won in part, the reimbursement for costs may be adjusted correspondingly. According to the main rule, the reimbursement ordered fully corresponds to the costs for counsel, the

[121] See Nylund in this book, Sect. 3.10.2.

[122] Lappalainen (2003), p. 800, Leppänen (1998), p. 436.

[123] Chapter 21, Sections 5, 6 (FCJP), Leppänen (1998), p. 435.

[124] Chapter 21, Section 1 (FCJP).

party's own work and production of evidence.[125] According to Chapter 18, Section 6, the responsibility for legal costs can be a sanction for non-compliance of procedural rules even in Sweden, like in Finland.

There is and has been a wide discussion especially in Finland on legal costs. Especially after the procedural reforms, legal costs are very high. General fees for proceedings are not high at all but the costs of the parties are. The costs are so high that the claimants will no longer take the risk and take cases into court. This covers especially private persons whereas the reason to avoid courts in dispute resolution among firms is duration and publicity of court proceedings. Still, during recent years, there have been less civil cases in the Finnish courts nowadays and the reasons to this problem have been discussed in the legal literature. The economic crisis has from its part caused some increasing statistics because there are more debt cases, bankruptcies and applications for loan arrangements.[126] However, the basic problem still exists. People do not use court service that much any longer even if the amount of disputes is probably not decreasing in the society. On one hand, this kind of situation will effectively eliminate unnecessary law suits from the courts, but it will nowadays eliminate even necessary law suits and therefore prevent the realization of the access to court and further the access to justice.

The Finnish legislator is aware of this problem and the first step towards the solution was the taxation of the costs in the summary proceedings. Because of that problem of the costs, the court estimates *ex officio* the amount of the legal costs in the summary proceedings. In summary debt cases, the question is in fact in most cases more of the collection than controversy. Therefore, the legal costs can be more coherent and lower. The Ministry of Justice lays down provisions concerning the grounds for legal costs in these cases.[127] The fixed sums will also help the parties to estimate the costs and the possible risk beforehand. The second step towards the solution was the wider possibilities to get legal aid in 2002.[128] However, the legal aid does not cover the costs of the opposing party and the liability for them, but it will cover the party's own costs and that way help a little. This aim to cover even people with middle-income has partly realised thanks to the reform.[129] The latest step was the court-connected mediation, which should be cheaper than the traditional civil proceedings because both parties will pay their own costs. In spite of these steps taken by the legislator, the final solution is still failing.

---

[125] Chapter 18 (SCJP).

[126] Lesknen (2002), pp. 632, 638–641, Autio (2014b), pp. 227–228 and Saarensola (2014), p. 246. Due to the economic crisis, the amount of debt cases became much higher from 2005 until 2010; the latter was again a more normal year but, in 2011, the amount was again increasing whereas in 2013 there were only about 2000 new debt cases more than in 2012. In 2013, 68 % of civil cases were debt cases and district courts decided in 2013 299,000 debt cases, which was 11 % more than they decided in 2012. http://tilastokeskus.fi/til/koikrs/2013/koikrs_2013_2014-04-02_tie_001_fi.html, visited 2015-08-11.

[127] Chapter 21, Section 8c (FCJP), Ervo (2001), p. 123.

[128] More about that reform for instance in Nylund (2002), pp. 279–294.

[129] Litmala et al. (2007), p. 84.

In Sweden, there has not been that much discussion about legal costs so far.[130] It is difficult to guess the reason for this silence but at least arbitration is a very common way to solve business cases and, therefore, access to courts in Swedish business litigation is not a current problem.[131]

2.5 The East-Scandinavian "Disclosure"

The East-Scandinavian preparatory system derives from the continental tradition, which has the premise that the parties in a civil case must find the necessary evidence outside the legal procedure and through their own private investigation. The East-Scandinavian system does not offer the parties significant procedural coercive means to find evidence. Another feature is that the entire preparatory proceedings are before a court and there is no official role for direct contacts between the parties.[132] Of course, it belongs into attorneys' duties to seek settlement and negotiate with the opposite party[133] at the pre-action phrase but otherwise that stage is not very essential in the East-Scandinavian countries. The Swedish rules on "disclosure" are close to Finnish ones. That is the concept of full disclosure is as yet unknown, but many other rules can be found, which cover the same area and will help in organising the testimony and in finding out the facts beforehand or during the trial including the preparatory stage.

The normal practice in the preparatory proceedings in Sweden and Finland is to hear the parties only and they are not heard for the purpose of taking evidence at that stage. The East-Scandinavian system does not recognise the concept of disclosure of documents either. If requested by one party, the other party is obliged to inform whether or not he/she is in possession of a written piece of evidence or an object that may have significance in the case. This obligation to inform and, correspondingly, the obligation to produce the document or the object require that the other party specifies the document to an adequate detail.[134]

In the East-Scandinavian countries, there has not been much discussion on the need to adopt the disclosure model. *Leppänen* argued already in the end of 1990s that here is no reason to carry out major changes to advance towards the disclosure or the disclosure system. Nevertheless, he suggested some minor revisions. First, the obligation of one party to inform the other party should, according to *Leppänen*,

---

130 Almkvist and Elofsson (2013), p. 150.

131 SOU (1995:65), p. 115, Autio (2014a), p. 29.

132 Leppänen (1998), p. 437.

133 The Code of Conduct (Finland), rule 5.6. Available on the web: http://www.asianajajaliitto.fi/files/1044/B_01_Code_of_conduct_for_lawyers_%2815.1.2009%29.pdf, visited 2015-09-09, The Code of Conduct (Sweden), rule 5.2.1. Available on the web: https://www.advokatsamfundet.se/Documents/Advokatsamfundet_sv/Advokatetik/V%C3%A4gledande%20regler%20med%20kommentarer%20december%202012.pdf, visited 2015-11-07.

134 Chapter 5, Section 20 (FCJP), Chapter 42, Section 8(SCJP), Leppänen (1998), pp. 437–438.

be strengthened for the evidence of which that party has knowledge but which he does not intend to present. Second, the possibility to present oral evidence as a preliminary measure in the preparatory proceedings should be expanded to a degree.[135]

Leppänen's suggestions did not spark on any wide discussion.[136] It seems not to be a problem in practice that a disclosure system does not exist or the other explanation for no discussion can be that the parties and other actors are not enough aware of the possibilities and positive sides of the disclosure system. Just recently, a big reform of the law of evidence has been finished in Finland and the new Chapter 17 (FJCP) on the evidence entered into the force on 1 January 2016. Despite a wide reform there were no proposals for disclosure or any discussion on that need. The current system seems to be satisfied.[137]

Still, many other rules that serve the similar purposes can be found. For example, the parties in Swedish (and Finnish[138]) civil litigation and their representatives may not lie during the proceedings. However, they are under no obligation to disclose facts that he/she considers unfavourable to him/her voluntarily. It is for each party to detect identity and the facts that he/she wishes to rely on. If he/she suspect that relevant facts are being withheld the party may try to induce or force the other side to disclose those facts using the following methods. Firstly, the party can put questions to the opposite side. Then the party can ask the disclosure of documents and even the preparatory examination of witnesses is in extraordinary circumstances possible.[139]

The parties are free to put questions at each other during the preparatory proceedings. However, there is no general sanction available to force an answer. Swedish either Finnish law does not know the concept of the contempt of court. Thus, if a party to whom a question is directed does not wish to answer he or she may refuse to do so. It is for the court to draw its own conclusions from the fact that no answer is given. A party is, however, under the duty to state what evidence he or she relies upon. In respect of written evidence, the party is also required, at the request of the opponent, to state what further evidence he/she possesses.[140] This rule is rarely used and it is not properly sanctioned. Moreover, its scope of application is unclear.[141]

---

[135] Leppänen (1998), p. 438.

[136] There is not much discussion in Sweden either. Peter Westberg has touched the topic from the perspective of fishing expeditions. Westberg (2013), pp. 443–448.

[137] Todistelu yleisissä tuomioistuimissa, OMM 69/2012, Vertailua eräistä todistusoikeudellisista kysymyksistä Suomessa, Ruotsissa, Norjassa ja Tanskassa 31.10.2012 (Oikeusministeriön selvityksiä ja ohjeita 65/2012), Lausuntokooste (Oikeusministeriön mietintöjä ja lausuntoja 30/2013), HE 46/2014 vp, PeVL 39/2014 vp, and LaVM 19/2014 vp.

[138] Chapter 17, Section 26 (FCJP), Chapter 37 (SCJP).

[139] Lundblad (1990), pp. 151–152.

[140] Chapter 17 Sections 6, 40, Chapter 42 Section 8 (SCJP).

[141] Lundblad (1990), p. 151.

East-Scandinavian law permits the disclosure of written evidence to a fairly large extent. Not only is a party obliged to produce written evidence in his/her possession. Disclosure may also be ordered against any holder of a document that may be presumed to have evidentiary value. This obligation applies also to persons who are not parties to the dispute. The difficulty is, however, that to obtain a court order the applicant will have to identify the document with such clarity that, if need be, the order can be enforced by a bailiff. The courts tend to uphold the identification requirement to prevent fishing expeditions. The result is that disclosure of unknown documents becomes difficult. One of way in which the identification problems may be solved is for the requesting party to ask the court for permission in the course of the preparatory proceeding to call witnesses who may be privy to the existence and the contents of relevant documents. This approach has gained increasing popularity in recent years. It tends to make the documentary disclosure rules more efficient.[142]

Before the main hearing, a witness cannot be compelled to disclose what his or her testimony will be. The principle is that the witness is heard at the main hearing and may be forced to give testimony only at the main hearing. The only exception is where the court grants a request that for special reasons a witness should give testimony before the main hearing. Such special reasons include witnesses who for good cause are unable to attend the main hearing or where the cost of bringing the witness to appear at the main hearing would be exorbitant relative to the value of the testimony. This possibility is infrequently used as the courts are reluctant to deviate from the basic procedural rule that the main hearing should be confined to one hearing and that the judgment should be based solely on what transpires in the course of the main hearing.[143]

2.6 Settlements

2.6.1 Judicial Settlement Efforts in Finland

In the reform of 1993 one of the main aims there was to promote settlements during proceedings. Especially the preparatory stage was seen as a suitable playing ground for judicial settlement efforts and settlements. Even one of the functions of the preparatory proceedings can be named to be aiming at the friendly solution of the case.

Of course, the negotiations for the settlement happen usually even before the court proceedings. It is even the duty of the advocate to start the case with the negotiations of that kind. The Finnish Bar Association has adopted the rules of

[142] Chapter 17 Sections 9, 40 (FCJP), Chapter 42 Section 8, Paragraph 1 (SCJP) and Lundblad (1990), pp. 151–152.

[143] Chapter 17 Section 56 (FCJP), Chapter 36 Section 19 (SCJP), Lundblad (1990), p. 152.

proper professional conduct for advocates. According to Section 34, prior to taking legal action an advocate must notify the opposing party of his client's demands and give the opposing party reasonable time to consider the claims and an opportunity to reach an amicable settlement. However, when these negotiations have been terminated and the case brought into court, there are possibilities to new negotiations and to settlement as a solution of the case.

The dispute and its limits will become clearer when the case is brought into court. The party has the better possibilities to compare the values between the judgment and the settlement and he/she can take his risk for dismissing the case and for the compensation of the costs of the opposite party in an easier way into consideration when the proceedings have already started. This can be an explanation for the very many settlements made during the preparation in spite of the fact that the earlier negotiations have been terminated.[144]

Through the reform in 1993, the judge was assigned the duty to promote a settlement between the parties. If a settlement cannot be reached, the judge proceeds with the case and adjudicates upon the matter. A settlement can be confirmed by the court, after which it may be enforced.[145]

Nowadays the role of the Finnish judge should also be seen as a peacemaker. During the preparatory stage, the judge should establish whether any prospects of judicial settlement efforts exist. The judge can also put forward proposals for settlement. However, a good trial judge is not always a good peacemaker. This new judicial role requires new characteristics or, at least, new ways in which the judge can work.[146] At the last, the judge must remain a good and neutral judge, whether he or she had made a proposal for settlement or not. When making the final judgment as a judge, he/she should, of course, step away from any previous role as a peacemaker.[147]

Some has seen these two main tasks of the judge in collision. The conflict between promoting settlements and adjudication, that is, how the judge can simultaneously act in the role of a mediator and a judge.[148] Especially the duties of the judge to be impartial and to promote settlements have sometimes seen to be in conflict. Therefore, there has been a wide discussion in Finland on the limits of the promoting of settlements. The question has been how far the judge can go without becoming partial and disqualified.[149] Another question is if the skilled judge is a skilled mediator. The skills for both professions are not always the same.

The third question is that court proceedings and alternative dispute solution—for instance, mediation—are based on different principles and aims.[150] Traditional

---

[144] Lappalainen (2003), p. 796.

[145] Ervasti (2004), pp. 505, 507.

[146] Lesknen (2002), pp. 635–636, 645.

[147] Ervo (1995), p. 61.

[148] Ervasti (2004), p. 506.

[149] Lappalainen (2003), pp. 810–811.

[150] Salminen and Ervasti (2015), pp. 591–592.

court proceedings are based on specific procedural rules that are considered representing formal justice. A court judgement is considered right and legitimate when arrived at by applying the appropriate norms and procedural rules. Conflict resolution, again, is characterised by variable and flexible procedures, aimed at enhancing a settlement between the parties or inducing the parties' co-operation to settle their conflict. The legitimacy of the settlement is in this case measured by the degree of acceptance by the parties or inducing the parties' co-operation to settle their conflict. It is seen that conflict resolution often satisfies the requirement of perceived procedural justice better than do formal court proceedings. In a conflict resolution perspective, traditional court proceedings have been criticised for solving only the legal dispute, whereas the conflict that resides behind the dispute persists. Within legal theory, again, conflict resolution has been criticised for its lack of the guarantees of formal legal certainty.[151]

The Finnish legal rules concerning the promotion of a settlement is fairly scarce, and in legal literature varying views have been advanced concerning the settlements of kind judges should promote, and in what way. If the object is conflict resolution, the settlement aimed at should reflect the will of the parties. The aim is thereby to eliminate the conflict between the parties and restore amicable relations between them. If the goal is dispute resolution, the settlement should be in accordance with substantive law.[152]

Out of the civil disputes that had reached the oral hearing stage in district courts, approximately one-third had resulted in a settlement confirmed by the court. The settlements were mostly arrived at during the preparatory hearing. It is, however, impossible to say if the settlements are attributable to the involvement of the court and to what extent a settlement was reached in negotiations between the parties themselves. The settlements that were confirmed by the courts generally appear to have been genuine compromises, where both parties waived part of their claims.[153]

There have been great variations in judges' practice promoting settlement, and equally so in their understanding of what means they can use to promote a settlement. Judges can be divided into three groups: (1) those that hold a negative attitude towards conflict resolution, (2) those with a moderate approach and (3) those who favour conflict resolution. Judges generally favour conflict resolution and only a few of them are negative about the procedures. The strategy for promoting a settlement used by many of the judges can be described as moderate. The judges actively promote a settlement between the parties, but they avoid measures that might jeopardise their impartiality. For instance, they take a negative attitude towards separate negotiations with the parties (caucuses) and are reluctant to propose a settlement—especially if the parties had not requested one. Caution is

[151] Ervasti (2004), p. 506.
[152] Ervasti (2004), p. 507.
[153] Ervasti (2004), p. 507.

also revealed towards the question what judges may reveal about the position of the parties at the preparatory stage.[154]

Many judges are of the opinion that the difference between adjudication and seeking a settlement is not as great as indicated in theoretical discussions. Judges consider that they, both when they adjudicate and when they promote a settlement, try to solve the conflict between the parties in such a way that it leads to a fair solution that is both just and equitable.[155] One of the problems is that judges' do not always see the differences between court-connected mediation and its possibilities compared with the judicial settlement efforts which have some other positive sides. Both are needed and judges should not neglect any chance to settle whenever parties so wish or there seems to be capacity for such negotiations or other type of settlement activities. Still, the extreme situation is where a judge is too active and eager in settling the case instead of adjudicating it and almost pushes the parties to settle.[156] The reasons can vary, maybe judges wants to keep the desk clean and minimise their workload and even such suspicions have sometimes been presented. Still, to see the limits and chances requires professional eye but those chances should be used whenever they exist. According to the legislator, it is a duty of judges to settle cases in an active way during the preparatory stage and this in normal cases does not make the judge impartial.[157]

2.6.2 The Finnish Court-Connected Mediation

In the spring of 2003 a committee appointed by the Ministry of Justice proposed that a system of court-connected mediation should be introduced in Finland, based on the Norwegian example. The proposal came into force at the beginning of 2006.[158] According to that system, a district court judge may, with the parties' consent, transfer the case to mediation. At this stage, the civil suit would be suspended. The mediator is another judge. If mediation failed, the civil proceedings would continue.[159] The new system was introduced in addition to the earlier system for judicial settlement efforts. So, it is not replacing it.[160]

[154] Ervasti (2004), p. 509.

[155] Ervasti (2004), p. 510.

[156] About the differences between the judicial settlement efforts and the court-connected mediation see Salminen and Ervasti (2015), pp. 598, 610.

[157] HE 78/2000, p. 47.

[158] Court-connected mediation is discussed widely and in details for instance in Ervasti and Nylund (2014).

[159] Sections 4, 5, 9 in the Act of Mediation of Civil Cases in General Courts.

[160] Ervasti (2004), p. 511.

Court-connected mediation[161] in a dispute may be instituted if both parties to the dispute so wish. A further condition is that the dispute is suited to mediation and that mediation makes sense considering the requirements presented by the parties. The court decides whether or not a mediation procedure shall be initiated.[162]

Court-connected mediation can be applied to disputes that also otherwise are brought before court. The difference of opinion between the parties concerned may relate to some dispute over a contract, legacy or injury indemnification.[163] Concerning the mediation in family cases Finland adopted also a specific model—similar to the Norwegian one—as a part of the child-friendly justice project.[164]

In court-connected mediation, a judge of the District Court acts as mediator. Mediation is a part of the ordinary tasks of a judge. If the case requires specific knowledge of some area, the mediator may, with the agreement of the parties, engage an assistant whose fee is paid by the parties. Otherwise, each party pays only his or her own costs and is not obliged to pay the costs of the opponent.[165]

One of the parties to a dispute or both parties may together request the initiation of mediation. Mediation in a dispute may be request already before the case becomes pending. The party who is interested in mediation files an application for that with the court. The application may be freely formulated but should contain a short description of the dispute and the parties involved and the applicant's view of chances to solve the dispute by mediation.[166]

The parties to a dispute may request mediation in a case already subject to legal proceedings before the court. In such a case, no specific application is needed. In addition, the court may suggest mediation in a pending case. The suggestion should be made during the preparation.[167] Successful mediation requires an honest effort by both parties to reach an amicable solution. It is not the mediator who must find a solution to the dispute but the parties themselves. However, upon mutual agreement between the parties, also the mediator may render a proposal for resolution of the dispute.[168]

Mediation takes the form of discussions between the judge and the parties involved. The judge discusses either with both parties present or with one of the parties at a time. Also other persons may be heard, when necessary. The mediation

161 This English information on mediation can be found on the websites of the Ministry of Justice (http://www.om.fi, visited 2015-05-12).

162 Sections 3, 4 in the Act of Mediation of Civil Cases in General Courts.

163 Section 18 in the Act of Mediation of Civil Cases in General Courts.

164 HE 186/2013.

165 Sections 5, 14 in the Act of Mediation of Civil Cases in General Courts.

166 Section 4 in the Act of Mediation of Civil Cases in General Courts.

167 Section 4 in the Act of Mediation of Civil Cases in General Courts.

168 Section 7 in the Act of Mediation of Civil Cases in General Courts.

process should not go on unduly long without producing a result, and therefore intensive mediation should be conducted during, for instance, for two days.[169]

Mediation is usually public, i.e. the general public may be present at mediation. However, the general public is not admitted into the negotiations between the judge and one of the parties. Also, other phases of the mediation process may be closed for the general public, if one of the parties so wishes and the mediator so decides. Requirements for the closed mediation process are that it would prefer the aim of mediation and the fairness of the mediation can be truly achieved without open process and there is no other reason for the public process.[170]

No minutes are taken during mediation and the discussions are neither recorded on tape nor saved in some other way. If the mediation is successful, the conditions can be set down in an agreement. The result can be, for instance, financial compensation, work to be done or the transmission of property.[171]

At the request of the parties involved, the court may confirm the settlement agreement. In that case, the agreement constitutes an enforceable judgement, which provide the basis for recovery of, for example, a payment or compensation for damage or maintenance payment by enforcement order.[172] In case the settlement has not been confirmed, the settlement agreement constitutes an ordinary agreement between the parties and is legally binding on them.

One problem from the parties' perspective is the publicity of confirmed settlements. There is no specific rule for confirmed settlements. They are court documents like all other material, and the regular rules on publicity are valid.[173] If they include for instance trade secrets, the parties may prefer not to ask the court to confirm it to keep the secrecy.[174]

Mediation can be terminated if one of the parties so wishes. It is also possible for the judge to terminate the mediation procedure if there is no real prospect for settlement.[175]

After the termination of mediation, the parties may—if they so wish—initiate court litigation proceedings. If a litigation procedure was started already before mediation, it is continued. The judge presiding over the civil proceedings is not the same person as the judge acting as mediator. Circumstances put forward by a party during the mediation shall not be invoked before the court.[176]

Mediation may also be applied at the Court of Appeal to cases decided by a District Court. The Act covers all general courts.[177]

---

[169] Section 6 in the Act of Mediation of Civil Cases in General Courts.

[170] Section 12 in the Act of Mediation of Civil Cases in General Courts.

[171] Section 8 in the Act of Mediation of Civil Cases in General Courts.

[172] Section 8 in the Act of Mediation of Civil Cases in General Courts.

[173] HE 114/2004.

[174] Tuominen (2008), p. 73.

[175] Section 9 in the Act of Mediation of Civil Cases in General Courts.

[176] Sections 9, 13 and 15 in the Act of Mediation of Civil Cases in General Courts.

[177] Section 1 in the Act of Mediation of Civil Cases in General Courts.

2.6.3 Sweden: Judicial Settlement Efforts Instead of Court-Connected Mediation

In Sweden, about 60 % of civil cases are settled by a friendly settlement during the preparatory stage.[178] However, the "court-connected mediation"[179] is not that common.[180] Still, arbitration has a long tradition in Sweden and is a popular way to solve especially business disputes, as already explained above.[181] Still, in non-mandatory cases even the mediation is possible. In such a situation, the court may decide the special mediator will continue the mediation. Mediation is possible in large and complicated cases. The requirement is that the parties agree that the mediation will be the next step in proceedings. The mediator can be even an expert—such as an engineer or economist—but it must be underlined that it is important that the mediator has judicial knowledge as well. Therefore, it is also possible to use many different persons as mediators in the same case.[182]

Also in Sweden, a judgement may also be pronounced in certain other cases without going to the main hearing. Such is the case if the event the plea of the claimant is acceded to or if the parties to a dispute reach a settlement and wish the court to give legal status to such judicial settlement efforts.[183] According to the government's bill, the session by phone is not allowed to organise in the situations of judicial settlement efforts.[184] The reason for this regulation is that during judicial

[178] According to court statistics, the amount of civil cases at district courts where the case has been decided by a judgment are the following: (per cent) in 2008, 40.5 %; in 2009, 40.2 %; in 2010, 40.4 %; in 2011, 42 %; and, in 2012, 41.2 %, 2013, 43.5 % and in 2014, 43.4 %. http://www.domstol.se/Publikationer/Statistik/domstolsstatistik_2014.pdf, visited 2015-11-08, http://www.domstol.se/Publikationer/Statistik/Domstolsstatistikpercent2012.pdf, visited 2015-11-08. Similar results also in Lindell (2012), p. 303, and in SOU 1982:26, p. 137, which shows us that the trend has quite long traditions by now.

[179] The term 'court-connected mediation' is in parentheses because some scholars are of opinion that there is no court-connected mediation in Sweden compared with Finland, Norway and Denmark. See Salminen and Ervasti (2015), p. 592. It is true that the court-connected mediation is more common, discussed and perhaps developed in the other Nordic countries, especially if the word court-connected is stressed. Still, the EU mediation directive (Directive 2008/52/EC of the European Parliament and of the Council of 21 May 2008 on certain aspects of mediation in civil and commercial matter) has been implemented also in Sweden and the mediation exists. However, the implementation was made with the minimum changes into the earlier legislation. More about the implementation and its effects see, Ervo and Sippel (2012) pp. 389–391, Dahlqvist (2014), pp. 137–155.

[180] Dahlqvist (2014), p. 139. Ficks was already in 2008 rather negative and discussed the Swedish mediation from critical perspective. His criticism is directed especially on lacks in process models concerning the judicial settlement efforts and court-connected mediation. Fics (2008), pp. 493–523.

[181] SOU (1995:65), p. 115, Autio (2014a), p. 29.

[182] Sippel (2014), p. 188.

[183] Chapter 42, Section 18 (SCJP).

[184] Prop. 1986/87:89, p. 200.

settlement efforts the parties should have a personal contact with each other. In such circumstances, the climate for the friendly settlement is the best. On the other hand, it would also be difficult to conciliate in an equal way between parties by phone.[185]

According to Chapter 42, Section 6 (SCJP), the court shall investigate if there are possibilities for settlement in the case. This rule covers both mandatory and non-mandatory civil cases. However, in non-mandatory civil cases the court has a wider duty to promote settlement. In mandatory cases, the judicial settlement efforts can mean the discussion on the facts, for instance, which would be the best resolution for the child in the custody cases.[186]

The judge may argument during judicial settlement efforts with precedents and judicial doctrines. The arguments should be clear and simple. The judge should, however, bear in his mind that he/she cannot be sure on the judicially right decision yet at this stage: he/she has not, for instance, heard the testimony and the advocacy yet.[187] According to many Swedish judges, the judge has to be also careful because of the risk of becoming disqualified on the basis of too active and too substantive a judicial settlement efforts. It must also be pointed out that the parties may as well wonder why the judge is so passive and quiet and why he/she does not discuss on some points at all. Even that kind of behaviour can make the judge untrustworthy and partial in the parties' eyes. Brolin and others will, therefore, recommend the open discussion, where the judge may be active and even to some extent substantive, if he/she tells in an open way, what and why he/she is doing and discussing.[188]

The "climate" has become friendlier to judicial settlement efforts in Sweden during after the Code of 1948. The legislator had quite a negative attitude towards judicial settlement efforts in the 1948 reform. The reason was that the proposal for settlement made by the court would destroy the parties' trustworthiness towards the court. Nowadays it is quite acceptable to make proposals for settlement. One of the reasons is that the judicial settlement efforts have been seen more effective and cheaper way of the procedure than the traditional court proceedings would be.[189]

Earlier some were of the opinion that only judicial points can be discussed in judicial settlement efforts and the judge may not take external points into discussion at all. Nowadays when the climate has become more positive, it is quite possible to take some external points—such as procedural economy or even good relationships in the family or in business—into discussion.[190]

[185] Brolin et al. (1997), p. 92.
[186] Brolin et al. (1997), p. 135.
[187] Brolin et al. (1997), p. 130.
[188] Brolin et al. (1997), p. 134.
[189] Lindell (2003), p. 271.
[190] Brolin et al. (1997), p. 129.

2.7 Conclusions: Efficiency and Flexibility

In Finland, the reformed civil procedure has brought about essential changes in the nature of the work of judges and lawyers as well as the nature of court's activities, affecting the whole court culture. The former civil procedure was mainly based on written documents. The parties played a minor role whereas lawyers dominated the proceedings. In contrast, the preparatory hearing and efforts to promote settlements in district courts offer flexibility and give the parties an opportunity to take part in process. The procedure now gives room for more co-operation. There is further more interaction and dialogue in civil proceedings than was the case earlier. The new procedure has set novel preconditions, but it equally possesses new qualitative requirements for the work of judges and lawyers. Much more skills for handling human relations and communicative skills are today required from lawyers, although all judges and lawyers do not yet possess such skills.[191]

In Finland, the role of conflict resolution outside courts has been increasing and more emphasis is placed on alternative procedures[192] like conflict resolution even in courts. With this trend, the personality and professional skills of judges are accentuated and equally so their personal responsibility for their decisions. In addition, there is a stronger focus on the subjective experience of procedural justice. All these changes reflect a changed role for courts and civil proceedings.[193]

It could be said that the application of law in courts and the entire Finnish court culture has undergone a radical change.[194] There is growing emphasis on procedural justice, on a client-centred approach, as well as on communicative skills and interaction. Increasing focus is placed on conflict resolution and means are devised for alternative procedures alongside traditional adjudication. In essential ways, all these factors influence the traditional work of the courts and their personnel. Justice cannot be based merely on formal legal rules and procedures. Instead, the changing environment where courts operate requires a new kind of professionalism and proficiency involving ethical and moral dimensions.[195]

In its modern form, also the adversarial principle (*audiatur et altera pars*) bears with it, as a human and fundamental right, the chance for active involvement in a trial. The parties have to have an equal opportunity to present their case and to

---

[191] Ervasti (2004), p. 511.

[192] The mediation is possible in the general courts and the role of settlements during proceedings has become important after the reform of 1993. There are also mediation processes outside the court. The Finnish Bar Association has the mediation system and services. For further information see http://www.asianajajat.fi, visited 2015-05-12. Outside the court there is even another mediation system in Finland. It is possible in criminal litigation and in cases concerning damages with minor interest. The mediator is a voluntary layman and the service is normally organised by communities. See the Act on Judicial settlement efforts in Criminal matters and in some civil cases (9.12.2005/1015).

[193] Ervasti (2004), p. 512.

[194] Ervo (2013), pp. 51–71.

[195] Ervasti (2004), p. 512.

participate in the proceedings. The in-quality of the starting-point has to be brought into a rightful balance by emphasising the legal security of the weaker party. The parties in the case have to be guaranteed sufficient practical means for their participation so as to put forward their side of the matter. Neither lack of resources nor ignorance should serve to hinder the exercise of their adversarial right. Nor should participation of this kind be prevented or restricted by the imposition of too strict a set of procedural limitations upon the hearing of the case. Nowadays the adversarial right covers much more than the provision of a formal opportunity to be heard in answering the contentions of the other side.[196]

The other main trend, especially in Finland, namely, an alternative conflict resolution mechanism—for example, court-connected mediation—has sometimes been considered as a more discursive procedure than the traditional trial form. It may, indeed, be true that discourse through the court-connected mediation may constitute a more communicative milieu than the traditional trial, which is more formally bound. Likewise, for example, an outburst of moral feelings can be borne more readily in unofficial proceedings. However, there are many perils, too, in an unofficial milieu and these can reduce the scope of discursiveness. Procedural rules and methods are not entirely to be understood as limitations on the maximising of discursiveness: they can also have protective and enhancing significance. A more regulated approach, bound to a specific and well-known form, is not inevitably a hindrance, but may also be a safeguard for a many-sided communicative activity. It is only necessary to think, for instance, of the protection of the weaker party against the manipulation of the stronger. Procedural forms that guarantee the participation of all parties constitute in situations of this kind a bulwark for a many-sided and coercion-free communication.[197]

To sum up, a system based on the concept of a fair trial is a communicative one. A fair trial, in particular, communication has an important procedural role. The adversarial principle and the other principles that enhance communicativeness serve to strengthen the chances of realizing a fair trial. Indeed, they constitute its very core.[198] Especially, the Finnish proceedings can be seen more communicative than earlier and the preparation is a very important phase in order to maximize the discursive nature of the procedure. Where the Swedish preparatory stage is concerned, the increasing value of the delegation principle in the name of the party-autonomy and the flexibility in forms are the main features. On the one side, they serve the efficiency and are linked with the State economy. On the other side, they are manifestations on the same phenomenon where the parties can be seen as clients and the adjudication can be called court-service.

Orality and immediacy are naturally key principles as far as a trial is looked at as a communicative activity between the parties involved and the court itself. Written communication or communication through an intermediary is inevitably poorer

[196] Ervo (2005), p. 451.
[197] Ervo (2005), pp. 457–458.
[198] Ervo (2005), p. 458.

forms if compared with oral communication.[199] However, these fundamental principles have recently been radically reduced in the East-Scandinavian countries, especially in Sweden, to give more space for flexibility in the case. This means that actors can choose the best forms to handle the case in the most rational and functional way. Still, the court can make the final decision on the procedural form (for instance, choose between written and oral preparation) but usually the parties wishes play a significant role in this consideration. This development can be seen as a positive if it really guarantees the best way to handle the case. There should, namely, not be any forms without an acceptable aim and in the case of civil proceedings the aim is always to guarantee the most effective procedure. Still, the most effective procedure includes the balance between the judicial relief and effectiveness as commonly known. However, the East-Scandinavian, party autonomy plays nowadays a more significant role in this balancing than before. It is typical, especially in Sweden but also in Finland, to think that the parties know best their needs and they should get that service they wish even at courts. So, for instance, the modification of judicial relief is acceptable if the parties prefer conflict resolution and therefore appreciate some other interests to better continue their lives for example as business partners.

The other reason for this flexibility in procedural forms is, however, the State economy. Even the Nordic countries, especially Finland, struggle with the European and to some extent global economic crisis, which means that the State budget must be strongly reduced to make ends meet needs. To be successful in this aim, the public services, included courts, have to work in a more intensive way than before. There is no longer time or human resources for endless proceedings but the cases should be decided quickly and mainly at the early stages of procedures. To reach this aim, the East-Scandinavian legislators have intensified especially the preparatory stage by many procedural tools to activate the parties to co-operate in an effective and active way, to sanction those parties who stay as passive, to decide the case as soon as it matures for the decision despite of the procedural stage, and finally to give space for tailored solutions during the preparation to prepare the single case in a way which is the most effective in the current circumstances.

What the practicalities are concerned, the Swedish and Finnish preparatory proceedings are very similar and based on the same main procedural principles namely orality, immediacy and concentration. This is no wonder because the Swedish system has been a model for Finland. Even the historical development has been much closed to each other. Finland has namely started with the same starting points and strict rules in order to respect these principles named above even when Sweden has already ceased to use them as a whole and made some exceptions because of the reasonableness and the practical needs. Later the same need for re-reform with exceptions and rules with more discretion came current also in Finland.

---

[199] Ervo (2005), p. 454.

It is typical for the civil proceedings in these both countries that there are two different stages, namely the preparatory stage and then the main hearing. In this system, the preparatory hearing plays a very important role. The function of preparation is to serve the main hearing. The other function is to have a possibility to decide clear and simple cases as soon as they are ready for decision. Therefore, there are many possibilities to decide the case finally already during the preparatory stage and without the main hearing. The trend has been to add these possibilities. Nowadays even the decision based on documentary merits is possible in some situations during the preparatory stage.

The main difference in general is that in Sweden there is even more discretion in procedural rules covering the preparatory stage. Especially the principle of orality has been modified more than in Finland in the name of reasonableness. However, the Swedish procedure as a whole is based on the orality which has been seen as a very important and valuable principle also in post-modern proceedings, where the technical possibilities, that is phone and video conference, are increased the possibilities refuse to organise the face-to-face sessions. In spite of these modern possibilities the oral hearing, where all the parties and the members of the court are at present at the same time, has been seen very important in order to maximise the communication in the proceedings. The best possible communication is important because it serves the effectiveness of the proceedings including time, costs and legal certainty.[200]

References

Almkvist G, Elofsson N (2013) Rättegångskostnader i förenklade tvistemål. Svensk Juristtidning 150–168

Autio A-L (2014a) Lainkäyttö yritysten riidanratkaisussa. Talentum, Helsinki

Autio A-L (2014b) The main problems in access to court regarding the dispute resolution of Finnish companies. In: Ervo L, Nylund A (eds) The future of civil litigation: access to court and court-annexed mediation in the Nordic countries. Springer, Cham, pp 213–229

Brolin T, Rehnström Å, Widebeck M (1997) Tvistemålsprocessen I. En handledning för förberedelsen, 2nd edn. Norstedts Juridik AB, Stockholm

Bylander E (2004) Processuella handlingsformer. Muntlighet, skriftlighet och ny teknik. Rhetorica Scandinavica. Tidsskrift för Skandinavisk Retorikforskning 31:60–64

Bylander E (2005) Muntlighetsprincipen vid domstol i Sverige. In: Bylander E, Lindblom PH (eds) Muntlighet vid domstol i Norden. En rättsvetenskaplig, rättspsykologisk och rättsetnologisk studie av presentationsformernas betydelse i förfarandet vid domstol i Norden. Iustus Förlag, Uppsala, pp 95–131

Bylander E (2006) Muntlighetsprincipen. Iustus Förlag, Uppsala

Bylander E (2007) En modernare rättegång och bättre? Svensk Juristtidning 516–526

[200] See, for instance, Bylander (2006). The author of this fresh thesis deals with the opinion summarised above.

Dahlqvist A (2014) Mediation in the Swedish courts: change by EU directive? In: Ervo L, Nylund A (eds) The future of civil litigation. Access to court and court-annexed mediation in the Nordic countries. Springer, Cham, pp 249–280

Ekeberg K-G (2013) En ännu modernare rättegång? Svensk Juristtidning: pp 169–175

Ekelöf PO, Edelstam H, Pauli M (2011) Rättegång. Femte häftet. Åttonde upplagan. Nordstedts Juridik, Stockholm

Ervasti K (2004) Käräjäoikeuksien sovintomenettely. Empiirinen tutkimus sovinnon edistämisestä riitaprosessissa. Oikeuspoliittinen tutkimuslaitos, Helsinki

Ervasti K, Nylund A (2014) Konfliktinratkaisu ja sovittelu. Edita, Helsinki

Ervo L (1995) The reform of civil procedure in Finland. Civ Just Q 56–64

Ervo L (2001) Order for payment in Finland. In: Rechberger WH, Kodek GE (eds) Orders for payment in the European Union / Mahnverfahren in der Europäischen Union / L'Injonction de Payer dans l'Union Européenne. Kluwer Law International, The Hague, pp 121–129

Ervo L (2005) Oikeudenmukainen oikeudenkäynti. WSOY, Helsinki

Ervo L (2011) The role of judges and party-autonomy in settlement in litigation – a Scandinavian perspective. In: Stürner R, Kawano M (eds) International contract litigation, arbitration and judicial responsibility in transnational disputes. Mohr–Siebeck, Tübingen, pp 336–357

Ervo L (2013) Changing civil proceedings: court service or state economy? In: Recent trends in economy and efficiency of civil procedure. Vilnius University Press, Vilnius, pp 51–71

Ervo L (2014) Nordic court culture in progress: historical and futuristic perspectives. In: Ervo L, Nylund A (eds) The future of civil litigation. Access to court and court-annexed mediation in the Nordic countries. Springer, Cham, pp 383–407

Ervo L (2015) Comparative analysis between East-Scandinavian countries: Scandinavian Studies in Law. Comp Law 61:135–152

Ervo L, Dahlqvist A (2014) Delays in civil proceedings: comparative studies between Finland and Sweden. In: Ervo L, Nylund A (eds) The future of civil litigation. Access to court and court-annexed mediation in the Nordic countries. Springer, Cham, pp 249–280

Ervo L, Sippel L (2012) Scandinavian countries. In: Mota CE, Buhigues JLI, Moreno GP (eds) Civil and commercial mediation in Europe, I. Intersentia, Mortsel, pp 371–426

Fics E (2008) Om domstolarnas förlikningsverksamhet i Sverige. Australien och Japan – en kritisk utvärdering av det svenska systemet Svensk Juristtidning 493–523

Fitger P (1993) Domstolsprocessen. En kommetar till rättegångsbalken. Norstedts Juridik, Stockholm

HE 114/2004 Hallituksen esitys Eduskunnalle riita-asioiden sovittelua ja sovinnon vahvistamista yleisissä tuomioistuimissa koskevaksi lainsäädännöksi

HE 15/1990 Hallituksen esitys Eduskunnalle riita-asiain oikeudenkäyntimenettelyn uudistamista alioikeuksissa koskevaksi lainsäädännöksi

HE 186/2013 Hallituksen esitys eduskunnalle laeiksi lapsen huollosta ja tapaamisoikeudesta annetun lain, riita-asioiden sovittelusta ja sovinnon vahvistamisesta yleisissä tuomioistuimissa annetun lain 5 ja 10 §:n sekä sosiaalihuoltolain 17 §:n muuttamisesta

HE 32/2001Hallituksen esitys Eduskunnalle laiksi oikeudenkäymiskaaren ja eräiden muiden lakien riita-asiain valmistelua, pääkäsittelyä sekä hakemusasioiden käsittelyä koskevien säännösten muuttamisesta

HE 46/2014 Hallituksen esitys Eduskunnalle Oikeudenkäymiskaaren 17 luvun ja siihen liittyvän todistelua yleisissä tuomioistuimissa koskevan lainsäädännön uudistamiseksi

HE 78/2000 Hallituksen esitys Eduskunnalle tuomarin esteellisyyttä koskevaksi lainsäädännöksi

Lagrådsremiss En modernare rättegång II, 13 maj 2015

Landström S, Willén R, Bylander E (2012) Rättspraktikers inställning till modern ljud- och bildteknik i rättssalen – en rättspsykologisk studie. Svensk Juristtidning 197–218

Lappalainen J (2002) Siviilijutun käsittely käräjäoikeudessa vuoden 2002 uudistuksen mukaan. Helsingin yliopiston oikeustieteellinen tiedekunta, Helsinki

Lappalainen J (2003) Siviilijutun käsittely. In: Lappalainen J, Frände D, Koulu R, Niemi-Kiesiläinen J, Rautio J, Sihto J, Virolainen J (eds) Prosessioikeus. WSOY, Helsinki, pp 773–817
LaVM 19/2014 Lakivaliokunnan mietintö hallituksen esityksestä eduskunnalle oikeudenkäymiskaaren 17 luvun ja siihen liittyvän todistelua yleisissä tuomioistuimissa koskevan lainsäädännön uudistamiseksi
Leppänen T (1998) Riita-asian valmistelu todistusaineiston osalta. Suomalainen Lakimiesyhdistys, Vammala
Lesknen M (2002) Käräjäoikeus riidan ratkaisijana. Defensor Legis 2(2002):630–646
Léven S, Wersäll F (2011) En modernare rättegång – hur har det gått? Svensk Juristtidning 18–31
Lindell B (2003) Civilprocessen, 2nd edn. Iustus Förlag, Uppsala
Lindell B (2012) Civilprocessen, 3rd edn. Iustus Förlag, Uppsala
Litmala M, Alasaari K, Salovaara-Karstu C (2007) Oikeusapu-uudistuksen seurantatutkimuksen osaraportti II. Research Communications 77. National Research Institute of Legal Policy, Helsinki
Lundblad C (1990) Sweden. In: Platto C (ed) Preparatory and pre-hearing procedures worldwide. Graham & Trotman and International Bar Association, London
Nylund A (2002) Rättshjälp och rättegångskostnader. Tidskrift utgiven av Juridiska föreningen i Finland 3(2002):279–294
Oikeusministeriön selvityksiä ja ohjeita 65/2012, Vertailua eräistä todistusoikeudellisista kysymyksistä Suomessa, Ruotsissa, Norjassa ja Tanskassa 31.10.2012
OMM 30/2013. Todistelu yleisissä tuomioistuimissa. Lausuntokooste. Oikeusministeriön mietintöjä ja lausuntoja
OMM 69/2012. Todistelu yleisissä tuomioistuimissa, Oikeusministeriön mietintöjä ja lausuntoja
PeVL 39/2014. Perustuslakivaliokunnan lausunto hallituksen esityksestä eduskunnalle Oikeudenkäymiskaaren 17 luvun ja siihen liittyvän todistelua yleisissä tuomioistuimissa koskevan lainsäädännön uudistamiseksi
Prop. 1986/87:89. Proposition 1986/87:89 om ett reformerat tingsrättsförfarande
Prop. 2004/05:131. En modernare rättegång – reformering av processen i allmän domstol
Saarensola S (2014) The risk of legal costs and its effects on access to court. In: Ervo L, Nylund A (eds) The future of civil litigation. Access to court and court-annexed mediation in the Nordic countries. Springer, Cham, pp 231–248
Salminen K, Ervasti K (2015) Tuomioistuinsovittelun yleistyminen ja tuomioistuimen tehtävät. Lakimies 5(2015):591–612
Sippel L (2014) Comparative aspects between the Nordic countries and Austria: court mediation in or out? In: Ervo L, Nylund A (eds) The future of civil litigation. Access to court and court-annexed mediation in the Nordic countries. Springer, Cham, pp 185–209
Sippo J, Välimaa A (2003) Siviiliprosessin muutetut säännökset. Talentum, Helsinki
SOU 1982:26. Statens offentliga utredningar. Översyn av rättegångsbalken. I. Processen i tingsrätt. Del B. Motiv mm. Delbetänkande av rättegångsutredningen
SOU 1995:65. Statens offentliga utredningar. Näringslivets tvistlösning
SOU 2012:93, del 1. Statens offentliga utredningar. En modernare rättegång II - en uppföljning, del 1 huvudbok
SOU 2012:93, del 2. Statens offentliga utredningar. En modernare rättegång II - en uppföljning, del 2 bilagor.
Tuominen, J (2008) Sovinnon vahvistamisen edellytykset ja vaikutukset tuomioistuinsovittelussa. Pro gradu, The University of Lapland, Rovaniemi. Available on Edilex, 26.5.2008. www.edilex.fi/lakikirjasto/5198, visited 2015-11-12
Westberg P (2013) Nordiskt fiskafänge. Svensk Juritstidning 443–448

Chapter 3
Preparatory Proceedings in Norway: Efficiency by Flexibility and Case Management

Anna Nylund

Abstract Active use of the preparatory stage to promote a concentrated main hearing is a key element in Norwegian civil procedure. The judge actively manages the cage and prepares it for the main hearing. Judicial discretion is an important tool to allow the judge to tailor the proceedings to the need of the parties. If an issue or question is unclear, the judge has a duty to help the parties clarify the issues and provide guidance by helping parties identify disputed and undisputed facts and argument and to separate core questions from questions that are more peripheral. The judge has a duty to promote settlement either by judicial settlement efforts or by diverting the case to court-connected mediation. When appropriate, the case can be disposed of during the preparatory stage. The format of preparatory proceedings is flexible: the judge has discretion to combine written and oral proceedings and use telephone hearings. The 2008 reform of Norwegian civil procedure, which emphasised the role of preparatory proceedings, has made civil litigation swifter and cheaper. It has also enhanced the quality of proceedings and the outcome. In the final part, Finnish and Norwegian preparatory proceedings are compared. Norway has a long tradition of concentrated oral hearings, promotion of settlement and an active judge, whereas these ideas were introduced in Finland only in 1993. The comparison explores how the underlying structure and culture of civil proceedings influence the implementation of the main hearing model in countries with a similar (legal) culture.

A. Nylund (✉)
Faculty of Law, University of Tromsø – The Arctic University of Norway, 9037 Tromsø, Norway
e-mail: anna.nylund@uit.no

L. Ervo, A. Nylund (eds.), *Current Trends in Preparatory Proceedings*,
DOI 10.1007/978-3-319-29325-7_3

3.1 Introduction

In this chapter, the preparatory proceedings in the Norwegian civil justice system are disseminated. Norway has one of the most efficient civil justice systems with an average disposition time of slightly over five months for litigious civil cases. In 2008, the Norwegian laws on civil procedure were completely modernized and a pure main hearing-model of civil justice was introduced.

The main features of the reform of the preparatory proceedings will be discussed and the impact of the reform on the functioning and result of civil proceedings will be analysed. In the next part, a short introduction to the Norwegian civil procedure system is given. Then, the structure and goals of the preparatory proceedings are disseminated. After that, the different tools available during the preparatory proceedings and the significance of the end of the preparatory proceedings are examined in closer detail. The tools available and the rules on ending the preparatory stage are the core elements of the Norwegian system. Subsequently, two separate tracks of civil proceedings, court-connected mediation and the small claims track, are discussed. Lastly, the Norwegian system is evaluated and contrasted with the current Finnish system.

3.2 The Structure and Principles Norwegian Civil Procedure

Norway is a part of the Nordic legal family, thus is civil justice system has many typical features of other Nordic legal systems.

Norway has a very simple *structure of the court system*. There is only one set of courts, handling administrative, civil, commercial, and criminal cases. The same courts and the same judges sit all kinds of cases. The court system is three-tiered with almost all cases starting in one of the 66 *District Courts*, which decisions can be appealed to one of six *Court of Appeal*. The *Norwegian Supreme Court* hears mainly cases which can serve as precedent. There are almost no special courts and no constitutional court. All courts have powers to perform judicial review, and the Norwegian Supreme Court regularly assesses the constitutionality of laws.

The *Conciliation Boards* (forliksråd) are a special feature of the Norwegian court system. The Conciliation Boards are not courts by definition, yet they are the mandatory first instance for claims with a primarily pecuniary interest of no more than NOK 125,000 (about EUR 15,000). Family law and administrative law cases are exempted, as are cases where both parties have legal representation. The Conciliation Boards have a panel of three lay members, and have only limited powers to decide a case. About 70 % of cases are solved by a default judgement. The Conciliation Boards have limited powers to decide a case. Only if both parties agree to let the Board decide the case, and the case is simple, may the Board decide a litigious case. There is a judgment in less than 5 % of all cases. The judgment can be appealed to the District Courts.[1]

Norwegian civil procedure is based primarily on the Austrian code of civil procedure from the late nineteenth century, mixed with old Nordic traditions and Danish procedural law. The previous *Civil Procedure Act* (tvistemålsloven), which was valid from 1915 to 2007, was influenced to a high degree of the ideas of Franz Klein. Although the concepts, structure and theories of civil procedure are clearly from the Germanic civil law tradition, the proceedings themselves reflect the common law tradition. The oral "trial" has been the core of the hearing, the proceedings can be described as more adversarial than "inquisitorial", and lay judges have an important role in the system. The judge has had the right to promote settlement. The court culture is very pragmatic, with a tendency to seek for the most practical solution rather than the solution fitting the theories and constructions of the law. The procedural rules are seldom formalistic, giving extensive discretion to the judge.

The *Civil Procedure Act* had rules on the preparatory stage. Usually the preparatory stage was written. The aim of the stage was to ensure that the main hearing could be conducted in a single session, but the purpose was still very vague. However, in practise the preparatory stage was often very limited, as it only consisted of asking the defendant to present claims, defences and other contentions in writing. In other words, the preparatory stage was in fact the pleadings stage. In more complicated cases, the court could ask the claimant to prepare a summary of the facts of the case regardless of whether the facts were disputed. The defendant would then comment on the summary. If a preparatory hearing was conducted, the parties could discuss the case and the judge could promote settlement.[2]

At the end of the 1990s a full reform of the civil procedure was initiated by the government. The proposal for new rules on civil procedure, published in 2001, was heavily influenced by the 1998 reform of English civil procedure. *The Act relating to mediation and procedure in civil disputes, the Dispute Act*[3] (hereinafter DA) was enacted in 2005 and entered into force in 2008. It is based on main hearing model of civil procedure, where the preparatory stage has an important role. According to the preparatory works *(travaux preparatoires)*, the main aims of the reform was to ensure that the courts would provide *adequate, fairly cheap and swift dispute resolution* and to ensure *effective and uniform application of laws*. The courts must be accessible, providing "correct" solutions swiftly and cheap.[4]

Although the regulation of civil procedure is very modern and Norway in general is technologically advanced society, the courts have outdated information

[1] The total annual number of cases is higher than 110,000. The statistics are on file with the author.

[2] Skoghøy (2001) pp. 486–500.

[3] Lov 17.6.2005 nr. 90 om mekling og rettergang i sivile tvister (tvisteloven). Unofficial English translation available at http://www.ub.uio.no/ujur/ulovdata/lov-20050617-090-eng.pdf. An English and a German translation is available in Lipp and Fredriksen (2011), p. 135 et seq.

[4] NOU 2001: 32, pp. 127–129.

technology systems. Documents, including the statement of claim can be sent by e-mail, but otherwise access to modern technology is limited to word processing, e-mail, internet, electronic databases and case registration systems. Video conferencing, video or audio recording of evidence and electronic processing is not available.

3.3 Preparatory Proceedings in Norway: Structure and Goals

Civil proceedings start with the *pleadings stage*. The proceedings start when the *statement of claim* arrives at the court. The statement must include the name of the court; the names and addresses of parties and their representatives and counsel; the claim that is made and the prayer for relief which is requested; the factual and legal basis for the claim; the evidence which the claimant intends to present; and the claimant's view on the organisation of the proceedings (DA section 9-2). Written evidence must be attached to the statement of claim.

The court proves that the statement of claim fulfils the legal requirements and that the claimant has a legal standing against the defendant. If the statement of claim does not fulfil the requirements the claimant must be given an opportunity to correct it (DA section 16-5) or the case is dismissed. The statement of claim is then served to the defendant. When the statement of claim has been served, the claimant is no longer free to withdraw the case. The case is assigned to a judge who will be responsible for preparing the case for the main hearing. The judge responsible for the preparatory proceedings will usually hear the case in the main hearing. The largest District Courts often assign the case to a different judge for the main hearing to allow for more efficient scheduling.

The *preparatory stage starts* formally when the statement of claim is served to the defendant. The court must decide if the statement of defence is requested in writing, or if it should be presented in a preparatory hearing. In practice, oral replies are almost never used. Self-represented parties can, however, present the statement of claim and the statement of defence orally at the court. A judge will write the statement of claim or the statement of defence for the party. This makes the judge partial and disqualified from deciding the case. The content of the statement of defence must fulfil the same requirements. If a statement of defence is not filed or it is filed after the time limit, a default judgment may be issued. If the defendant admits the claim, or the factual and legal argumentation, the court may decide the case immediately.

The preparatory stage ends two weeks before the main hearing. The main hearing should be held within six months after the court has received the statement of claim. The main hearing is conducted as a single hearing. If the case is complex or if there is much evidence, the case may be heard on several consecutive days. The judge who has been responsible for presiding over the preparatory stage will, in most cases, hear the case in the main hearing. Most cases are heard by a single judge.

The *purpose of the preparatory stage* is to ensure that the case is "heard in a swift, cost effective and sound manner" (DA section 9-4). Four main methods of gaining efficient proceedings and substantially correct results were introduced to reach the goal. All measures require an active judge. First, the judge must involve in active *case management* to avoid delays. Time limits are a tool to enhance clarity and expediency. Second, the judge must help to *clarify issues*, among others, where specific prayers for relief are sought, and on which grounds, facts, pieces of evidence and legal argumentation the claims made are based on. The judge must arrange for clarification of which of the relevant facts that are disputed. Third, the judge must provide *guidance* to the parties when needed and appropriate. Fourth, *amicable solutions* should be promoted by the judge during the proceedings. Settlements are also promoted by encouraging the parties to use mediation and other alternative means of dispute resolution before they file the case.

Fifth, the claims, the factual background of the case, the pieces of evidence presented and the persons which will be heard during the main hearing are "fixed" at the end of the preparatory proceedings by using *preclusion and written closing statements*. An efficient procedure requires that the parties identify the relevant and disputed legal and factual issues early on, and no later than by the start of the main hearing. The legal and factual arguments and the evidence is presented during the main hearing, but the boundaries of the case and identification of the pieces of evidence and the persons to be heard is done during the preparatory stage.

In addition, the proceedings should be *flexible*. The proceedings should be tailored individually to each case. The judges are given discretion to choose if and how they use their powers, as long as the primary goals of efficient proceedings and substantially correct results are achieved. Finally, in a typically Norwegian way, it was stressed that over formalism should be avoided.[5]

The court proceedings are seen as a *cooperation* between the judge and the parties. The parties decide the scope and object of the proceedings, as they have the sole right to decide on the prayers for relief and for introducing the facts and the main legal arguments. The judge presiding over the case has a duty to discuss the organisation of the proceedings with the parties (usually their legal representatives). The parties and the judge cooperate to clarify the case and to identify the main legal and factual issues and the disputed facts and legal arguments.

Paragraph 2 of DA section 9-4 states which methods the judge can use during preparatory proceedings for case management. The list includes:

- court-connected mediation and judicial settlement efforts,
- preparatory hearings,
- the need for written statements,
- deciding the case, or parts of it, during the preparatory stage,

[5] NOU 2001: 32, pp. 132, 140–141.

- how evidence should be presented, secured or produced; use of expert witnesses,
- if lay judges or expert judges should participate in deciding the case,
- the need for special proceedings,
- setting time limits and a date for the main hearing,
- the need to split the case,
- the need for closing statements,
- other issues of importance.

Hence, the judge has many alternatives to consider. The decision on the preparatory proceedings is made after the judge has consulted the parties by telephone or, in some cases, in writing or even in person. The plan for the preparatory proceedings may be adjusted as needed. The judge must hear the parties before adjusting the plan. As the preparatory proceedings should be tailored to the individual case, there is no general pathway for the conduct of preparatory proceedings.

The court may choose between a *written, oral, or a combination of oral and written proceedings*. Written proceedings are cheaper and should therefore be preferred. Hearings should generally be conducted by telephone, as conference calls with the judge and the lawyers attending. *Telephone hearings* are often most convenient way to discuss issues such as the timetable for the hearing at court, use of expert witnesses, on-site inspections, and clarification of claims, facts and evidence.[6]

The concept of a hearing is partly indeterminate during the preparatory proceedings. If a hearing is considered a court hearing *(rettsmøte)*, the court has several obligations, such as to document the meeting and to ensure the presence of the parties, and the public has normally access to the hearing. According to the preparatory works, preparatory hearings during the preparatory stage are court hearings, but there are a few exceptions. The language used in the preparatory works makes the role of the hearings unclear. Telephone conferences between the judge and the parties are not always a court hearing. If the judge only calls to schedule a meeting or to address some other purely technical question, the call is not a hearing. Although the telephone conversation would be considered a hearing, the general public does not have access to the hearing, as it is conducted inside the judge's chambers. Further, the preparatory works state that the judge is supposed to have a planning meeting to plan the preparatory proceedings at the beginning of the preparatory proceedings. However, in practice, there is no hearing *stricto sensu*, in most cases the judge only needs to call the parties (more precisely their legal counsel) to set the date for the main hearing, and to discuss diverting the case to court-connected mediation. The judge usually also encourages the parties to try to settle the case. The term "hearing" might, therefore, seem misleading and turgid.

Judicial settlement efforts and judicial guidance often require that the judge discusses the case with the parties in a preparatory hearing.[7] With judicial guidance,

---

[6] NOU 2001: 32, pp. 710–713 and 749–750, Skoghøy (2014), pp. 620–627.

[7] NOU 2001: 32, p. 750.

parties may drop claims of minor importance or modify their claims. Therefore, the court should consider having a preparatory hearing, instead of a telephone hearing when appropriate. This is especially true with self-represented parties.[8] Disposal of a case often requires a preparatory hearing to satisfy the basic requirements of a fair trial. In practice, preparatory hearings are not very common.[9] Most of the oral communication is done by telephone. Judges use about 10 % of their time in preparatory hearings.[10]

3.4 The Active Role of the Judge

3.4.1 Clarification and Judicial Guidance

One of the aims of civil procedure is to provide for substantially correct judgments. Correct judgments are understood as judgments that are based on true facts and the correct application of law (substantive truth). To achieve the aim, the parties must make the right claims and submissions, and provide appropriate evidence. The court must provide the parties with guidance to prevent errors and to make the parties able to attend to their interests in the case (DA section 11-5). The court will promote clarification of disputed issues, elucidation of the contentions and positions of the parties, and clarification of factual and legal issues. The purpose of clarification and guidance is to ensure that the main proceeding is concentrated on the relevant disputed factual and legal questions.

The court will, in particular, give *guidance* to parties without legal counsel. If there are considerable differences in power between the parties, the court should to some extent try to level out the playing field by giving more guidance to the weaker party. Guidance does not mean that the court can give advice to the parties on which procedural steps they should take or which position they should take. However, the court may ask if a party has evidence to prove a claim, thus inducing the party to present new evidence. The proceedings are party-initiated, and the parties still determine which claims, defences, contentions and evidence they provide.[11]

When giving guidance, the court must refrain from actions that may interfere with its impartiality. The balance between giving enough guidance and ensuring impartiality may sometimes be difficult to strike. The tone of voice or the choice of wording a question may be decisive.[12]

[8] Schei et al. (2012), comment for § 9-5, comment 2. For a different opinion, see Skoghøy (2014), p. 625.

[9] Skoghøy (2014), pp. 627–629.

[10] Evaluering av tvisteloven (2013).

[11] See also Robberstad (2015), 189.

[12] NOU 2001:32, pp. 138–140, 708–710.

Clarification of the key questions and evidence, which questions and arguments are most relevant and which legal questions and facts are disputed, is very important. When the case becomes clear, some of the issues become undisputed or the parties may drop claims, defences or evidence of minor importance. Parties may also realise that a claim or defence will most likely be dismissed, and choose to drop it. They will also become aware of misunderstandings or errors at an early stage. The legal questions often become more defined and pointed. The more concentrated and well-defined the case is, the less likely a party will need to change submissions later, the shorter and more concentrated the main hearing will be, and the less likely the parties will appeal. The preparatory proceedings will also be swifter and the litigation costs will be lower.

Clarification of key legal questions and disputed facts enhance the quality of the argumentation of the parties and the evidence presented during the main hearing. The court may reject evidence that does not appreciably strengthen the case of the party or if the evidence offered is not proportionate with the case (DA sections 21-7 and 21-8). Consequently, the court has a better foundation for its decision and the goal of substantially correct results is promoted.[13]

Before the reform, the case could change throughout the proceedings in the District Courts and well into the Court of Appeal. Sometimes the parties understood what was disputed and which legal questions were the most relevant only after the District Court had decided the case.

The rules on guidance and clarification may require a preparatory hearing. Depending on the case, the quality of the written statements by the parties, issue (s) in need of clarification or correction, and the complexity of the case, clarification and guidance can be given in writing, on the telephone or in a preparatory hearing. Self-represented parties will more often benefit from a preparatory hearing, as will cases with many or complex issues in need of clarification. In many cases, judicial settlement efforts can be combined with guidance and clarification. The parties may understand that the dispute is based on a misunderstanding, or they may realise that the case will be expensive due to a need for extensive evidence. Consequently, the parties may wish to settle the case.

3.4.2 Early Disposal of Cases

Early disposal of cases is important to save the resources of the parties and the court. In order for the courts to save resources, they may decide a case or part of it during the preparatory stage. The judgment may be delivered after purely written proceedings, or the court may decide that a preparatory hearing is necessary to guarantee the parties the right to a fair trial.

[13] NOU 2001: 32, pp. 133–138.

Deciding the case on procedural grounds during the preparatory stage is one of the key tools to ensure efficient proceedings. The court must rule on procedural issues as early as possible (DA section 9-6). The parties are asked to raise any objection to procedural steps by the other party as soon as possible. The time limit is flexible. It depends on the complexity of the procedural step taken, on how obvious the issue is and how complex the issue is. The court cannot rely on the parties finding and reacting to possible problems; active case management requires that the judge in charge reads the statements of the parties and reacts accordingly to any mistakes, unclear actions or problems.

If it is evident that the *claim or part thereof cannot succeed* or the defences presented are unsustainable, the court may decide the case during the preparatory stage in written or oral proceedings (DA section 9-8). The provision should only be used when the court is completely certain of the legal shortcomings of the claim or defence. The simplified judgment proceedings can only be used upon request of the party. The decision is made in written proceedings, but the parties can request a preparatory hearing. The hearing should be limited to the most pertinent questions.[14]

The court may also decide a case on formal grounds if one of the *requirements of justiciability lacks*. If the problem can be corrected, the parties must be given an opportunity to correct the problem. If it is unclear if the case is justiciable, the court must usually hear the parties in writing, by telephone or in a preparatory hearing. If the issue of justiciability is difficult and connected to the claims, the decision can be postponed to the main hearing. If the claim clearly cannot succeed, the court may rule on the claim for the defendant. Thus, the court will not use resources on a difficult procedural question when the outcome of the case regarding the claim is clear in favour of the defendant.[15]

If the court decides to have a *preparatory hearing*, the court may decide the case after the hearing. The requirement is that the court considers itself to have solid basis for doing so and the parties have consented. The parties must have had a sufficient opportunity to present evidence. The relevant written evidence is usually already available, as written evidence is submitted as an appendix to statement of claim and statement of defence. If a preparatory hearing has been held, the court may have sufficient information to decide the case. Deciding the case during the hearing is mostly for simple cases or cases that became simple after partial settlement or successful clarification.

[14] Skoghøy (2014), pp. 630–631.

[15] Skoghøy (2014), p. 620, NOU 2001: 32, pp. 145–146.

3.4.3 *Judicial Settlement Efforts*

Conciliation has been part of the Norwegian legal culture for centuries. One of the aims of the civil justice reform of 2008 was to provide for more settlements *inter alia* by increased use of judicial settlement efforts. Judges had had the right to *promote settlement* under the Civil Procedure Act of 1915, but some judges did not use their powers. Others were active conciliators; some even had *ex parte* meetings, which could be detrimental for the impartiality of the judge.

The judge has a *duty to consider the possibility of* a full or partial *settlement at each stage* of the proceedings (DA section 8-1). Judges have a duty to promote judicial settlement. Judges should not try to settle their cases at every stage of the proceedings, rather they must consider when and how to promote settlement in each case.

The judge can suggest the parties negotiate or encourage settlement by pointing out common ground or the costs and delays resulting from a main hearing. The judge can point out the benefits of a settlement or stress the risks of the legal decision. However, the judge must refrain from actions endangering impartiality. The judge may not have private meetings, suggest (specific) solutions or receive information that cannot be communicated to all parties involved (DA section 8-2).

The outcome of judicial settlement efforts may be settlement, partial settlement or no settlement. If the parties settle, the parties may decide that the settlement should be a court settlement. This means that the settlement is entered into the court records and that it is enforceable as a judgment. If the case is not settled, or the parties reach a partial settlement, the proceedings continue. If the parties settle the content of the case but cannot agree on who pays for the litigation costs, the court has an *ex officio* right to decide on the costs (DA section 9-7). The parties know they do not negotiate about the costs, as long as they can agree on the rest.[16]

The content of the settlement and the role of the judge have been discussed. The question is if the judge can contribute to a settlement that is against the law. Naturally, the content of the settlement does have to be identical with the probable outcome if the case were decided by the court. The question is rather how much may the settlement depart from the law, before the judge must withdraw from the case, tell the parties that the negotiated outcome is not in accordance with the law, or reject the parties the possibility to register the settlement as a court settlement. Different views have been expressed, most commentators are quite liberal but emphasise that public policy considerations and the protection of the weaker party form restrictions.[17]

The judge has the duty to consider if the case should be diverted to court-connected mediation. The question should also be discussed with the parties. Court-connected mediation is discussed *infra*.

---

[16] Nylund (2014); Bernt (2011), p. 111, NOU 2001: 32, pp. 217–218.

[17] Skoghøy (2014), p. 38 Bernt (2011), pp. 446–447.

3.4.4 Summary of Facts, Written Statements and Closing Statements

Norwegian courts may ask the parties to provide written summaries of facts, claims and relevant legal issues. The summaries or statements help the parties and the court to clarify the case and identify the key issues and facts and to distinguish disputed facts and issues from undisputed ones. At the end of the preparatory stage, the parties file written summaries.

In complex cases, the court may order the claimant to submit a *brief chronological* or other systematic *summary of the facts* of the case (DA section 9-9 subsection 4). To avoid unnecessary costs, this opportunity is limited to cases with complex facts. The defendant must submit a reply stating which parts of the summary of facts are accepted and which parts are contested. The defendant must give a brief account of the contested facts. The court may encourage the parties to cooperate, to make a single summary where disputed facts are clearly labelled and provided in two different versions.

The summary helps to cement the main facts of the case. Once the main facts are presented in a systematic manner, the undisputed facts of the case are set. The summary gives the parties and the court the opportunity to evaluate if the disputed facts are essential or incidental for the case, and which evidence is needed to prove the disputed facts. The court and the parties may also compare the facts with the claims and the legal argumentation: Are the claims appropriate for the facts of the case, or should they be adjusted or even dropped? Does the argumentation of the parties fit the facts and the claims?

Evidence is only to be presented for disputed facts and the parties must state what they want to prove with each piece of evidence (DA section 21-6). The court may disallow evidence that is not purported to establish disputed facts or evidence, which is disproportionate to the importance of the dispute (DA sections 21-7 and 21-8). In practice, the courts seldom decide to disallow evidence. The main method to reduce evidence is to use judicial guidance and ask the parties if they believe all the evidence is necessary to establish the disputed facts.

The parties have a duty to provide truthful accounts of the facts even if they would have to testify against themselves. The parties also have a duty to *disclose* the existence of important evidence that is not in their possession. The duty to disclosure applied when the party has reason to believe the opposing party does not know of. Third parties have a duty to testify and to give access to other pieces of evidence, unless they are exempted by law (DA sections 21-4 and 21-5).

If there are many pieces of written evidence, the court may request the parties that these are provided as a booklet with consecutive numbering. During the main hearing, finding the document referred to by one party is easy: the party can refer to the bill on page seven.

In particularly complex cases, the court may order the parties to provide *written statements on a specific issue*. If the legal question is complex, the parties can be ordered to provide an overview of preparatory works, case law and legal literature on the topic. In a case with complex technical details, the parties can be ordered to provide an overview of them. The overview will help the court understand the case. In addition, the material provided can be actively used in the main hearing. The parties can refer to the material, knowing that the opposing party and the court have access to the same documents. The documents are usually numbered sequentially, helping the parties and the court find the right place.[18]

Both parties generally submit *written closing statements* at the end of the preparatory stage. The summaries state the claims of the parties, including the relief and the grounds for the relief, the legal rules that are invoked and which pieces of evidence the party will present (DA section 9-10). The statements form the basis for the main hearing. They set the legal and factual limits of the case and define the dispute. The closing statements can be very brief, consisting primarily of keywords briefly stating the main ideas.[19]

The closing statements are submitted at the end, or after the end of the preparatory proceedings, which is, according to law, two weeks before the main hearing will be opened. Therefore, the parties and the court can prepare the main hearing knowing which claims and defences will be evoked, which factual and legal questions are disputed and which pieces of evidence will be presented.[20]

The summaries and statements help the parties and the court to organise their work and prepare for the main hearing. When the statements have consecutive numbering, the parties can refer to a page number, making it easier for the court and the opposing party to find the relevant document. However, in small and simple cases summaries and closing statements may be superfluous and cause unnecessary cost and delay. Thus, they should only be used when they can provide additional support for the court and the parties.

3.5 The End of the Preparatory Stage

3.5.1 A Plan for the Main Hearing

One of the goals of the preparatory stage is to make a plan for the main hearing. The main hearing must be held within six months of filing of the case (DA section 9-4). Not all cases are disposed of within six months, due to court congestions, holidays, illness and the complexity of the case. The managing judge has the duty to set dates as early as possible to enable a swift proceeding.

The judge must plan the main hearing in consultation with the parties. A timetable should be used to determine the approximate times for presentation of the case, testimony, hearing of witnesses and experts, discussing written evidence

[18] Schei et al. (2012), comment § 9-9.

[19] Skoghøy (2014), pp. 629–630.

[20] Schei et al. (2012), comment § 9-10

and closing speeches. The order of the witnesses should be decided in addition to approximate duration of the hearing of each witness. The parties may also decide to set time limits for the presentation of cases and closing speeches. The parties submit their suggestion for the timetable with the written closing statements.[21]

3.5.2 The Closing the Preparatory Stage and Preclusion

The preparatory stage is closed two weeks before the main hearing. The parties have time to prepare the main hearing, as they have the *written closing statements* at hand. The closing statements combined with the two week period between the end of the preparatory stage and the main hearing are one of the main tools to combat problems of a case that evolves throughout the proceedings in the District Court. It allows the parties to prepare the main hearing in an efficient way. At the same time, the period is a procedural void between the preparatory stage and the main hearing stage of the proceedings.

The closing of the preparatory stage is closely connected with *preclusion*. *Before the end of the preparatory stage*, the parties are free to change their claims, the grounds for the claims and the evidence invoked. If the changes made expand or change the object of the proceedings, a document including those changes must be served to the opposing party in the same manner as the statement of claim and statement of defence. The court may also choose not to allow the changes, or decide to deal with part of the case in a different proceeding. This depends on the changes the party wishes to make, the impact of the possible change and the stage of the proceedings.

In the *two-week period between the closing of the preparatory stage and the commencement of the main hearing* a party may submit new claims or evidence if the opposing party does not object (DA section 9-16). The opposing party must actively object: passivity counts as an acceptance of the changes.

If the opposing party objects, the court will allow changes in certain cases. Changes are automatically allowed if they are a consequence of the written closing statements of the opposing party. Changes will be also allowed if the party cannot be reproached for the late amendment; if the proceedings will not be delayed or become more costly; or if the refusal would lead to a considerable loss for a party. Typically new evidence is allowed, as is a minor modification of the claim or the grounds for it. If the buyer of goods has claimed damages, but realises that rectification or delivery of substitute goods will be more appropriate, the buyer

[21] Under the Civil Procedure Act the Gulating Court of Appeals in Bergen had a scheme of giving priority to short hearings to dealing with court congestion. If the parties agreed to limit the hearing to a single day in court, the hearing would be held within a few months of the appeal. The parties were responsible to limit the length of the presentation and closing speech and the number of witnesses to fit in a short hearing. So far no court has to the author's knowledge tried a similar scheme under the Dispute Act.

may add a payer for rectification or delivery of substitute goods. For the buyer, not allowing the addition could result in loss. For the seller, who claims the goods delivered are in conformity with what was agreed, the change will not result in any major changes. For the proceedings, the result is only a minor delay.

The rules are very flexible giving the judge ample discretion. The court has discretion to allow changes even though the requirements are not fulfilled. It has also discretion to reject the amendment even if the requirements are fulfilled, if the amendment would result in unreasonable costs for the opposing party. It seems that courts usually give parties the right to make amendments, as long as they do not result in extensive new preparation and do not cause a significant delay.

The rules on preclusion of new claims and evidence are typical for Norwegian legislation. The rules set conditions for amendments, but give the courts wide discretion. The approach is flexible and pragmatic. If rejecting a change could result in a new court case, and allowing the change would result in only a minor delay and minor additional costs, the court should allow the change.[22]

The rules reflect the goal of a cost- and time-efficient civil procedure. The court should avoid incurring cost and delay, but if the impact on cost and delay is limited, there is no reason to refrain from a measure. The cost of the change must be weighed against the benefit of claims and evidence matching the need of the parties.

Finally, discretionary rules on preclusion work against front-loading the case. Strict rules on preclusion are an incitement to bring forward all thinkable claims, arguments and evidence early on. The case can become far more complex, as both highly relevant issues and only remotely relevant issues are presented. The court must use resources to find out what is relevant.

3.6 Court-Connected Mediation as a Parallel Track

Court-connected mediation was introduced in Norway in the mid-1990s when a group of lawyers suggested a trial period for court-connected mediation in selected District Courts. From 2008, court-connected mediation has been available for all general civil cases. In administrative cases and cases with mandatory rules, court-connected mediation is often not appropriate. Court-connected mediation should not be used in the small claims track, thus, judicial settlement efforts are the key to settlements.[23] The fear of loss of time and money if court-connected mediation is unsuccessful and the problem of having self-represented parties with little knowledge of their legal rights in court-connected mediation, are the main reasons for rejecting court-connected mediation for small claims.

Before suggesting court-connected mediation in a pending case, the judge must consider if mediation is appropriate. Earlier attempts at mediation, large differences

[22] Schei et al. (2012), comment § 9-16, nr. 1, NOU 2001: 32, pp. 759–761.

[23] Schei et al. (2012), comment § 10-2.

in relative strength of the parties and the general interest of the case are factors against court-connected mediation. Cases should not be mediated if one of the parties actively objects to court-connected mediation. The initiative to mediate can come from the parties, but the judge decides if court-connected mediation is used.

With few exceptions, a judge serves as the mediator. All courts are obliged to have a panel of external mediators, but many courts do not have one, or they do not use the mediators on the panel. If a mediator from the panel is used, the parties pay the remuneration to the mediator in question according to a pre-established fee schedule or as agreed (DA section 8-4).

Court-connected mediation is not part of the court hearings. This means that the rules on court records and access for the general public to the hearings are not applicable. Neither does the rules on the powers, duties and role of the judge applicable.

The mediator must seek to clarify the parties' interests in the dispute to help them reach settlement (DA section 8-5). The role of the mediator is according to the law primarily facilitative and mediation should be interest-based, not rights-based. The mediator decides the mediation process in consultation with the parties. There are almost no restrictions as to the mediation process so long as the mediator is impartial. The guidelines given in the preparatory works are very liberal and include both narrow evaluative mediation and purely facilitative interest-based mediation. The mediator may suggest solutions, and discuss strengths and weaknesses of the legal and factual argumentation of the parties. Evidence may be presented in court-connected mediation at the discretion of the mediator. A party can demand that an offer of settlement is recorded in the mediation record. In other words, court-connected mediation can be highly evaluative, or even a mini-main hearing or a non-binding quasi-arbitration. In practice, the role of the mediator, the mediation process and the quality of the outcome varies to a high degree.[24]

Court-connected mediation is confidential (DA section 8-6). The parties and the mediator cannot testify on what was said and done in mediation. However, parties can use information of the existence of specific evidence that they learned of during mediation. A settlement recorded in the mediation records may be used as evidence in later proceedings.

If the parties reach agreement, they can decide the settlement is binding as a judgement. If the parties do not reach agreement, or they reach partial agreement, the case continues at the court. The judge who mediated the case is normally barred from hearing the case (DA section 8-7).[25]

Court-connected mediation has become popular, with about 15–20 % of all cases going to mediation. The mediation rate varies from court to court. Settlement is reached on the average in 70–80 % of mediated cases.[26]

[24] Mykland (2010).

[25] See Bernt (2011) and Nylund (2014), pp. 111–113.

[26] Numbers are from the Norwegian Courts Administration (Domstolsadministrasjonen), and are on file with the author.

Although judicial settlement efforts and court-connected mediation provide for swift settlements, the practices and methods used vary greatly between judges. In court-connected mediation, some judges seek for interest-based solutions, while others offer the parties an abbreviated trial. The content of court-connected mediation and the mediation process varies considerably, and mediation can be anything from passive shuttle mediation, "muscle" mediation where the judge-mediator pressures the parties to settle, highly evaluative mediation, to a process where the judge facilitates discussion, empowers the parties and helps the parties find creative, mutually satisfactory solutions. The variation in practices reduces the quality of court-connected mediation, as it reduces foreseeability. Unless one knows who will mediate the case, one does not know what mediation will be like or what the results will be. The parties may also be pressured to accept dissatisfactory solutions and a process that is not satisfactory to them. They cannot appeal the process or the result and the Supervisor Committee for Judges does not consider direct pressure unethical. Yet, the parties are deprived of their right to a trial. If the case is not settled, court-connected mediation often causes costs and delay.[27]

Court-connected mediation has become popular because it offers at least some potential for interest-based solutions and constructive dispute resolution.[28] Yet, in many cases court-connected mediation is not about just settlement, it is just about settlement. Mediation training is very short, and many judges keep to their role as a judge when mediating. The limited use of external mediators may hamper the quality of mediation. When mediation is court-conducted, the parties may not understand the difference between the role of the judge and the role of the mediator, between the litigation process and the mediation process. External mediators can be helpful in certain types of cases, for instance, construction disputes, not because they can evaluate the case, but because they understand which problems and questions are the most important to solve. Hence, the quality of court-connected mediation could be enhanced in several different ways.

3.7 Preparatory Proceedings in the Small Claims Track

Cases with a value under NOK 125,000 (about EUR 15,000) are generally directed to the small claims track. Some of the cases have already been decided by the Conciliation Board, and are, in fact, an appeal, others have been redirected from the Conciliation Board to the District Court. As there are many exemptions from the Conciliation Boards, many claims go directly to the District Courts and the small claims track.

In the small claims track a *preparatory hearing should not be held*. The rule was established to ensure fast and cheap proceedings. In small claims procedure the

[27] See Nylund (2014), pp. 113–117.

[28] Adrian and Mykland (2014).

rules are designed to allow parties to be fully or partially self-represented. Self-represented parties often need more help and guidance to clarify issues, match evidence and argumentation with the claims made, to drop or adjust claims and evidence and more help to understand if there is common ground to make a settlement feasible. Therefore, the parties will often need judicial guidance, which in turn, should be given in a preparatory hearing. In general civil cases, a preparatory hearing is recommended whenever at least one of the parties is self-represented.[29]

The ban on preparatory hearings in the small claims seems illogical. It would be more appropriate to make a preparatory hearing the norm, and reduce the main hearing and lower the boundary between the two hearings. The eagerness of the legislator to reduce costs has gone too far, and might reduce the access to justice, prolong the main hearing and hinder settlement.

3.8 Cost Rules

In Norwegian civil procedure the *loser pays for litigation costs*, as the main rule (DA section 20-2). This rule is applied regardless of the stage of proceedings. There are numerous exceptions from the rule. Only just and reasonable costs are compensated. This gives the judge discretion to adjust the compensation to less than the full amount. Often a party will not win completely on all details, thus, the question is if one of the parties has won to a significant degree to make the opposing party compensate all or some of the costs. Conduct before and during the preparatory proceedings, *inter alia*, changes in claims, ground for claims and evidence, negotiations, and settlement offers, may be considered when deciding on the costs. The parties are hence encouraged to aim for clarity and to consider the costs invoked. A party who frivolously causes lengthier and more extensive court proceedings can be punished by making that party responsible for the extra costs.

The cost rules are also used to balance flexible rules. A party can be afforded the opportunity to introduce new evidence or to make changes after the end of the preparatory stage, because the court can decide that the party making the change will be responsible for the extra cost occurred.

During both judicial settlement efforts and court-connected mediation procedures, a party can request the court include a settlement offer in its records (DA section 13-6). If the case is settled later during the proceedings to similar terms as in the offer, of if the judgment is similar to the settlement offer, the party who made the offer may ask the other party is partially responsible for litigation costs. Hence, the costs awarded to the winning party may be reduced or increased. The aim is to encourage settlement, by making an incentive for the parties to consider the likely outcome of the case early.

[29] Schei et al. (2012), comment for § 10-2, NOU 2001: 32, pp. 341–342.

3.9 An Evaluation of Preparatory Proceedings in Norway

The civil procedure reform was evaluated in 2013. The results show that the 2008 reform has been successful. The number of civil cases disposed of per judge had increased with 7.5 %. The *average time* of the proceedings has been reduced from about 6.3 months to 5.5 months (four months for small claims). The total length of meetings at the courthouse has been slightly reduced from an average of almost 11 hours to about nine hours (slightly less than 11 hours for full cases and slightly more than three hours for small claims cases). *The costs have been reduced* by more than 30 % (67 % for small claims).[30] At the same time judges and advocates believe that *the quality of the hearing and the decision has improved slightly*, as the key legal and factual issues have been identified before the main hearing starts. Thus, the argumentation and presentation of evidence is more structured and focused on the disputed questions. Simultaneously, the amount of cases filed has increased.[31] In total, there were almost 17,000 civil cases in 2014.[32] Norway spends little money on the courts as percentage of GDP per capita and has fairly few judges. However, the expenditure on legal aid is high.[33]

The preparatory proceedings with active judicial case management have proved to be a success in Norway. The rules function well, and provide for efficient civil proceedings where the key questions are identified and clarified at an early stage. Norwegian rules on preparatory proceedings provide for swift, cheap and substantially correct results.

3.10 The Impact of Regulation and Legal Culture on Efficiency: A Comparison Between Finland and Norway

3.10.1 Differences in Court Culture Between Finland and Norway

Both Finland and Norway are part of the Nordic legal family. Both have a main hearing-type model of civil procedure. The societies, the history and culture are similar. However, Norwegian civil procedure was modernised already in 1915, the

[30] The average cost in 2009–2011 was NOK 15,962 (about EUR 1,800) for small claims and NOK 110,392 (about EUR 12,300) for regular cases. The number includes the total costs for the claimant and defendant. Evaluering av tvisteloven (2013).

[31] Evaluering av tvisteloven (2013). The numbers are from the period 2006–2012.

[32] http://aarsmelding.domstol.no/#!/oversikt/tingrett. Norway has the second lowest litigation rate in Europe, surpassed only by Finland.

[33] CEPEJ (2014), p. 32, 48, 158. Norway has the second lowest number of civil litigious cases per 100,000 inhabitants in Europe (p. 203).

Finnish almost 80 years later in 1993. The Norwegian civil procedure system is more close to an English trial-system, where the main hearing has been the most important element, whereas the Finnish model was the piecemeal trial. In Norway, the legal representatives have a stronger position in the civil justice system, and the societal role of advocates has been far stronger. Despite relatively similar societies and cultures, until 1993, the civil procedure systems of Finland and Norway differed significantly.

In this final part, the current systems of Finland and Norway are compared to shed light on how the underlying civil procedure system influences implementation of a full main hearing-based structure of civil procedure. The aim is to explore how different underlying cultures require different type of regulation, and how slightly different ways of regulation an issue can lead to same or different outcomes.

Norway has a very efficient civil procedure system. The length of proceedings is about twice as long in Finland as in Norway, with about 10 months compared to 5.5 months. The average costs of litigation for first courts is about the same in both countries (about EUR 12,100 in Finland[34] and NOK 110,400, or EUR 12,700 in Norway[35]) but the average salary is far higher in Norway (about EUR 38,500 in Finland and EUR 65,000 in Norway). As percentage of average income, civil litigation is almost twice as expensive in Finland. Finnish courts handle fewer litigious civil and criminal cases than Norwegian courts (10,320 respectively 18,123 incoming cases in courts of first instance in 2012). The number of judges is significantly higher in Finland, with 18.1 judges per 100,000 inhabitants compared to 11.0 in Norway.[36] However, Finland has administrative courts, Norway has only general courts. Thus, when comparing the workload of judges, administrative court cases must also be taken to account for Finland. The figures indicate that Norwegian civil proceedings are faster and cheaper than Finnish civil proceedings.

The *court culture* is different in Finland and Norway.[37] Norway has had a legal culture and a civil procedure system based on main hearings, the main purpose of which are to allow the lawyers to present and discuss their legal and factual arguments. The culture is lawyer driven. Finnish lawyers are not used to extensive use of hearings except in District Courts. Hearings are held in about one third of the cases is Courts of Appeal, in a few percent of cases in Administrative Courts, and very seldom in the Supreme Court and Supreme Administrative Court.[38] The role of the judge was passive in terms of managing the proceedings. Because preparatory hearings and case management were not familiar to Finnish court culture, there needed to be clear rules mandating preparatory hearings and active case

---

[34] Ervasti (2009a), p. 21. The numbers are from 2008.

[35] Evaluering av tvisteloven (2013), pp. 136–137. The numbers are from 2009–2011. The amount is only about NOK 16,000, or EUR 1,780 for small claims.

[36] CEPEJ (2014), p. 12, 195 and 202.

[37] Ervo (2014) Ervo (2015).

[38] Information is based on the annual reports from the courts, available on www.oikeus.fi.

management. In the first ten years of the Finnish reform, the main hearing could be held directly after the preparatory proceedings. The parties did not have to repeat what had been said during the preparatory stage.

3.10.2 The Preparatory Stage in Finland and Norway

As discussed in Chap. 2, the preparatory stage is massive in Finland, and its scope has been reduced to some extent. Thus, its role is far more important in Finland. The role of the preparatory stage is reflected in the duration of it and *the balance between oral and written format*. In Finland, a preparatory hearings are held in almost all cases. In 50 % of all cases, two hearings are held, and in 10 % of cases, three or more hearings are held.[39] Although preparatory hearings contribute to clarification, judicial settlement efforts and enable the judge to give guidance to the parties, they also account for increased costs and delay. One can ask if having preparatory hearings is important in all cases, and if hearings should as a general rule be limited to a single hearing.[40] In Finland, the preparatory hearing has often in practice become the acme of civil proceedings, and the main hearing remains underdeveloped. The result is a front-loaded proceeding, where the preparatory hearing is too substantial causing extra costs and delay.[41]

However, one may ask if the opposite is true for Norway, if there are too few preparatory hearings. The advantage of preparatory hearings is the possibility for clarification, guidance and judicial settlement efforts. Part of these advantages may be lost if fear of costs prevent judges from conducting preparatory hearings.

Another significant difference between Finland and Norway is the *allocation of duties between the parties and the court*. In Norway, the parties, in practice their counsel, write summaries of fact and legal arguments when needed. In Finland, the judge summarises the case based on the pleadings and the discussions during the preparation..[42] From the point of view of the parties, having the judge perform the work is advantageous, as the judge does not charge the parties by the hour. However, because the legal counsel does not have to refine the material and to work to find out if there are misunderstandings or common ground, the counsel has reduced incentives to do in-depth work before filing the case. When judge write summaries, they have less time for other duties.

Strict rules on preclusion add to the aforementioned problem. As discussed in Sect. 2.4 Finland has strict rules on preclusion giving little discretion to the judge. Strict rules were perhaps necessary in the beginning when the old system with short consecutive hearings, where the counsels submitted written evidence or arguments

---

[39] Ervasti (2009a), p. 9.

[40] See also Stürner (2002), p. 504.

[41] See Sect. 2.2.1.

[42] See Sect. 2.3.1.2.

was replaced by a system with a concentrated main hearing where all arguments and evidence were to be presented orally in a single hearing. However, strict preclusion can have adverse effects in the long run, as cases become front-loaded to avoid preclusion.

Finland does not have *a small claims procedure*. Small claims cases have in practice almost disappeared from the courts.[43] The reason is thought to be high costs. Most commercial cases have also disappeared from the courts, and are now solved by negotiation, arbitration or other dispute resolution procedures. In Norway, the small claims procedure is seemingly a success and there are fairly many small claims cases. However, the question remains if the procedural rules for small claims are adequate and provide for good solutions as the preparatory stage should be as short as possible.

In terms of court-connected mediation and judicial settlement efforts, Finland and Norway are quite similar. In Norway, there is a longer tradition for both out-of-court mediation and judicial settlement efforts.[44] However, the *duty to judicial settlement efforts* has existed longer in Finland. In practice, judges actively promote settlement in both countries. In Finland almost half of all cases are settled during the preparatory stage or the main hearing stage.[45] The role of Finnish District Court judges is to be a peacemaker.[46]

Norway introduced *court-connected mediation* about 10 years earlier than Finland. Thus, court-connected mediation has become an integral part of the Norwegian civil justice system. In Finland, court-connected mediation is still in the process of consolidating its position. In few a few years, court-connected mediation will probably be ubiquitous in Finland as well. One reason for the slow start of court-connected mediation in Finnish courts is that the duty to judicial settlement efforts was introduced in 1993, 13 years before court-connected mediation was introduced. In Norway, the trial on court-connected mediation started in 1997 and the duty to judicial settlement efforts entered into force in 2008. Finnish judges and lawyers were already accustomed to judicial settlement efforts on a large scale when court-connected mediation was introduced. The extensive use of preparatory hearings in Finland probably reduces the need for court-connected mediation, as the judge can actively promote settlement during the hearing.[47]

---

[43] Ervasti (2009a).

[44] Nylund (2014).

[45] Ervasti (2009b), p. 51. In 2008 almost 2,500 cases were settled in oral preparatory hearings and main hearings. Annually about 5,000–6,000 cases are heard in oral preparatory hearings or main hearings or both.

[46] See Sect. 2.6.1.

[47] Judicial settlement efforts and court-connected mediation are compared in more detail in Chap. 9.

3.10.3 *Outcome of Preparatory Proceedings in a Nordic Perspective*

Preparatory proceedings are considered a success in both Finland and Norway. However, they function more efficiently in Norway than in Finland. Norway has more discretionary rules on the choice between oral and written format, and on preclusion. Some of the tasks performed by Finnish judges, such as writing the summary, are performed by the party counsel in Norway. The process is more counsel driven in Norway, easing the workload of the judges and forcing the party counsel to work through the case in more detail.

The transition to the main hearing model has been easier in Norway than in Finland. The reason is probably the distance between the former system and the main hearing model. In Finland, preparatory hearings were a new concept, and the judges had a passive role. Finnish lawyers were not used to a concentrated main hearing where evidence and arguments were presented directly to the presiding judge. Thus, the transition to the main hearing model involved fundamental changes in the role and tasks of the judge and the conduct and structure of civil proceedings. For Finland the main hearing model was a revolution, for Norway it was more as an adjustment. Therefore, the criticism of the Finnish rules and the need for later modification, should not be surprising.

The comparison of Finland and Norway indicates that preparatory proceedings contribute to efficient proceedings mostly in countries with a strong tradition for a hearing. The courts and lawyers must be used to a main hearing format to make preparatory proceedings efficient. Oral preparation can be a good tool for gaining more efficient proceedings, but it requires the right mixture of oral and written proceedings. In Finland, civil proceedings are front-loaded, in Norway preparatory hearings could be held more often. Rules on preclusion and practices regulating the division of duties between the court and the parties have an impact on the efficiency of the preparatory stage. Efficiency in preparatory hearings is a matter of both legal culture and regulation.

The comparison of Finland and Norway shows that the main hearing model is indeed no quick and easy solution to more efficient proceedings in countries with no tradition for a single, immediate, concentrated final hearing. Despite problems with comparably slow courts and the criticism of some of the details of the system, the main hearing model provides a more flexible and settlement oriented procedure, and probably also leads to more accurate judgments.

References

Adrian L, Mykland S (2014) Creativity in court-connected mediation: myth or reality? Negot J 30 (4):421–439

Bernt C (2011) Meklerrollen ved mekling i domstolene. Fagbokforlaget, Bergen

CEPEJ (2014) European judicial systems – Edition 2014 (2012 data): efficiency and quality of justice., Council of Europe

Ervasti K (2009a) Käräjäoikeuksien riita-asiat 2008. Oikeuspoliittisen tutkimuslaitoksen tutkimustiedonantoja, vol 93. Oikeuspoliittinen tutkimuslaitos, Helsinki

Ervasti K (2009b) Riita-asiat tuomioistuimissa. In: Lasola M (ed) Oikeusolot 2009. Katsaus oikeudellisten instituutioiden toimintaan ja oikeuden saatavuuteen, vol 244, vol. Oikeuspoliittisen tutkimuslaitoksen tutkimuksia, Helsinki, pp 43–64

Ervo L (2014) Nordic court culture in progress: historical and futuristic perspectives. In: Ervo L, Nylund A (eds) The future of civil litigation. Access to court and court-annexed mediation in the Nordic countries. Springer, Cham, pp 383–408

Ervo L (2015) Comparative analysis between East-Scandinavian countries. Scand Stud Law 61:135–152

Evaluering av tvisteloven (2013) Justis- og beredskapsdepartementet, Oslo

Lipp V, Fredriksen HH (eds) (2011) Reforms of civil procedure in Germany and Norway. Mohr Siebeck, Tübingen

Mykland S (2010) Særmøter som rasjonelle myter? Tidskrift for Rettsvitenskap 123:288–326

NOU 2001: 32 Rett på sak. Lov om tvisteløsning (tvisteloven) Norges Offentlige Utredninger 2001:32

Nylund A (2014) The Many Ways of Civil Mediation in Norway. In: Ervo L, Nylund A (eds) The future of civil litigation. Access to courts and court-annexed mediation in the Nordic countries. Springer, Cham, pp 97–120

Robberstad A (2015) Sivilprosess, 3rd edn. Fagbokforlaget, Bergen

Schei T, Bårdsen A, Nordén DB, Reusch C, Øie TM (2012) Tvisteloven: Kommentarutgave Bind I, vol 1, 2nd edn. Universitetsforlaget, Oslo

Skoghøy JEA (2001) Tvistemål, 2nd edn. Universitetsforlaget, Oslo

Skoghøy JEA (2014) Tvisteløsning, 2nd edn. Universitetsforlaget, Oslo

Stürner R (2002) Zur Struktur des europäischen Zivilprozesses. In: Roth H, Gottwald P (eds) Festschrift für Ekkehard Schumann zum 70. Geburtstag. Mohr Siebeck, Tübingen, pp 491–505

Chapter 4
Reform and Development of Preparatory Proceedings in the Danish Civil Justice System: Towards (Even) More Efficient Courts

Jakob Juul-Sandberg

Abstract Regulation of civil procedure in Denmark is based on a long history of national legislation. The Danish civil justice system is one of the most well functioning in Europe and the Danish courts have evidently become more effective over the years. Through several reforms in the last decade, the civil justice system has been changed and restructured in order to adopt new digital technology. Structural reforms have also made the courts more efficient without compromising the basic principles on rule of law, access to courts and justice for all parties involved in a civil proceeding. Large parts of the reforms have focused on preparatory proceedings and the use of new technology as means to access the courts easier, get cases tried faster and lower the costs for parties. This article explores the implementation of reforms to the preparatory proceedings in the Danish justice system. It seeks to determine whether the actions have fulfilled their purposes, if the system is working sufficiently and discover whether there still are possible ways of making the process in civil cases more effective and less expensive without compromising rule of law or principles of access to courts and justice.

4.1 Introduction

4.1.1 The Danish Civil Justice System and Its Main Principles

The history of the Danish courts goes back several hundred years, and their duties and role reflect the socio-historical development of Danish society. Since the

J. Juul-Sandberg (✉)
Department of Law, University of Southern Denmark, DK 5230 Odense, Denmark
e-mail: jju@sam.sdu.dk

L. Ervo, A. Nylund (eds.), *Current Trends in Preparatory Proceedings*,
DOI 10.1007/978-3-319-29325-7_4

enactment of the Danish Constitution (1849), the judiciary has gradually assumed the responsibilities of the overall and regulatory authority of the Danish Parliament (the legislature) and the Queen (the government).

This development allowed the judiciary to garner more independence and, by implication, safeguard public due-process protection.[1] In 1999, the Danish Court Administration and the Danish Judicial Appointments Council were formatted to ensure the organisational independence of the judiciary. From then there are no direct ties between the judiciary and the Ministry of Justice. The main purpose and aim of the civil justice system in Denmark—from the legislator's point of view—has been that the system should to be well functioning and effective to secure law enforcement. The rulings from the Danish Courts must be materially correct and of a high professional quality.[2]

In line with the jurisprudence of The European Court on Human Rights, the general understanding is also that each party must have the possibility to become familiar with and comment on all written material and all pieces of evidence that are brought forward at trial, regardless of whether these items do not appear to be new or capable of changing the case.[3]

4.1.2 The Administration of Justice Act

Civil proceedings included the regulation of preparatory proceedings are regulated in the Administration of Justice Act (*Retsplejeloven*). The first Administration of Justice Act came in to force in 1919.[4] The Act gives a legal home to a number of principles of procedural law that have either previously existed in Danish law or immigrated to Denmark from German procedural law, where Danish procedure takes much of its inspiration from.[5]

It follows from some of the early motivations behind the Act that Danish courts should step into character exercising a "gap-filling" function when necessary, when the text of the law is unclear in the sense that judges should have a more active role in cases brought before the courts.[6]

Throughout the years the Act and the provisions on preparatory proceedings has been changed several times—sometimes due to common developments in society

---

[1] The Scandinavian Court Administrations (2007).

[2] See e.g. Udvalget om bedre og mere effektiv behandling af civile sager ved domstolene (2013) Bedre og mere effektiv behandling af civile sager ved domstolene. Ministry of Justice.

[3] Rammeskov Bang Pedersen and Højlund Christensen (2015), p. 72.

[4] See Gomard and Kistrup (2013), p. 21 for an overview and Werlauff (2010), pp. 11–12.

[5] This can be seen in the first draft of the Danish Administration of Justice Act from 1869, which was strongly influenced by German procedural law. Waage and Herborn (2015). On the German influence, see e.g. Taksøe Jensen (1976), p. 96.

[6] Nellemann (1869), p. 87.

or specific political agendas, but in recent years mainly with a purpose to achieve a better, more effective and flexible processing of civil cases.

Most important have been the changes made with effect from 1 January 2008, where a number of significant changes of the Administration of Justice Act came in to force with the purpose of "streamlining" the courts in order to ensure more strict and at the same time flexible rules of procedure in the preparatory phase of the court proceedings and to make it easier for people to have their case processed in court.

The main objectives of the reform were: shorter case processing time, less vulnerable and more efficient courts, more emphasis on leadership and management of courts, and more uniform application of law by improved possibilities of knowledge sharing and specialisation. The changes, among other things, included a small claims procedure, the possibility of class actions and mediation as an alternative to a traditional adversarial lawsuit. Analysing the effects of this reform is the main issue in the following parts of this article.

Some of the provisions on preparatory proceedings and the provisions on the right to appeal were revised (again) in 2014. The purpose of this limitation was primarily to reduce the load of smaller claims on the High Courts to ensure that larger and more principle cases are solved faster and more effectively.[7]

Further changes have come into force from January 1st 2016 (see below).

4.1.3 General Principles

The contradictory principle, plays an important role in Danish civil procedure. According to the traditional definition of this principle, the parties must have access to all the facts, including the claims and arguments that are a part of the case.[8] In practice, lawyers inform each other about any relevant correspondence with the court. Otherwise, the court is responsible for ensuring that the information is brought to the attention of each party.[9]

The principle also have the effect that unilaterally obtained documentation, in most cases, only have a limited value as evidence—because the opposite party have not had the chance to present a point of view to the person who is responsible for the evidence in question; for example, a report on a defect in a building.[10]

---

[7] Act no. 84 of 28 January 2014. Cases with a value of less than DKK 20,000 (EUR 2,684) cannot be appealed. The maximum was changed from DKK 10,000 (EUR 1,342). These changes were based on recommendations from: Udvalget om bedre og mere effektiv behandling af civile sager ved domstolene: Bedre og mere effektiv behandling af civile sager ved domstolene. Ministry of Justice (2013).The Appeals Permission Board may still grant permission to appeal judgments if the case concerns fundamental legal questions or if special circumstances so warrant. See Højgaard Pedersen (2009), pp. 31–35.

[8] E.g. von Eyben (2008), p. 223.

[9] Rammeskov Bang Pedersen and Højlund Christensen (2015), pp. 456–457.

[10] See Sect. 4.4 below as well.

The procedure in civil cases is distinctly contradictory—only facts and evidence places before the judged by the involved parties will be taken in to consideration. The court does not conduct its own investigations. This means that the object of the court is not to establish an absolute objective (material) truth, but rather a relative or subjective truth on the basis of the material produced by the parties involved and presented before the judge.[11]

The party-presentation principle is codified in section 338 of the Administration of Justice Act, which states that the court's judgment must be exclusively based upon the claims of the parties and pieces of information that are brought before the court by the parties.

The court is free to access the value of the evidence presented. The court may not give a party to the proceedings more than he has claimed (*ne ultra petita partium*) and it can only assess arguments that the party has brought before the court, or arguments that are mandatory under the law for the court to consider, cf. section 338.[12]

According to section 339(3) of the Justice Administration Act, the court may invite the parties to present certain pieces of evidence that are available to them. In general the court does not have the power to bring further pieces of information into the case, but in cases with big consequences for one or both parties involved the court may urge the parties to present pieces of relevant and available evidence so that a decision based solely on the burden of proof will not have to be made.

The provision aims at ensuring the elucidation, or clarification of claims and arguments that may be a precondition to rational arrangements of the proceedings.[13]

The court can also *ex officio* cut off evidence that it deems to be irrelevant in deciding the case, cf. section 341, but courts are very cautious on using this prerogative.[14] The courts are, generally speaking, reluctant to ask the parties to present evidence or cut off evidence in order to safeguard its impression of impartiality.

Danish civil procedure is also centred upon the principle of free disposition. In the context of Danish civil procedure, free disposition is defined as a principle that "in general expresses the right of the parties to freely dispose over the case and—to some degree—also the form of the procedure".

A distinction is made between the principle of free disposition and the principle of officiality. The principle of officiality applies in cases where the court on its own

---

[11] Gomard and Kistrup (2013), p. 577, Rammeskov Bang Pedersen and Højlund Christensen (2015), p. 90, Lindencrone and Werlauff (2014), p. 295, Administration of Justice Act section 338: "The court cannot grant a party more than he has claimed and can only take into consideration such allegations as the party has made, or which cannot be withdrawn".

[12] Jochimsen (2012), pp. 28–33.

[13] Gomard and Kistrup (2013), p. 597, The Danish Standing Committee on Procedural Law (Retsplejerådet) report no. 698/1973, p. 22, UfR 1981.101 H (Supreme Court decision) and U 1982.171 H (Supreme Court decision).

[14] Rammeskov Bang Pedersen and Højlund Christensen (2015), p. 484.

initiative retrieves information or decides to investigate a question on its own. A few examples of this exist in Danish civil procedure law, primarily in family law matters, but this must be seen as the exception to the main rule of free disposition in civil cases.

Decisions on procedural matters are not dealt with in accordance with the rule of free disposition. The parties involved cannot make decisions on how the court works or how the court organises their cases.[15]

All court hearings employ free speech including party and witness examination.[16]

4.1.4 The Danish Court System

Denmark has one of the highest numbers of incoming civil, commercial, administrative and other cases per 100 inhabitants in the European Union.[17] The figures cover all cases though, including contentious and non-contentious cases, which has an effect on the numbers from Denmark, as there are no administrative courts. Violations of fundamental rights can be brought before the ordinary courts, as Denmark has neither a constitutional court nor special courts dealing with questions concerning human rights.[18]

Danish courts uphold a society founded on the rule of law and is the present-day and primary forum of conflict resolution.[19] The Danish courts are—by themselves—considered a highly respected and confidence-building organisation, which discharges its duties at the highest level of professional competence, service and efficiency. Users of the Danish courts are also very satisfied with the service they get.[20]

---

[15] Gomard and Kistrup (2013), p. 589.

[16] Administration of Justice Act section 148 (2). The court may permit written statements from witnesses (Administration of Justice Act section 297).

[17] 41 in 2013. See "The 2015 EU Justice scoreboard" from the European Commission on quality, independence and efficiency of justice systems in the European Union. http://ec.europa.eu/justice/effective-justice/files/justice_scoreboard_2015_en.pdf (figure 2).

[18] The whole organization is composed of the Courts (districts, high and supreme), the Appeals Permission Board, the Danish Judicial Appointments Council and the Danish Court Administration. The organization has separate appropriations in the State budget. The board of the Danish Court Administration shall ensure that the courts are run and developed in an adequate and proper way.

[19] The Scandinavian Court Administrations (2007).

[20] Due to a study done by Oxford Research in 2013 amongst 8,000 users of the court system (to be found on the Danish courts webpage www.domstol.dk). See also "The 2015 EU Justice scoreboard" from the European Commission on quality, independence and efficiency of justice systems in the European Union. http://ec.europa.eu/justice/effective-justice/files/justice_scoreboard_2015_en.pdf.

The Danish court system today consists of 24 district courts (down from 82 before the reform in 2008),[21] two high courts and the Supreme Court. Besides this, there are two specialised courts: the Maritime and Commercial Court and the Land Registration Court. The Court of the Faroe Islands, the Court of Greenland and the High Court of Greenland are also part of the Danish court system—but not regulated by the Danish Administration of Justice Act.[22] [23]

Unless otherwise provided in the Administration of Justice Act or other enactments civil cases are tried in the district court in the first instance. The Danish civil justice system is based on a right to appeal once—referred to as the "two instance" principle. Claims or pleas and allegations or submissions that have not been made before the lower court may under appeal, only be taken into account with the court's permission if the opposing party objects.[24]

4.1.5 Communication with the Courts

Public authorities in Denmark have in recent years increased their digital communication with citizens and they now very often use systems based on, for example, electronic signatures in order to the ensure privacy and security of transactions, communications, and so on. Digital communication with the courts has, however, for many years been restricted by various legislative regulations, for example, the *sine qua nons* of written proceedings and signatures on documents.

Current reforms have also focused on more flexible approaches to new communication technologies.[25] The courts have also agreed on a set of guidelines for the

[21] The Bailiff's courts and probate courts are departments of the district courts.

[22] The court of the Faroe Islands in Torshavn jurisdiction comprises all of the islands. The court hears the same cases as do district courts in other regions of Denmark. Appeal lies to the High Court of Eastern Denmark. The courts of Greenland are composed of the High Court of Greenland and 18 magistrates' courts. Appeal against a decision made by a magistrates court lies to the High Court of Greenland. Major cases are, however, may be brought directly before the High Court of Greenland. Appeal lies to the High Court of Eastern Denmark. Pre-trial procedures in The Court of the Faroe Islands, the Court of Greenland and the High Court of Greenland will not be described or be part of the analysis in the following sections.

[23] A number of special courts are functioning partly on the basis on legislation separate from the Justice of Administration Act: The special court for impeachment (*Rigsretten*), The Industrial Tribunals (*Arbejdsretten*) and the Housing Courts (*Boligretten*). Disputes arising from tenancy agreements are brought before special divisions of each of the District Courts called the Housing Courts. The only difference between the Housing Court and an ordinary court is that the Housing Court consists of three judges instead of one. Two of them are lay judges nominated by tenants and landlords associations respectively. All three judges have a vote on decisions regarding evidence and other procedural steps during pre-trial. Juul-Sandberg (2012), p. 591, Juul-Sandberg and Godsk Pedersen (2013), pp. 251–276.

[24] Jochimsen (2012), p. 246.

[25] The Danish Standing Committee on Procedural Law (Retsplejerådet) report no. 1401/2001.

use of e-mail or other digital communication between the court and its users.[26] Starting from 1 January 2015, the courts are individually authorized to decide whether documents may be send to the court by e-mail during preparatory proceedings.[27]

Under the Administration of Justice Act, section 154, communications from the court is given in the way that the court decides unless the form of communication is given by law.[28] Today most courts use e-mail as the general form of communication when accepted by the parties involved. This also encourages effectivity and improves the users' experience, as following the technical evolution is expected in a modern society as exists in Denmark.

By January 1st 2016 the Administration of Justice Act has been changed so that it is possible to handle a civil case solely digital without any paper being exchanged between the court and the parties involved. This will not change the content of preparatory proceedings, but it will definitely make access to courts easier. The possibilities for exchanging documents and statements digitally will also make processes in the court operate faster and smoother.

4.2 Preparatory Proceedings in the First Instance

Preparatory procedures are mandatory in civil cases in the first instance. The regulations on preparatory procedures are, therefore, mainly focused on the procedure in the district courts, but the Act also includes sections on pre-trial procedures in the high courts and before the Supreme Court. When a civil case is appealed new preparatory proceedings start in the appeal court.

The structure of civil procedure in Denmark is in accordance with the "Nordic model"[29] using a main hearing model consisting of three stages. In the following the first two phases—the "pleadings stage" and "the preparatory stage"—will be described together, as these stages in Denmark are defined as the pre-trial process in civil case and not clearly separated in the Administration of Justice Act. This means that both stages are considered as part of the preparatory proceedings.

Even though the principle of party representation applies, the parties themselves do not control the preparatory proceedings. The tasks of court in the preparatory stage include, amongst others, the enforcement of the rules in the Administration of Justice Act, determination of time of meetings and hearings, time of delivery of written documents.

---

[26] http://www.domstol.dk/om/Digitalpost/professionelle/retningslinjer/Pages/default.aspx.

[27] By Act no. 737 of 25 June 2014 introducing section 148b to the Administration of Justice Act.

[28] Already in 2004 section 148a of the Administration of Justice Act was adopted stating that digital information may be exchanged with the courts even if documents had to be in writing or with a signature. This section of the Act has not come in to force yet though.

[29] See Chap. 1.

According to section 344 of the Administration of Justice Act, the court decides which facts must be properly established before the case can be tried. The preparatory stage is in some of the courts (approximate one-half of the 24 district courts) administered by a certain unit of the courts including not only a judge but also other legal staff. This means that the judge who tries the case often do not see the documents or evidence more than a week or two before the main hearing.

This administrative procedure has been developed after the court reform in 2008, making the preparatory proceedings more effective and making it possible for the judges to concentrate on deciding cases on basis of the main hearing.

In the other half of the courts the case is handled by one judges department from filing the statement of claim until the cases are settled or a decision is made—eventually after the main hearing.

It is not easy to determine which solution is the better one. When the judge who tries the case at the main hearing is not involved in the preparatory stage this particular judge might not have the same insight into the evidence of the case or the same encouragement to try to settle the case. As well as the person who is preparing the case do not have the encouragement to try to settle the case or to try to "streamline" the case and speed it up during pre-trail.

On the other hand, there are good arguments for the opposite solution—as mentioned just above. In small claims (see Sect. 4.3 below) a centralised handling of the preparation of cases seems like the most effective solution.

4.2.1 Proceedings in Court

Proceedings are instituted by the filing of a statement of claim[30] with the court. The statement of claim is the document initiating the court proceedings and is obligatory to get a court case on the way.[31]

After receiving the statement of claim the court will serve these on the defendant based on the information provided therein. The court will direct the defendant to file

[30] In the Administration of Justice Act section 348 it is said that the statement must: (i) state the name and address of the parties, including a postal address in the European Economic Area for the sending of procedural notices to the claimant and for service of documents; (ii) name the court in which the proceedings are instituted; (iii) state the claimant's claim; (iv) include the detailed submissions on points of fact and law made by the claimant in support of his claim; (v) set out the documents and other evidence on which the claimant intends to rely; and (vi) include the claimant's proposal for the hearing of the case.

[31] Administration of Justice Act section 349. Standard forms for statements of claim and statements of defence can be downloaded from the Court Administrations Boards homepage: http://www.domstol.dk/selvbetjening/blanketter/staevningogsvarskrift/Pages/default.aspx. Lindencrone and Werlauff (2014), p. 274 goes through the formal requirements to a statement of claim and statement of defence.

a statement of defence[32] with the court within a specified period of time, generally at least 2 weeks. This may be extended on request if the defendant, for instance, needs to talk to a lawyer and/or the defendant's lawyer will file the defence but most courts will try to make the case proceed as soon as possible.

When the case has been brought and the statement of defence has been filed the case will precede through the exchange of pleas and hearings, unless there are grounds for rejecting the case or settling it out of court. Civil procedural law in Denmark does not recognise "striking out" orders by the court as in other legal systems mainly under Common law.[33]

As it is required that the process is concentrated in order to reduce costs and save time for the parties and the court, arguments, documentation and claims should be brought before the court as soon as possible and new claims and arguments should only in exceptional circumstances be allowed when the preparatory stage is closed. This is the aim of the Administration of Justice Acts regulation on preparatory proceedings.

Proceedings are based on active management by the court and time schedules including deadlines for the parties involved. If a party fails to comply with deadlines, this may prevent the party from making new claims or even dismiss the case or deliver judgment by default.[34]

A party[35] to a case may attend the entire trial proceedings. This also applies to the preparatory hearings. But most often the party to a civil case will have legal representation and lawyers often attend oral preparatory hearings alone on mandate from their clients, because no evidence or statements are presented here. The court has the right to request that the party attend a preparatory hearing in person or by a person who is authorised to make decisions on the party's behalf if the court finds that this may be demanded, for instance, in order to find a settlement to the case.

Lawyers most often have the authority to make decisions regarding the case on the spot –at times it can relate to issues besides agreeing to settlements.

---

[32] The statement of defence must: (i) state the defendant's plea; (ii) state any counterclaims; (iii) include the submissions on points of fact and law made by the defendant in support of his plea and any counterclaims; (iv) set out the documents and other evidence on which the defendant intends to rely; (v) where such address has not already been provided, provide a postal address in the European Economic Area for the sending of procedural notices to the defendant and for service of documents; and (vi) include the defendant's proposal for the hearing of the case. Administration of Justice Act section 351.

[33] Werlauff (2010), p. 61.

[34] Petersen (2014), p. 297. Administration of Justice Act sections 358, 360, 362 and 363.

[35] If the party is a legal person, for example, a limited liability company, the party can be represented "in person" by someone with the requisite authority to make decision on behalf of the company, such as a majority shareholder.

4.2.2 Preparatory Hearings

The aim of the provisions on preparatory proceedings in the Administration of Justice Act is to make preparation of cases fast, effective and thorough, as case administration time in court should be as brief as possible.[36] A mean to meet these prerequisites is the preparatory hearing, which is held at a time set by the court most usually when the court has received a statement of defence. The court then sends out an order to convene the parties to an oral hearing, unless the court finds such hearing unnecessary (which is very rare).

The purpose of the preparatory hearing is to determine which evidence has to be produced, which documents that has to be filed, which witnesses who has to be heard and how the parties involved wish proceed with the preparation of the case.

Section 353 of the Administration of Justice Act contains a list of items that—when relevant to the particular case—will be discussed at the hearing. At the hearing, the parties' positions on the points of fact and law will be clarified, and in this process the points which are not disputed and the points for which evidence must be produced will be sought to be clarified. In addition, the parties must give an account of any discussions having taken place between the parties prior to the issue of proceedings, including of the possibility of reaching a settlement. The court may order the parties to give an account of any initiatives having been taken prior to the preparatory hearing.

At the hearing, the court must also—after consultation with the parties—determine the further process, where possible, including the time frame of an extended preparatory proceedings, if applicable, but the parties have influence on the course, form, content and length of the preparatory stage. If the opposing party does not object—or the parties involved agree on the timeframe and steps of preparation of the case—the court most often will allow it, so long as it seems reasonable from an overall perspective.

There are no specific time limits for when the hearing will be held. The court decides discretionarily on this—normally after consulting the involved parties by telephone. At the hearing the court must fix a date or period for the main trial hearing. If the time frame of the extended preparatory proceedings or the date or period of the main hearing has not been fixed at a preparatory hearing in accordance with section 353, the court must decide on this issue as soon as possible.[37]

Requests for evidence that will extend the preparatory stage significantly should be submitted at the hearing.

The court has a discretionary right to set another oral hearing during the preparatory phase if further important questions about the handling of the case arise after the first hearing.

---

[36] See The Danish Standing Committee on Procedural Law (*Retsplejerådet*) report no. 1401/2001.

[37] Administration of Justice Act section 353 and 354. Dalager (2015), p. 73.

4.2.2.1 The 2008 and 2014 Reforms

The preparatory hearing (section 353 of the Administration of Justice Act) was introduced at the court reform in 2008 as an instrument to speed up the case by securing that proceedings where agreed upon at the earliest possible stage.

These new provision replaced provisions on non-obligatory hearings held in court when decided on by the court or on demand of one of the parties involved. These hearing were not used that much as they would often mean that the case would be put "on hold" for a longer period of time because it could be difficult to find a date and time for the meeting where both the judge and one or two layers involved could attend.

The preparatory hearing is today most often held as a telephone conference call between the judge or court clerk responsible for the case and the parties involved or persons duly authorized to make decisions with regard to the proceedings. This is time saving and works very well as opposed to before 2008 where all court sessions in civil cases where held at the courthouse as mentioned above.

In 2013—five years after the reform was implemented—the average use of (time) resources on a normal civil case by the court has been estimated to be 720 min per case from institution of legal proceedings until the case is closed by the court after the end of the main hearing and service of the judgment.[38]

This means that the court and the lawyers involved find it easier to find an available time slot for the hearing. This has probably been one of the most effective changes to the preparatory proceedings from the reform, though no statistics show how much shorter this may have made the preparatory stage in general.

A downside to carrying out the hearing by telephone might be that settlement negotiations or conciliation is more difficult when the parties do not meet face-to-face.[39]

In 2014, the Administration of Justice Act section 343 was changed again, as yet another attempt to ensure that the hearing was exploited in the best possible way to make further preparation of the case even more effective. For example, at the hearing the parties to a case must be represented by a person who has authority to make decisions on the further handling of procedural steps to the case and the parties might be asked to explain which actions had been taken to try to settle the case before submitting a statement of claim.[40]

The regulation on interlocutory appeal came into force in 2014 as another means to relieve the high courts from a large amount of cases (before 2014 almost all decisions on procedural steps from the district courts could be appealed) and to

---

[38] Deloitte Consulting (2013). The processing time is estimated by identifying the first and the last registration of activity in case through the Court Administration databases. The statistics no not include a comparison with the time used on a civil case before the reform.

[39] Backhausen and Lundblad (2009), p. 240.

[40] Act no. 737 of June 25 2014.

make processing time in the district courts shorter, as interlocutory appeal would almost certainly delay preparatory proceedings to a case.

These changes also impact the preparatory proceedings, as these might be stopped every time a decision by the court was appealed. This means that if there is a dispute regarding court orders or decisions during preparatory proceedings regarding procedural steps—for instance, on exclusion of evidence—interlocutory appeal can, as the main rule, not be made to the high court.[41]

Time will show whether this newest regulation has any effect. It is clear that this to a great extent will depend on the judge who handles the case. If the judge does not use the "tools" in section 343, no improvements will be made. See Sect. 4.6 below for additional discussion on this topic.

4.2.3 *Presentation of Evidence*

All factual allegations must be documented through evidence presented during preparatory proceedings. Both audio and visual evidence—film, video, or otherwise digitally produced—can be part of a civil case and will often be considered just as important as written documents.

Traditionally, no distinction is made between private and public documents in relation to evidence. Whether a specific piece of evidence carries sufficient weight to carry the case will always depend on a free evaluation made by the court. When deciding the case the court will take the circumstances under which the evidence has been produced into consideration. Unilaterally obtained documents do generally not have any large value as evidence.[42]

Parties and witnesses are heard at the main hearing. While both the claimant and defendant during the preparatory proceedings may announce which witnesses they will hear, witnesses are not involved during the pre-trial phase.

A "survey" can be conducted during the preparatory proceedings on decision by the court after requests from one of the parties involved. In most cases, a request is given at the preparatory hearing but sometimes even earlier if the survey is most evident for the case.

The reasoning behind this procedural step is that the court does not have the expertise to assess all kinds of evidence that may be presented before the court. Therefore, in Danish civil procedure, specific experts with the relevant technical or

---

[41] Administration of Justice Act section 389a. Orders and decisions on costs fixed at a maximum amount of DKK 20,000 (EUR 2,684) are non-appealable. The Appeals Permission Board may permit an interlocutory appeal though if special circumstances so warrant.

[42] UfR 2007.2040 H, UfR 2008.2193 H, UfR 2008.2393 H and UfR 2011.151 H (Supreme Court decisions), Gomard and Kistrup (2013), p. 708 and 724; Sommer Jensen (2011), Amstrup Fournais and Aschou Johannesen (2012), pp. 498–504, Juul-Sandberg and Godsk Pedersen (2011), pp. 109–128.

academic knowledge participate as co-judges, are appointed to conduct an independent survey of the issue or are questioned as expert witnesses.[43]

Surveys under Danish civil procedure are defined as one or more independent court-appointed experts' objective inspection combined with their professional appraisal of how the objects inspected compares with certain standards.[44] Surveys are often used as evidence in various types of civil cases as they are recognised as valuable documentation for difficult technical issues that the judge does not have any insight in.

In civil proceedings, a party may request the court to commission an expert report on one or more questions; for example, on the state of a property, machine, or a product batch or the quality and price of a tradesman's work.[45]

The court-appointed experts may not give their opinion on points of law. Aside from investigating the main object of dispute at the trial, the expert who has performed the survey may, for instance, inform the court about market standards, best practises within the area, or other similar areas.

A survey can only be requested by the parties. The experts who conduct it must live up to a number of requirements of impartiality in accordance with the Administration of Justice Act.

The court sets the fee payable to the court-appointed expert for his report and attendance in court as well as for reimbursement of any expenses incurred. Before the decision, the court will ask the parties for their comments. At the same time, the court will decide how the fee is to be allocated between the parties.

The provisions in the Administration of Justice Act on surveys were also revised in 2014. The purpose of the revision was to modernise the language used and to create a better context between the different sections of the Act on surveys. The changes will only to a limited degree have any effect on time spend on preparatory proceedings in court.

Conducting a survey during the preparatory stage is often the procedural step that will take the longest time—from getting the expert appointed by the court until the report is filed. Cases involving surveys will, therefore, affect statistics on the average processing time of a court case.

Besides the changed mentioned just above, some changes to the Administration of Justice Act were also made at the revision in 2014 to make it easier to expedite survey proceedings during pre-trial as yet another attempt to make court cases go even faster through the court system.[46]

---

[43] Gomard and Kistrup (2013), p. 720, Werlauff (2010), p. 122.

[44] Werlauff (2010), p. 122.

[45] Werlauff (2010), p. 122.

[46] Act no. 737 of 25 June 2014 based on The Danish Standing Committee on Procedural Law (Retsplejerådet) report no.1543/2013.

Co-judges with knowledge on relevant technical matters may be appointed, but they also only appear at the main trial-hearing (except in the Housing Courts).[47] This was introduced in 2008.[48] Formerly, before the court reform in 2008, multi-member courts were not an option and assistance by expert judges was only allowed in very few case types.

4.2.4 Conclusion of Preparatory Proceedings

After the preparatory hearing the preparation of the case continues as agreed at the hearing usually with further written statements from the parties. This is a part of the preparatory proceedings that is individual from case-to-case. The court may set timetables and deadlines and decide if and when written statements or pieces of evidence must be put forward at the latest. The length of the preparatory proceedings in all is set by the court, but the court will often hear the parties involved on timeframes, evidence and other procedural steps, such as surveys.

Unless otherwise directed by the court, the preparatory procedure will be deemed closed 4 weeks before the date fixed by the court for the main hearing.

If, within the specified period, a party fails to take a procedural step that the party is required to take in accordance with the timetable set by the court for the preparatory proceedings,[49] the court may close the preparatory proceedings, unless such closure is outweighed by the interests of the opposing party.

A summary of claims, arguments and evidence is not made during or at the end of the preliminary procedure, but the court may direct the parties to file a summary of their final claims or pleas with the court within a period specified by the court which precedes the main hearing. The court may also invite the parties to file a summary of pleadings with the court within a period specified by the court which precedes the main hearing.[50] This is done in almost all civil cases both in first instance and under appeal.

While the parties are free to expand their claims and present new arguments and evidence before the end of the preparatory stage, new arguments and evidence can

[47] Disputes arising from tenancy agreements are brought before special divisions of each of the district courts called the Housing Courts. The only difference between the Housing Court and an ordinary court is that the Housing Court consists of three judges instead of one. Two of them are lay judges nominated by tenants and landlords associations respectively. All three judges have a vote on decisions regarding evidence and other procedural steps during pre-trial. Juul-Sandberg (2012), p. 591, Juul-Sandberg and Godsk Pedersen (2013), pp. 251–276.

[48] Administration of Justice Act section 12 (3) and section 20.

[49] According to the Administration of Justice Act section 353(5) and section 354.

[50] Administration of Justice Act section 357.

only be brought before the court under exceptional circumstances once the court has decided to end the preparatory stage.[51]

If the court finds additional preparatory proceedings necessary, it may direct the proceedings to be reopened. The consequence of this is in principle that new evidence—as a starting point—cannot be presented to the court after the preparatory stage has ended. One of the important reasons behind this preclusion is that a party should not lose a case because it has been taken by surprise by new evidence that it had no time to prepare for.

On the other hand, evidence that is likely to be decisive to the case should not be excluded only because it is presented after a certain deadline, as this could lead to an appeal that is not in the interest of the court nor the parties involved.

But the decision on submission is a prerogative to the court not stated directly in the Administration of Justice Act.

If a party wishes to expand the claims or pleas made during the preparatory proceedings procedure or to make submissions that have not been made during the preparatory proceedings or to produce evidence that has not been specified during the preparatory procedure, the party must notify the court and the opposing party.

If the opposing party objects to the presentation of new evidence after the preparatory stage has finished[52] the court may allow a party to expand his or her claims or pleas, make new allegations or submissions or produce new evidence if there are special reasons why the failure to make a request at an earlier point in time may be deemed excusable; the opposing party may adequately safeguard his or her interests without the main hearing being adjourned; or refusing permission may inflict a disproportionate loss on the party.

The court may refuse a request to expand claims and pleas, make new allegations or submissions or produce new evidence if granting a request may be assumed to necessitate an adjournment of the main hearing.

4.3 Small Claims Proceedings

In 2008, a new regulation—including simplified preparatory proceedings—were introduced for small claims disputes after the possibilities had been discussed for many years.[53]

---

[51] Cf. section 358 of the Administration of Justice Act. Gomard and Kistrup (2013), p. 327. Gomard et al. (2013), p. 864.

[52] The opposing party has 1 week to submit his comments to the court and the other party, after which the court will make its decision whether it will be allowed in accordance with the Administration of Justice Act section 358.

[53] See the legislative remarks to Act no. 538 of 8 June 2006 and The Danish Standing Committee on Procedural Law (Retsplejerådet) report no. 1436/2004. Rammeskov Bang Pedersen and Højlund Christensen (2015), p. 391. Jochimsen (2012), p. 200.

The procedure applies to claims that do not exceed DKK 50,000 (EUR 6,710)—or if agreed by the parties involved.

In small claims the court is in charge of the whole preparatory preparation of the case after the statement of claim has been filed. This means that the parties requires permission from the court to present evidence and a simplified procedure for the use of surveys also applies. The court may also give advice to the parties involved on the law as well as procedural matters e.g. the burden of proof.[54]

The procedure is simplified to make proceedings faster and less complicated but without compromising basic principles on law enforcement or access to court. At the same time, the aim was to make size of costs more predictable and more modest (compared to "ordinary" civil cases).

A main purpose of the small claims procedure is also to make legal representation under the preparatory proceedings unnecessary. This is reflected in the above mentioned very active role of the judge in these cases and also in the regulation on cost payable to the winning party. A lawyer or other legal representation can only recover a part of his or her fee fixed in accordance with the specific guidelines for small claims cases.[55]

For a small claims civil case the average time from institution of legal proceedings and until service of the judgment to the involved parties has been estimated to 353 min—which proves that preparatory procedures in these types of cases are faster than in "normal" civil cases (720 min—see Sect. 4.2.2.1 above) and that the adoption of this regulation has been a success from this point of view.[56]

The system seems to be well functioning and effective even though many lawyers representing parties to a small claim find that the modest cost distribution is a problem. Some judges might also find that the handling of the small claim procedure is unattractive as the judge—and not the lawyers often involved—must be in charge of the preparation of the case as opposed to other civil cases.[57]

The number of small claims has been decreasing over the last few years. In 2012, the districts courts finished 25,251 cases registered as small claims. In 2013, the numbers of cases registered under the small claims procedure were 23,783 in total. In 2014, the total was 22,411.[58] The total number of civil cases has dropped in the same period, which probably is the main explanation for the decrease in small claims cases, as well.

[54] Dalager (2015), p. 72 and e.g. UfR 2014.1697 Ø (Eastern High Court decision).

[55] Administration of Justice Act section 408.

[56] Deloitte Consulting (2013), p. 7. Petersen (2014), p. 295.

[57] Juul-Sandberg (2013), p. 193.

[58] www.domstol.dk.

4.4 Judicial Settlement Efforts and Court-Connected Mediation

The CCBE code of conduct[59] is implemented in the Danish code of conduct for lawyers guiding a lawyer to "... at all times strive to achieve the most cost-effective resolution of the client's dispute and provides guidelines on how a lawyer should advise the client at appropriate stages as to the desirability of attempting a settlement and/or a reference to alternative dispute resolution".[60]

In accordance with section 336a in the Administration of Justice Act, the claimant has an obligation to—before bringing the case to court—investigate whether the case can be settled before going to court and when filing the case to contribute to fast and effective handling of the case in court.[61] The rule is not sanctioned directly, but the court may take the claimants handling of the case into consideration when deciding on costs.[62]

Mediation is not obligatory during the preparatory phase, but the court has a duty to conduct judicial settlement efforts and try to settle the case during preparatory proceedings, before or at the main hearing.[63]

4.4.1 Judicial Settlement Efforts in Court

The Administration of Justice Act Chapter 26 holds the regulation on judicial settlement efforts in court. The regulation was amended in 1951 and has not been changed since. The sections of the Act do not regulate how or when the court may conciliate and try to settle cases. A definition is not inserted in the sections of the Act nor was it defined in the legislative work.[64]

The benefits of judicial settlement efforts for the courts can be that time and resources used preparing the case and writing a verdict when the case is stopped at an earlier stage is saved.[65]

The court most often takes the initiative to start settlement negotiations in court. The lawyers do not play a very active role without any encouragement when

[59] The Council of Bars and Law Societies in Europe (CCBE): Charter of Core Principles of the European Legal Profession and Code of Conduct for European Lawyers. http://www.ccbe.eu/fileadmin/user_upload/NTCdocument/EN_CCBE_CoCpdf1_1382973057.pdf.

[60] Charter of Core Principles of the European Legal Profession and Code of Conduct for European lawyers. Section 3.7.1.

[61] Enforced by Act no. 737 of 25 June 2014. A similar rule applies under appeal.

[62] See Sect. 4.6 below.

[63] Administration of Justice Act section 268. Lindencrone and Werlauff (2014), p. 340.

[64] Adrian et al. (2015), Adrian (2012), p. 87.

[65] Backhausen and Lundblad (2009), p. 237.

settlement negotiations are held in the courtroom before the judge even though they are present.

Judicial settlement efforts may be done both during the preparatory proceedings and before or at the main hearing. At the preparatory hearing, the judge has the opportunity to ask the involved parties whether they are interested in a settlement or not. As mentioned above, the preparatory proceedings in civil cases are often (in approximately half of the district courts) administered by a certain unit of the courts including not only a judge but also other legal staff. This means that the judge who tries the case at the main hearing is often not the judge who is leading the preparatory hearing. This might have an influence on the settlement efforts. Even if the judge has handled the case up until the preparatory hearing, trying to settle the case might be difficult at this early stage where all evidence has not been produced and a final result of the case cannot be predicted at all.[66]

When trying to settle the case the court decides whether the parties should be present or if their legal representatives may negotiate on their behalf even though lawyers do not in general have a mandate to make binding agreements in court on behalf of their client.

Some judges play a more active role in trying to settle a case than others. Some judges try very hard to get a case settled during the preparatory proceedings, while others do not put a large effort in to it. As there is no regulation on how judicial settlement efforts should be performed, the judge has a discretionary right to decide what arguments a settlement to the case should be based on. The judge can use legal arguments—what would become the result of a verdict—a fair solution to either parties, or something different.[67]

It is difficult to say generally what encourages a judge to try to negotiate a settlement in court besides the fact that the Administration of Justice Act state that it is obligatory. Eventually one of the largest encouragements can be the possibility of closing the case—saving time and resources—but also the possibility of avoiding making a decision in a case where, for example, facts are missing so that the results would not be fair from the judges' point of view.[68]

No statistics are available on the actual efforts or results from judicial settlement efforts in court. There are no direct statistics available on how many civil cases that are settled after conciliation in court during preparatory proceedings. The only guideline is the Danish Court Administrations statistics on cases settled before the main hearing. In 2013, approximately 14 % of all civil cases ended with a settlement before the main hearing.[69] But these figures do not tell the actual effect of judicial settlement efforts. Cases are often settled out of court without the court being involved or after the court has encouraged the parties to find a settlement.

---

[66] Rammeskov Bang Pedersen and Højlund Christensen (2015), p. 382.

[67] Backhausen and Lundblad (2009), p. 238.

[68] Adrian et al. (2015).

[69] Out of 46,382 cases.

It is, therefore, not easy to determine the judicial settlement procedures and actual amount of settlements effect on the courts resources and effectiveness. But it is evident that more focused conciliation efforts might have an effect.

The Danish Court Administration is also focusing on judicial settlement effort procedures in their latest action plan with the aim of spreading the knowledge both internally and externally on conciliation in court as an alternative to getting a verdict from the court (after a main hearing) as more settlements before the main hearing will give space to more effective handling of other cases and eventually bring down the time used preparing cases as a whole and in a larger perspective.[70]

4.4.2 Court-Connected Mediation

Court-connected mediation is different from judicial settlement efforts done by the judge during ordinary proceedings in civil cases as described above. Court-connected mediation is based on voluntary settlement activities conducted by a neutral third party who assists the parties in reaching their own solution in a pending court case.[71]

Such procedures are also implemented in the Danish Administration of Justice Act. In accordance with chapter 27, district courts may offer the parties a court-connected mediation procedure both in first instance and on appeal.

The court-connected mediation procedure was introduced with the court reform in 2008.[72] Since 2003, a pilot scheme had been in action in four of the larger district courts and the Western High Court. The scheme was rated successful, and the period for the pilot scheme was extended.

In 2006, The Danish Standing Committee on Procedural Law (*Retsplejerådet*) gave their report no. 1481 on court-connected mediation. The provisions in chapter 27 of the Administration of Justice Act are primarily based on the recommendations from the committee.

The purpose of the mediation procedure is to give the parties involved in a court case the possibility for a solution not based on traditional conciliation using applicable law or a court decision. The parties should be given an opportunity to reach a solution that is more satisfactory to both parties involved because a solution

[70] http://www.domstol.dk/om/publikationer/HtmlPublikationer/Handlingsplaner/Danmarks%20Domstoles%20handlingsplan%202015/kap04.htm.

[71] See sections 1.5 and 9.2.

[72] Act no. 168 of 12 March 2008 given on the basis of the Danish Standing Committee on Procedural Law (Retsplejerådet) report no.1481/2006. Aagaard and Toftegaard Nielsen (2008), pp. 167–172. Gomard and Kistrup (2013), p. 636, Adrian (2012).

reached from mediation to a higher level makes it possible to have influence on the parties' interests, needs and future.[73]

There are no formal requirements as to when or how mediation should be offered. This is often done in writing after the case has been filed or at the preparatory hearing. The mediation process can be started at any time during preparatory proceedings or even at the main hearing. The judge might mention the possibility at the preparatory hearing if the parties have not refused mediation in the statement of claim or the statement of defence.

When the parties chooses court-connected mediation the ordinary preparatory proceedings stops and the provisions of the Administration of Justice Act will no longer have to be followed (besides Chapter 27). Instead, a mediator will be in charge of the process in consultation with the parties.

The mediator is appointed by the court. The mediator can be a judge, a deputy judge or a lawyer appointed by the Danish Court Administration.[74]

There are no strict guidelines for how the mediation process should proceed, but the process will normally be structured more or less by the recommendations from the Danish Standing Committee on Procedural Law (*Retsplejerådet*) report no. 1481 and the corresponding ethical guidelines.[75]

When mediation ends in a settlement, there will be no further proceedings in the case before the court. If the case it not settled through a mediation procedure, the case will proceed as a "normal" civil case and ordinary preparatory proceedings are resumed.

Court-connected mediation is offered free of any fees to the court, but, in accordance with section 278 of the Administration of Justice Act, the involved parties must pay their own expenses to a lawyer who are representing them, unless otherwise agreed on in the settlement that is reached. If the case is not settled through mediation and the case proceeds as a normal civil case, costs will be set as in other civil cases (see Sect. 4.6 below). Costs related to the parts of the mediation process that has completed been must be held by the parties themselves, unless otherwise agreed.[76]

Mediation can be a faster or more effective way to settle a case. Therefore, court-connected mediation is also interesting from the legislators' point of view—when the aims of legislation are focused on effectiveness and optimised use of resources.

---

[73] Gomard and Kistrup (2013), p. 636; Adrian (2012), p. 47 f., The Danish Standing Committee on Procedural Law (Retsplejerådet) report no. 1481/2006, p. 12 f. An example of mediation after a case was appealed can be found in UfR 2014.1334 Ø (Mediation in Eastern High Court)—on the case Rammeskov Bang Pedersen and Højlund Christensen (2015), p. 385.

[74] Administration of Justice Act section 275. Lawyers have to go through an education to be appointed—see Adrian (2012), p. 66. There is also a Code of Conduct for mediators made by the Danish Court Administration—can be found on www.domstol.dk.

[75] For a further description see Adrian (2012), p. 65. Backhausen and Lundblad (2009), p. 247, Rammeskov Bang Pedersen and Højlund Christensen (2015), p. 387.

[76] Dalager (2015), p. 83, Rammeskov Bang Pedersen and Højlund Christensen (2015), p. 388, UfR 2014.623 V (Western High Court decision).

In this context, the Danish Court Administration wishes court-connected mediation to be used more often even though there is no documentation implying the exact economic benefits from this. A recent study though has estimated that there is an economic potential in an increased use of court-connected mediation.[77]

Statistics imply that court-connected mediation is not commonly used today. In 2013, court-connected mediation where tried in only 2 % of all civil cases (865 cases). Approximately 1 % of these cases ended through the mediation process.[78]

4.5 Court Fees and Other Costs Related to Preparatory Proceedings

The question of distribution of costs is not related directly to the preparatory proceedings and the regulation will, therefore, only be described very briefly here.[79] It could be argued that this is only partly true because one of the aims of the system of costs is to encourage settlements before the trial.[80]

Distribution of costs under the Danish Civil Justice System is based on three principles: any person initiating legal proceedings carries the initial responsibility for the costs involved; when the court approves the taking of a particular procedural measure, the court can decide that the other party must, at least until the end of the case, carry the costs if it is in his interest that the measure is taken—or the court may decide that the cost is divided between the parties; the losing party will, in most cases, be ordered to pay costs to the winning party.[81]

When a case is fully or partially disposed of or if the parties settle the case during the preparatory proceedings, the court will also make a decision on the questions of cost unless the involved parties have agreed otherwise, for example, in a settlement.

Only actual expenses may be refunded, which may include different actual cost related to both preparatory proceedings and eventually the main hearing, such as expenses related to expert witnesses, other witness compensation and cost fees.[82]

When a case is settled, withdrawn or otherwise closed during preparatory proceedings the costs paid until this time may be paid by the losing party.

---

[77] Deloitte Consulting (2013).

[78] Statistics from the Danish Court Administration found on www.domstol.dk.

[79] The court fee consists of a basic amount (DKK 500 (EUR 67)) and—when the claim concerns money or its equivalent—the claimant must pay an additional fee of DKK 250 (EUR 34) + 1.2 % of the exceeding amount not including interest or collection costs. There is an absolute cap on court fees at DKK 75,000 (EUR 10,065). See Petersen (2014), p. 285 for a an overview in English on the legislation on this topic.

[80] See Petersen (2014), p. 296. Gomard and Kistrup (2013), p. 631.

[81] Werlauff (2010), p. 106.

[82] Gomard and Kistrup (2013), p. 774.

If the case is closed during preparatory proceedings the amount for legal fees will be calculated on the basis of the actual stage of the case. Often the fee will be calculated as a not so significant amount as it is assumed that the lawyer will spend most of his or her worktime with the case preparing and carrying out the main hearing. This is often also an aspect of motivation to settle a case before the main hearing This means that the main focus on settlements often will be related to a phase after the preparatory proceedings have ended (but before the main hearing).

The over-all conclusion is that the regulation on cost distribution is most often not the decisive factor if the parties decide whether to settle a case during preparatory proceedings.

4.6 Concluding Remarks and Outlooks

Preparatory proceedings in the Danish Court System are, as it appears, focused on efficiency through fast and consequent preparatory procedures without compromising the rule of law or principles of access to courts and justice.

The legal system in Denmark is well functioning and effective from a European perspective.[83] Corruption and other like-minded problems in society, in general, are almost non-existent. As such, the main object for improvements has been to make the court system more efficient as manpower (or rather the lack of manpower) and limited budgets are other aspects to take into consideration given the high volume of cases that are processed through the system annually.

During recent years there has been an ongoing effort to make procedures even more efficient through several changes to the Administration of Justice Act, including the introduction of the preparatory hearing and other changes to the provisions governing preparatory proceedings and the small claims procedure.

The reforms of the Danish Court system have resulted in substantial empowerment of the district courts, since almost all civil cases starts here. It has made it easier for the district courts to maintain a high professional level in their judicial work and to organise their procedural routines more efficiently. In addition, the courts have, in civil cases, been granted the requisite instruments to achieve more expedient management of the preparatory work.[84]

The reform of the provisions on preparatory proceedings in 2008 and 2014 has put more focus on getting civil cases prepared faster and more efficient by forcing the involved parties (and the courts) to "think ahead" when deciding how to approach the case.

[83] The Courts of Denmark are the most effective measured on time needed to resolve civil, commercial, administrative and other cases (First instance/in days). See "The 2015 EU Justice scoreboard" from the European Commission on quality, independence and efficiency of justice systems in the European Union. http://ec.europa.eu/justice/effective-justice/files/justice_scoreboard_2015_en.pdf (figure 4).

[84] The Scandinavian Court Administrations (2007), p. 586.

Especially the preparatory hearing has been a decisive factor in this development, as the hearing is milestone in the preparatory stage that sets the outline for the following steps of the case. The further clarifications in section 353 of the Administration of Justice Act in 2014 indicate just that.

From the legislators' point-of-view, the easiest way to reduce time used in preparation of the case is to make the parties involved (and their representatives) "do their homework" and think through all elements of a case at the earliest stage possible. This will, by implication, give the judge—as well as the parties—a better overview on the case and relevant procedural steps. It will also make it easier to act on any disputes arising so that cases actually will be tried faster. Nonetheless, judges must still play an active role and make sure that the parties involved actually follow the directions set in the Administration of Justice Act. The judge has the tools to force the parties to initiate the preparation of the case and keep the pace—and it is up to the judge to make sure this is happening. Some judges are better at this than others and this might be a small but anyway weak spot to the regulation that is not easy to fix.

An active judge is most often a benefit, but it can be a problem from a "rule of law" point-of-view where the differences between the way judges act in court becomes too large. This will, of course, have to be addressed when discussing further regulation on preparatory proceedings.

It is a fact that judicial settlement efforts and court-connected mediation do not play a larger role in the preparatory phase of civil cases today. There is still room for improvement here as studies show that there can be economic benefits achieved from a higher degree of settlements in court during preparatory proceedings before the main hearing.

Also, from the rule of law perspective, the way judicial settlement efforts are promoted in various ways and manners can be a problem. Forcing parties to settle cases during preparatory proceedings may not become a goal in itself. Personal benefits, statistical reasons, or economic benefits for the courts should not be the most vital considerations for a judge's eager to settle a case. There is no documentation that it is so, but there should not be further encouragements to it becoming so. Judges should not be put under pressure to settle more cases without directions under which circumstances it should be done. This does not mean that judge should not be aware of the duty to try to settle a case that they already have.

More cases could be settled through court-connected mediation if lawyers and judges promoted this solution more. But further development of the regulation on court-connected mediation should take into consideration that the process must be based on the same principles in all courts to secure transparency and equal treatment. This could be a minor opposition to the regulation applicable today.

Ordinary civil cases in Danish courts had an average processing time in court of 10.8 months in 2014, down from 11.2 months in 2013. Sixty-nine per cent of the cases were settled within a year (67.3 % in 2013). From these figures alone it seems the efforts are producing measurable results.

Dommerforeningen[85] have made some guidelines on the procedures in civil cases in first instance.[86] The high courts have also made guidelines for the procedure in cases before these courts.[87] The same thing has been done by the Supreme Court.[88]

These guidelines are made to create further uniformity and transparency for all users of the court system, so that cases can be treated equally and effectively.

The civil procedure system in Denmark is still in a period of change, mainly due to demand for keeping up with technological developments and further demands for public service in society.

As the objectives of Danish courts are to make procedures, decisions and other services meet the highest professional standards and provide friendly and fast services, the courts must adapt to modern technology.

An important element of judicial transparency is the public accessibility of the courts. Public authorities in Denmark have, in recent years, increased their digital communication with citizens. They now very often use systems based on, for example, electronic signatures, in order to the ensure privacy and security of transactions and communications.

As a result, the current reforms have also focused on more flexible approaches to new communication technologies.[89] The courts have also agreed on a set of guidelines for the use of e-mail or other digital communication between the court and its users.[90] In 2014, the Danish Court Administration started focusing on "digital procedures" with the purpose of establishing the possibilities for digital communication with all users of the courts in civil cases and making the whole preparatory process digitalised. The goal is that a civil case can be digitalised from filing the statement of claim and paying the court fee until the decision in the case is announced to the parties involved.

As the next step (as mentioned in Sect. 4.1.5 above) the Administration of Justice Act has been changed from January 1st 2016 so that it will be possible to handle a civil case solely digital without any paper being exchanged between the court and the parties involved. This may be a new small "revolution" in civil procedure, even though almost other parts of public administration in Denmark are communicating with the citizens on a digitalised basis only.

---

[85] An association for judges and clerks employed by the Danish courts.

[86] http://www.domstol.dk/saadangoerdu/tildigderer/advokat/civilesagervedbyretterne/Documents/Vejledning%20om%20behandling%20af%20civile%20sager.pdf.

[87] http://www.domstol.dk/VestreLandsret/Behandling%20af%20civile%20sager/Documents/Behandling%20af%20civile%20sager%20maj%202013.pdf.

[88] http://www.hoejesteret.dk/hoejesteret/vejledninger/Pages/Civilesager.aspx.

[89] The Danish Standing Committee on Procedural Law (Retsplejerådet) report no. 1401/2001. In 2014 The Danish Court Administration launched a new strategy for digitization of the handling of civil cases: "Danmarks Domstole Digitaliseringsstrategi 2014-2018" https://www.domstol.dk/om/publikationer/Publikationer/Digitaliseringsstrategi%202014-2018.pdf.

[90] http://www.domstol.dk/om/Digitalpost/professionelle/retningslinjer/Pages/default.aspx

From 1 January 2015, the courts were also authorized to decide whether documents may be sent to the court by e-mail during pre-trial proceedings.[91] These steps are, of course, made to make access to court easier, faster, and more up to date with modern technology. The main issue in the decision to allow the use of e-mails has been how to make sure sensitive and sometimes confidential data could be kept secure and that the exchange of data will be in accordance with The Act on Processing of Personal Data.[92]

In the future, Danish courts will aim to continue operating a smooth-running legal system with efficient resource management with judiciary transparency and open justice.

A recent study[93] has shown that even though the Danish courts have become more effective since the reform in 2008, there are still possible ways of making the process in civil cases more effective and less expensive without compromising law enforcement. This is also still the largest challenge.

The study indicated the fact that the case administration time should be as brief as possible. This is also embodied in the European Convention on Human Rights.

Besides this, other proposals have been made on grounds of the findings in this study as to how civil proceedings could be made even faster and more effective by further digitalisation and a tighter regulation on the progress of preparatory proceedings.

Keeping the main focus on high standards of court procedures may help maintaining standards in the future when efficiency still heads the agenda and limited resources are a fact.

The focus will be on digitisation as a mean to make preparatory proceedings even faster, easier to handle for the court and the users so that the whole process will become even smoother and more effective.

The Danish civil justice system is still one of the most effective in Europe. Standards are high—and the aim is to keep them high or become even higher. The demands for continuous improvements in procedural standards are a necessity if the court system is to keep up with developments in technology and the high expectations of all users.

References

Aagaard H, Toftegaard Nielsen C (2008) Nye regler om retsmægling. Juristen 2008:167–172

Adrian L (2012) Mellem retssag og rundbordssamtale – retsmægling i teori og praksis. Jurist- og Økonomforbundet, København

[91] By Act no. 737 of 25 June 2014 introducing section 148 b to the Administration of Justice Act.

[92] Act no. 429 of 31 May 2000.

[93] Deloitte Consulting (2013).

Adrian L, Bager S, Salung Petersen C (2015) Perspektiver på forligsmægling. Juristen 2015:98–106
Amstrup Fournais A, Aschou Johannesen C (2012) Et paradigmeskifte i retsplejens tilgang til sagkyndig medvirken. UfR 2012(B):498–504
Backhausen P, Lundblad C (eds) (2009) Proceduren, 3rd edn. Djøf Forlag, København
Consulting D (2013) Analyse af civile sager, Rapport fra udvalget for bedre og mere effektiv behandling af civile sager ved domstolene. Justitsministeriet, København
Dalager C (2015) Civile retssager, 2nd edn. Djøf forlag, København
Gomard B, Kistrup M (2013) Civilprocessen, 7th edn. KARNOV Group, København
Højgaard Pedersen M (2009) Procesbevillingsnævnet efter domstolsreformen. Juristen 2009:31–35
Jochimsen J (2012) Bevisførelse i retssager, 1st edn. KARNOV Group, København
Juul-Sandberg J (2011) Godsk Pedersen H V (eds). Adgang til fremlæggelse af ensidigt indhentede erklæringer for domstolene – med særligt henblik på boligretssager og tvister om mangler ved fast ejendom in Juridiske Emner ved Syddansk Universitet, København
Juul-Sandberg J (2012) Boligrettens saglige kompetence in Tidsskrift for Bolig- og Byggeret, 2012:591–599
Juul-Sandberg J (2013) Hvornår skal en sag udgå af småsagsprocessen i medfør af retsplejelovens § 402, stk. 1? in Fuldmægtigen 2014:193
Juul-Sandberg J, Godsk Pedersen HV (eds) (2013) Lægdommere – Boligrettens legitimitet? in Juridiske emner ved Syddansk Universitet, København
Lindencrone L, Werlauff E (2014) Dansk Retspleje, 5th edn. KARNOV Group, København
Nellemann J (1869) Foreløbigt Udkast til Lov om Rettergangsmaaden i borgerlige Domssager med Motiver. Trykt som manuskript, København
Nylund A (2014) European integration and Nordic civil procedure. In: Ervo L, Nylund A (eds) The future of civil litigation. Springer, Cham
Petersen CS (2014) A comparative perspective on recent Nordic reforms of civil justice. In: Ervo L, Nylund A (eds) The future of civil litigation. Springer, Cham
Pii N, Bagger T, Rasmussen K, Lindblom L, Kistrup M, Arnt Nielsen P, Jochimsen J, Møller J, Dybdahl O, Hertz K, Carlsen B, Rammeskow Bang-Pedersen U, Højlund Christensen L, Rothe H, Haargaard F, Kruse Mikkelsen J, Ellehauge M, Røn J, Dahl Sinding G, Hjortenberg J, Højgaard Mørup S, Lundblad C, Frost L, Talevski O, Andersen NM, Mavrogenis A, Backhausen P, Jensen T, Thønnings T, Juhl N, Møller Madsen R, Kernn-Jespersen L, Rørdam T, Danielsen S, Gammeltoft-Hansen H, Gomard B (eds) (2013) Retsplejeloven og Bruxelles I-forordningen med kommentarer I, 9th edn. Djøf Forlag, København
Rammeskov Bang Pedersen U, Højlund Christensen L (2015) Den civile retspleje, 3rd edn. Pejus, København
Sommer Jensen K (2011) Ensidige erklæringer i civilprocessen. Erhvervsjuridisk Tidsskrift 2011:317–332
Taksøe Jensen F (1976) Materiel Procesledelse. Juristforbundet, København
The Scandinavian Court Administrations (2007) The Danish courts - an organization in development. Scand Stud Law 51:581–590
Udvalget om bedre og mere effektiv behandling af civile sager ved domstolene (2013) Bedre og mere effektiv behandling af civile sager ved domstolene. Ministry of Justice
von Eyben WE (1998) Dommertilkendegivelser 1987 til 1997 in U 1998 B:51–55
von Eyben B (2008) Juridisk Ordbog, 13th edn. Thomson Reuters, København
Waage F, Herborn M (2015) Dimensions of evidence in European civil procedure: national report Denmark. DEECP, Slovenia
Werlauff E (1999) Common European procedural law. Djøf Publishing, København
Werlauff E (2000) Fælleseuropæisk procesret, 2nd edn. Jurist- og Økonomforbundet, København
Werlauff E (2010) Civil procedure in Denmark, 2nd edn. Djøf Forlag, København

Further Reading

Danish Court Administration's Homepage: http://www.domstol.dk/. Accessed 29 Jul 2015
European Commission's homepage: http://ec.europa.eu/. Accessed 29 Jul 2015
The Danish Standing Committee on Procedural Law (Retsplejerådet) report no. 698/1973
The Danish Standing Committee on Procedural Law (Retsplejerådet) report no.1481/2006
The Danish Standing Committee on Procedural Law (Retsplejerådet) report no.1543/2013
The Danish Standing Committee on Procedural Law (Retsplejerådet) report no. 1401/2001
The Danish Standing Committee on Procedural Law (Retsplejerådet) report no. 1436/2004
The Danish Supreme Court's Homepage: http://www.hoejesteret.dk/. Accessed 29 Jul 2015

Part II
Preparatory Proceedings in Former Communist Countries

Chapter 5
The Preparatory Stage of Civil Proceedings in Slovenia, the Czech Republic and Slovakia: Halfway There Yet?

Aleš Galič

Abstract Although the legislatures of the three discussed countries are aware of the importance of a focused and thorough preparation of the main hearing, the achieved results so far have not been satisfactory. The reasons for this are manifold, ranging from insufficient legislative reforms, inadequate application of these reforms in the case law to the persistent court culture, which favours neither thorough preparation before the main hearing nor the idea of judicial discretion and procedural flexibility. There are deficiencies concerning procedural sanctions for noncompliance with the requirement of timely presentation of relevant material, whereby certain tools for preparation of the main hearing are inexistent altogether. In addition, courts have difficulties in striking a proper balance between the required burdens of the court and those of the parties and their legal counsel, as well as a proper balance between the system of preclusions and the need of flexibility.

5.1 Introduction

There are several things that the three Slavic nations of Central Europe—Slovenia, the Czech Republic and Slovakia—have in common. They were all part of the Austrian-Hungarian Empire until the end of the First World War. The territories of what are nowadays Slovenia and the Czech Republic belonged to the Austrian part, where the famous *Franz Klein*'s *Zivilprozessordnung* was in force.[1] On the other hand, Slovakia was integrated in the Hungarian part of the Empire, where

I am indebted to Helena Podveská, judge of the *Hodonín District Court, the Czech Republic,* for her extensive and valuable comments on the draft of this chapter; all errors are, of course, my own.

[1] See e.g. Rechberger (2008), p. 108, Dvořák (2012), p. 123.

A. Galič (✉)
University of Ljubljana, Faculty of Law, Poljanski nasip 2, SI-1000 Ljubljana, Slovenia
e-mail: ales.galic@pf.uni-lj.si

L. Ervo, A. Nylund (eds.), *Current Trends in Preparatory Proceedings*,
DOI 10.1007/978-3-319-29325-7_5

Hungarian laws, ultimately the Civil Procedure Act of 1911, applied.[2] After the dissolution of the Empire in 1918, the paths of the three entities parted. The Czechs and Slovaks united in the Republic of Czechoslovakia whereas Slovenia became a part of the newly formed Yugoslav kingdom. However, the formation of new states did not bring about discontinuance in use of the above-mentioned Austrian and Hungarian laws in any of the three countries, although for different reasons. Yugoslav legislature, entrusted with the task of adopting uniform legislation opted for a transplantation of Austrian law, which it perceived to be because the most modern and advanced.[3] Thus, the Yugoslav Civil Procedure Act from 1929 was practically a literal translation of the Austrian ZPO. In Czechoslovakia, legal dualism (reception of Austrian law in the Czech part and of Hungarian law in Slovakia) continued to apply.[4] Although adoption of a uniform civil procedure act was attempted, it has never been accomplished.[5] The process was brutally interrupted by the German occupation of the Czech lands (Bohemia and Moravia) and the formation of a puppet Slovak state in 1939.[6]

After the end of the Second World War communist governments were installed in all of the discussed countries (i.e. in Yugoslavia, which Slovenia was a federal unit of, and in reunified Czechoslovakia—now the Czechoslovak Socialist Republic, hereinafter CSSR). However, in the era of communist regimes, there were perhaps as much differences as similarities between Slovenia (as a part of Yugoslavia), on the one hand, and the CSSR, on the other. At least after the late fifties' Yugoslavia opted for what could most easily be described as a 'milder version of socialism'. Yugoslavia managed to stay out of the Soviet Bloc and remained open to the Western countries with unrestricted and visa-free travel to these countries for individuals as well. The CSSR, on the contrary, found itself in the group of Soviet satellites and thus behind the "iron curtain".[7] Personal and academic contacts with Western Europe remained widely available and exercised on a regular basis in Yugoslavia, whereas in the soviet-bloc CSSR they were effectively cut-off.[8] There was no language barrier since, at least in the northern parts of Yugoslavia (Slovenia, Croatia), English (and not Russian like in the CSSR) was the foreign language taught in primary and secondary schools. The main source of knowledge and professional links in legal academic circles (books, monographs, commentaries) came from West Germany, Austria and even the United States (which were all

[2] The Hungarian Civil Procedure Act of 1911 was perceived as a "middle way" between the Franz Klein's concept of active judge, concentration, orality and co-operation between the court and the parties and the more adversarial traditional German model. See Rechberger (2008), p. 108, Kengyel (2000), p. 361

[3] Juhart (1961), p. 21.

[4] Cappelletti and Garth (1987), p. 13.

[5] Schelleová and Schelle (2005), p. 47.

[6] Winterová and Macková (2012), p. 14.

[7] Winterová and Macková (2012), p. 15.

[8] For Slovenia see Kranjc (1993), p. 413, for CSSR see Dvořák (2012), p. 124.

freely available in law schools' libraries), whereas there was, at least in Slovenia and Croatia, practically no trace of Soviet academic writing on civil procedure. Again, the situation in this regard was exactly the opposite in the CSSR.[9] In addition the system of a 'centrally planned state economy' did not apply in Yugoslavia and its major trading partners were (West) Germany and Italy. The CSSR on the other hand was firmly integrated in the Soviet economic zone.

These characteristics inevitably expressed themselves in the regulation and practice of civil procedure as well. Unlike in the Soviet Bloc countries such as Czechoslovakia, communist ideological principles and political slogans were left out of the Yugoslav Civil Procedure Act.[10] The principle (and main statutory instruments) of respect for party autonomy was recognised in the law (whereas it was a typical feature of soviet-bloc systems that the public prosecutor had standing to bring lawsuits on behalf of people who were unable or unwilling to do so by themselves).[11] Furthermore, a Slovenian judge of Yugoslav era, was bound by the relief sought and also could not introduce facts that were not asserted by the parties. Dispositive acts (settlement, acknowledgment of a claim, and relinquishment of a claim—all with a *res iudicata* effect) were available. On the contrary, in the CSSR's Soviet-style civil procedure these expressions of "bourgeois individualism", were either abolished or—as settlement in court—drastically restricted.[12] A judgment by default as a typical expression of party autonomy was retained in Yugoslavia, whereas it was abolished in "Soviet style" civil procedure of the CSSR where such "bourgeois" instruments were denounced as leading merely to a determination of a "formal" truth instead of "material" truth.[13] The possibility of the intervention of a public prosecutor in civil litigation was much more limited in Yugoslavia than in the CSSR, where the "omnipresence" of a public prosecutor was endemic.[14] For all the above reasons, civil procedure legislation of Yugoslavia during socialism did not suffer such deformation as in the CSSR. Yugoslav Civil Procedure Act of 1976 could thus still be perceived as a continuity of its Austrian predecessor. The situation in the CSSR was different; the (first uniform) Czechoslovak Civil Procedure Code of 1963[15] was closely tied to the Soviet law and the ties of civil procedure law in this country to the Central European traditions of (either former Austrian or Hungarian) civil procedure were broken. It is also telling that the Yugoslav Bar Association was the only one from the—then—communist

---

[9] Dvořák (2012), p. 124.

[10] There was merely one reference to "socialist morality"; Art. 3/3 of the CPA-1976.

[11] Nový (2009), pp. 530 ff.

[12] See Nový (2009), pp. 535–536. It was typical for the soviet-style civil procedure that that the judge could prevent parties from settling the case if he found that this contravened "their best interest or the general interest". *Cf. e.g.* Nový (2009), pp. 519 and 523.

[13] Nový (2009), p. 537.

[14] Cf. Nový (2009), pp. 524 ff.

[15] Občanský soudní řád, zákon č. 99/1963 Sb. (in Czech); Občiansky súdny poriadok, zákon č. 99/1963 Zb. (in Slovak).

countries that was considered to be sufficiently compatible with the western standards of independence and was, therefore, accepted into the International Bar Association. On the contrary, the bar as an independent profession disappeared in the CSSR and other soviet-bloc countries.[16]

This being said, it should also be stressed that civil justice in socialist Yugoslavia suffered from painful degradation. Distortions of civil justice were nevertheless implemented on a much subtler level than in the countries of the Soviet Bloc. For example, while the principle of respect for party autonomy was (almost) adequately recognised in the written law, practice often tended toward much more paternalistic, sacrificing the value of human self-responsibility. This was partly an expression of the ideological view that courts (that is: the state) are omnipotent and have the capacity to find the truth and to adequately regulate all spheres of society and human relationships.[17] Secondly, it was an expression of certain disrespect for the autonomy of the individual and her or his ability to be responsible for own actions and omissions. Thirdly, it was an expression of a certain scepticism regarding the Bar as an independent legal profession and lawyers' ability to effectively accomplish their role of protecting the rights of their clients. Hence, it is observed that in Yugoslavia, the elements of cooperation between the parties and the judge and judicial activism of the Austrian procedural legislation, while retained in the law, were not interpreted in the *Franz Klein*'s manner of being a warrant for concentration, publicity, directness and efficiency any more, instead they became instruments of socialist paternalism.[18]

After the downfall of communist regimes in the late 1980s and early 1990s the three countries meet again on a path towards a parliamentary democracy and rebuilding of their legal systems. The early era of transition of the political system in these three countries was even more turbulent then elsewhere, as it was linked also to calls for independence. New sovereign states ultimately emerged. Slovenia became an independent state in 1991 (just on time not to be involved in wars that later followed in other parts of former Yugoslavia), whereby a full international recognition followed in 1992. Czechoslovakia was consensually dissolved with effect as of 1 January 1993. All three countries joined the European Union in 2004.

The transition of legal systems and civil justice, in particular, in the discussed countries is an onerous and difficult process, which is far from over yet. In all three countries there exists a great public dissatisfaction with the functioning of civil justice due to excessive duration of proceedings and backlogs in courts. This still seriously undermines the trust in the judiciary in public opinion. The "EU justice scoreboard" shows that the situation in both respects is actually not overly critical in

---

[16] Bohata (2003), p. 15.

[17] For such an ideological foundation concerning the doctrine of the primacy of the material truth see Kamhi (1957), pp. 22–24.

[18] Uzelac (2004), p. 295.

the Czech Republic.[19] It is however, as the EU Commission keeps pointing out,[20] worrying both in Slovenia as well as in Slovakia. Nevertheless, at least there is a distinct positive trend in Slovenia, where backlogs have been gradually decreasing, the disposition time shortened and the "clearance rate" is slightly more than 100 %, which means that the situation is stable."[21] On the contrary, no such progress has been made in Slovakia, which continues to score poorly and where the length of civil proceedings has actually deteriorated over the recent years.[22]

Numerous attempts have been made by the legislature to tackle the problem of inefficiency in civil proceedings. In Slovenia, the Yugoslav Civil Procedure Act remained in force (with merely some minor changes) until 1999 when the first Slovenian Civil Procedure Act was adopted. Since (as it has been already been mentioned) the Yugoslav CPA remained closely linked to its Austrian predecessor, this reform did not need to be—and indeed it was not—particularly radical. Subsequently, the CPA has been amended on a couple of occasions, the most important amendments being made in 2002 (promotion of judicial conciliation and referrals to ADR) and in 2008 (strengthening of procedural obligations for the parties, emphasis on preparatory stage of proceedings, reshaping the access to the Supreme Court). One could expect that a more radical reform was needed and implemented in the Czech Republic and Slovakia, where Civil Procedure Acts were based on the Soviet model. However, this is not the case. The legislatures opted for continuity and the recodification of civil procedure law did not take place yet—the old Civil Procedure Code of 1963 remained in force in both countries. It was, however, subject to numerous amendments. Since the beginning of the 1990s, the CPA has been amended about 80 times in Slovakia[23] and 100 times in the Czech Republic.[24] It is obvious that such fragmented changes, implemented in a piece-meal manner, which merely tackled isolated features of procedural system, could not amount to a systemic and coherent reform and neither could they implement a more ambitious overall reshaping of the structure of proceedings.[25] However, the situation is about to change in the near future. Both countries have announced that

---

[19] The EU Justice Scoreboard (2015), pp. 8–10.

[20] Assessment of the 2013 national reform programme and stability programme for Slovenia (2013), p. 30, Assessment of the 2013 national reform programme and stability programme for Slovakia (2013), p. 30 and 31, The functioning of judicial systems and the situation of the economy in the European Union Member States (2013), p. 516.

[21] The functioning of judicial systems and the situation of the economy in the European Union Member States (2013), p. 516.

[22] Assessment of the 2013 national reform programme and stability programme for Slovakia (2013), p. 30 and 31. See also: The EU Justice Scoreboard (2015).

[23] See the text of the Act and the chronological list of amendments since 1963, available at: http://www.zakonypreludi.sk/zz/1963-99.

[24] Dvořák (2012), p. 123.

[25] Dvořák (2012), pp. 134–135, Nový (2009), pp. 550–552.

entirely new civil procedure acts will be adopted.[26] In time of finalising of this chapter (September 2015), this goal has almost been achieved in Slovakia. The new Civil Procedure Act (*Civilný sporový poriadok*) has been adopted on 15 May 2015 and it will come into force on 1 July 2016.[27] In the Czech Republic, the Commission for Recodification of Civil Procedure was formed in 2013 and became operable in 2014.[28] No law has been publicly submitted yet though and the work of the recodification commission has recently been practically stalled.

Finally, it should be noted that in the last two decades powerful new actors strongly influenced the development of civil procedure in all three discussed countries: namely the constitutional courts. They impacted both the legislation (numerous norms of civil procedure acts have been invalidated by the constitutional courts) as well as case law. The constitutional courts in all three countries have (*inter alia*) jurisdiction to examine constitutional complaints against the judgments of regular (ordinary) courts for alleged breaches of fundamental (constitutional) rights.[29] After the exhaustion of all available remedies, individual litigants can have the judgment reached in their case reassessed by the Constitutional Court. However, the Constitutional Court may only look into "constitutional matters", leaving the interpretation of ordinary law to the general courts.[30] Nevertheless, in case of very activist constitutional courts, a relation between the constitutional court and the ordinary courts, particularly the supreme court, can be very conflict-ridden. In this regard, there are considerable differences between constitutional courts. Especially the distrust of the Czech Constitutional Court toward the Supreme Court is well known, at least in earlier years.[31]

---

[26] For Slovakia see: Final Recommendation for a Council Recommendation on Slovakia's 2013 national reform programme and delivering a Council opinion on Slovakia's stability programme for 2012–2016, for the Czech Republic see: 2014 Office of the Government of the Czech Republic National Reform Programme of the Czech Republic, p. 31.and its Annex No. 3. See also Dvořák , p. 136.

[27] The text is available (in Slovak language) on: http://www.nrsr.sk/web/Dynamic/Download.aspx?DocID=414985. See also the explanatory memorandum: Ministerstvo spravodlivosti Slovenskej republiky, Návrh legislatívneho zámeru rekodifikácie civilného práva procesného, p. 77.

[28] See e.g. Válová (2014), p. 1, see also National Reform Programme of the Czech Republic 2014, p. 31 and its Annex No. 3 (Overview of impacts and a time schedule for the implementation of other measures).

[29] See e.g. the Study on Individual Access to Constitutional Justice (2010), pp. 24ff; see also Kühn (2011), p. 196.

[30] See Study on Individual Access to Constitutional Justice (2010), p. 55.

[31] Bobek (2009), p. 64. This prompted the Czech Supreme Court to openly revolt against the Constitutional court's decisions and its openly activist approach. Přibáň (2002), p. 380, Cf. Kühn (2011), pp. 138–141 and 159–161.

5.2 Disappearance of a Preparatory Stage as an Adverse Consequence of the Quest for Material Truth

In the era of communist rule, both in the CSSR as well as in Yugoslavia tools for concentration of proceedings of old Austrian and Hungarian tradition were effectively abolished. In spite of certain improvements (or at least attempted improvements) in recent years, there still exist serious deficiencies in the preparatory stage of litigation in the discussed countries. True, their civil procedure laws have always contained references to "preparation of main hearing". This, however, was not understood in the sense of substantive preparation aimed at timely gathering assertions of facts, adducing evidence, clarifying legal positions and determining what issues are really in dispute between the parties and, at the same time, relevant for determination of the case. Rather, it was restricted to formal aspects of proceedings, such as examination of jurisdiction, payment of court fees and other admissibility requirements.

Programmatic norms such as that "*litigation, whenever possible, should be terminated in one single main hearing*"[32] have little practical weight. The reality of litigation practice shows a different picture. Litigation usually consists of a number of consecutive ("piecemeal") hearings, many of which are immediately adjourned due to the parties' filing of new preparatory briefs. Moreover, the time intervals between sessions are often long. In the time period between consecutive hearings parties often file further preparatory briefs.

Both the accentuated responsibility of the judge, on the one hand, the non-existence of any binding time-limits for collection of procedural material and lack of sanctions against the parties' belated submission of facts, evidence and preparatory briefs were an expression of the paramount importance that the legislatures of the communist era placed on the "principle of material truth". However, the experience of the discussed countries from the period such a system was in force demonstrates that the high importance assigned to the material truth often led to results exactly the opposite of those it strove to achieve. The procedural system that enabled frequent adjournments of hearings, "piecemeal" manner of the presentation of facts and evidence, caused the goal of substantive justice to fade. Through such practice, proceedings often became too formalised and bereft of substance. It is disastrous, not just from the viewpoint of speed, but as well from the viewpoint of substantive justice, if new arguments and fresh evidence are adduced only at the hearing itself so that neither the opponent nor the judge could adequately reflect on them. In addition, since lawyers were aware that any insufficient diligence in preparing the case would need to be rectified by the (paternalistic) activism of the judge, they increasingly became completely inactive and negligent in the preparation and conduct of their clients' cases. This system that enabled lawyers to attend court hearings totally unprepared, whereby these hearings were reduced to a mere

[32] Art. 298/2 of the Si CPA, Cf. Art. 114a of the CzCPA. Art. 114 of the (old) SkCPA, Art. 157 of the new SkCPA.

formality with the exchange of further briefs, followed by another adjournment, inevitably also resulted in the passivation of judges. It simply did not pay either for judges to prepare diligently for the hearing, if it was very likely that the parties would put forward new material that would shed an entirely different light on the case.

5.3 Instruments Aimed at Ensuring Better Preparation of the Main Hearing: Between the Bold Proclamations and (Not so Bold) Reality

5.3.1 Preparatory Hearings: Promoted in Legislation, Rejected in Practice

The Yugoslav Civil Procedure Act, which retained the structure of its Austrian predecessor, provided for the instrument of a preparatory hearing. In the course of such hearing the judge was expected not only to examine procedural issues but also to determine, together with the parties, what issues are in dispute and material for the case, so that the subsequent main hearing should focus on them.[33] This could be a genuine preparatory stage in proceedings, however, the instrument—which was optional—has practically never been utilised in practice. So, when it was formally abolished by the first Slovenian Civil Procedure Act in 1999 this was not a real change at all—the law just adjusted to what has happened through practice already a long time ago.

The development in the other two countries was to some extent different but nevertheless led to similar results. Whereas the preparatory phase of civil procedure disappeared not only from practice but also from the letter of the law during the communist era, certain instruments were or are being (re-)introduced, however only recently. In the Czech Republic the possibility to schedule a preparatory hearing has been introduced with the CPA reform in 2005. The system was further elaborated with the CPA reform of 2009, which pursued the goal of "concentration of proceedings" and introduced a system of proper preparatory measures (Art. 114a CPA), including a possibility to schedule a preparatory hearing (*přípravné jednání*, Art. 114c CPA). Closely following the Czech example, the new Slovak Civil Procedure Act also provides for the instrument of a preparatory (preliminary) hearing (*predbežné prejednanie sporu*, Art. 168-172).[34] The activity of the judge and the parties in such preparatory hearings is not limited to the examination of procedural prerequisites but should focus also on substantive aspects of the dispute. The drafters of the 2009 reform of the Czech law expected that a preparatory

[33] Ude (1988), p. 218, Juhart (1961), p. 336.

[34] Šínová (2014), p. 1.

hearing would play a very important role in ensuring the concentration of proceedings.[35] Statements, accompanying the on-going reform in Slovakia, share this view; the preparatory hearing where a court and the parties would structure the proceedings and identify the disputed and relevant factual and legal issues is often singled out as the most important instrument of the proposed reform for achieving the goal of concentration of proceedings.[36] Practical experience in the Czech Republic, however, shows that such expectations were much too optimistic. It is realistically acknowledged that the expected results were not achieved. Some authors claim that preparatory hearings almost never take place in practice.[37] This statement may be somewhat exaggerated[38] but there is a general consensus that the instrument has not contributed to the concentration of proceedings.

5.3.2 The Introduction of the Judge's Power to Disregard New Facts and Evidence: Initially Applicable Only After the Commencement of the Main Hearing

The Slovenian Civil Procedure Act (1999) introduced the rule that the parties may assert new facts and evidence at the first main hearing at the latest, whereas at the latest stages the parties are allowed to present new facts and evidence only with a proper excuse for the belated submission (Art. 286 of the 1999 Civil Procedure Act). With the described system the 1999 CPA made some important steps towards the concentration of proceedings (comparing to the previously applicable regime, where no such time-limits existed). However, it remained "half-way". The system of procedural sanctions for facts and evidence submitted late applied only to phases of litigation *after* the first session of the oral hearing. In earlier stages of litigation (including the first oral hearing), there were no restrictions as to when the parties should put forward (and if necessary, clarify, supplement, and substantiate) facts and evidence they wanted to rely on. Understandably, if parties are free to bring forward any new facts and evidence during the first session of the main hearing, it is not possible to properly organise and prepare it. Since the parties were entirely free to put forward entirely new arguments, facts, and evidence (e.g. a proposal to hear an additional witness) as late as during the first oral hearing, the promoted goal that whenever possible the litigation should terminate after only one, but thoroughly prepared, oral hearing, was clearly frustrated. In such system, merely the first

[35] Winterová and Macková (2012), pp. 109–110, Dvořák (2012), p. 133.

[36] See e.g. Návrh legislatívneho zámeru rekodifikácie civilného práva procesného, Ministerstvo spravodlivosti Slovenskej republiky (2013), p. 77.

[37] Šínová (2014), p. 1.

[38] Some authors point out that a preparatory hearing due to its more informal setting, can be valuable for promoting settlements as well as for a more open discussion with the parties about further steps in a complex litigation. Cf. Drapál and Bureš (2009), p. 800.

session of the main hearing could, at best, serve as a "preparatory stage" in proceedings. This, however, does not correspond to an ideal division between the preparatory stage of proceedings and the main hearing. The main hearing should serve the purpose of establishing the relevant facts in dispute. However, which facts are relevant and in dispute and which evidence should be taken in order to establish them, should to the greatest possible extent be clear already before the main hearing.

The development in Slovakia and the Czech Republic was similar. The parties may, as a rule, bring forward new facts and evidence at the first main hearing at the latest, whereas only exceptionally at the later stages. Since 2009, this is a generally applicable rule in the Czech Republic (Art. 118b and 114c CzCPA), whereas in Slovakia it applies for certain types of disputes only; Art. 118a of the old SkCPA. For the same reasons as in Slovenia, this rule does not enable proper preparation of the main hearing. As mentioned above, the Czech law enables the judge to schedule a preparatory hearing, where parties are expected to submit all available facts and evidence (so they will not be able to submit them in the first session of the main hearing anymore).[39] However, as explained, this instrument is very rarely used.

In Slovakia, the drafters of the new law perceive the lack of proper system of preclusions, to be one of the most important reasons for the inefficiency of civil proceedings.[40] The new law therefore emphasises the need for timely bringing forward facts and evidence. Unlike in Slovenia and the Czech Republic where the main rule is rigid (the end of the first session of the main hearing as a cut-off date, in principle) the proposed new Slovak regime is more flexible. There is no fixed date in the Act itself as to when the parties may bring forward new material at the latest (however the court can set such binding time-limits; see *infra*), but rather a general clause that they are expected to do it "*in a manner that corresponds to the need to ensure concentration and acceleration of proceedings and diligent preparation of their cases*" (Art. 153). The rule is framed under a distinct influence of the German *Zivilprozessordnung*, which imposes the "*Prozessförderungspflicht der Parteien*" (Par. 282)—the obligation of the parties to contribute to efficiency of proceedings, linked to an adequate system of sanctions for belated submissions (Par. 296).

---

[39] Drapál and Bureš (2009), p. 778.

[40] Návrh legislatívneho zámeru rekodifikácie civilného práva procesného, Ministerstvo spravodlivosti Slovenskej republiky (2013), p. 32

5.3.3 The Attempts to Promote Written Preparatory Proceedings

In the Czech Republic the 2000 reform provided some (although very modest) tools for written preparatory proceedings. The judge was empowered, in cases of dilatory behaviour of a party, to set additional binding time limits for asserting facts and adducing evidence already at earlier stages of proceedings (so-called "court's concentration"; *koncentrace soudcovská* (or *vhodná*; appropriate); Art. 118c CzCPA).[41] If such time-limits were set by the judge, the other party was in principle prevented from bringing forward new facts and evidence later. The instrument (which, oddly, the judge could apply only upon a motion of the other party but not *sua sponte*) was meant to predominantly apply after the commencement of the main hearing, but at least in theory could be applied in earlier stages as well. However, the reform clearly proved to be a complete failure. The instrument of *koncentrace soudcovská* was therefore abolished in the 2009 reform (which introduced the instrument of a preparatory hearing instead that, as already mentioned, is equally rarely used in practice).

The Slovenian legislature approached the problem in a more systematic manner. The Slovenian CPA was substantially reformed in 2008. The system of procedural sanctions for delays in litigations was strengthened and more importance was given to the (written) preparatory stage of litigation.[42] In order to enable the other party's right to be heard and to organise his or her case, the first party is now obliged, whenever possible, to file new preparatory briefs in sufficient time for them to be served on the other party with adequate time before the main hearing. What is especially important from the viewpoint of distinction between the preparatory stage of proceedings and the main hearing is that judges now have the power to require (and to impose binding time limits) that parties make further submissions and clarifications concerning facts, evidence and legal positions in the set time limit (Art. 286a/1 of the 1999 Civil Procedure Act). The judge may exercise this discretion already in a written form before the main hearing. The discussed provision is framed following the example of Art. 273 of the German ZPO (according to which a court can demand from the parties to submit written statements on certain points that need to be clarified). If a court set the time limits for the filing of new preparatory submissions and this time limit is not met, new submissions made after the time period has expired are admissible only if the court is convinced that admitting them will not delay the resolution of the dispute or if the party provides

[41] The generally applicable rule was that the parties were free to put forward all facts and evidence until the end of the evidentiary (main) hearing (so called "statutory concentration"; *Zákonná koncentrace*). Merely for certain particular types of proceedings the more restrictive rule applied was introduced in 2000 that all facts and evidence must be adduced at the first session of the main hearing at latest.

[42] Amendment to the Civil Procedure Act (ZPP-D); Official gazette of the Republic of Slovenia, No. 45/2008 (in force since October 1, 2008).

an adequate justification for the delay in presenting them (Art. 286a/2, CPA). The discussed tools are optional, as the judge is empowered but not obliged to use them. Thus, in line with the world-wide trends in development of civil procedure, more room is now provided for the judge to adapt the unfolding of proceedings and its time-frame to the characteristics of each particular case. A judge can decide, according to the particularities of the given case, whether it will implement a written preparatory procedure or whether a main hearing will take place and the case will be discussed orally with the parties. The weak point of the reform, however, is that there is no possibility for the judge to implement oral preparatory proceedings (a partial exception is a possibility to schedule a settlement conference—*see infra*).

The described tools, introduced through the 2008 reform, could significantly contribute to the goal that procedural material should be as much as possible collected and clarified already before the main hearing. If the judges exercised the aforementioned powers, they could achieve that the standpoints of the parties would be clearer and more complete and that it would be clarified which facts are really at dispute and which questions the main hearing should be concentrated at.[43] However it must be realistically admitted that the introduced instruments, designed to promote a written preparatory stage in civil proceedings and aimed at achieving a comprehensive preparation of the main hearing, are still insufficiently used in practice. Although it would be wrong to think that the reform remained entirely unsuccessful, the expectations as to how much it would change the day-to-day practice in Slovenian courts were more optimistic.

The new Slovak Civil Procedure Act provides for a somewhat similar system as the Slovenian law. The court can set binding cut-off dates for adducing new facts and evidence (Art. 167 for the written preparatory proceedings; Art. 181 for the oral hearing and in general Art. 153; *sudcovská koncentrácia konania*). Belated evidence will, unless proper excuse is provided, not be admissible (*procesná preklúzia).*[44] The instrument is perceived as one of the main tools for ensuring concentration of proceedings, greater diligence of the parties and better preparation of the main hearing.[45] It remains to be seen whether these expectations, which very much resemble the statements accompanying the above described reform in Slovenia, will be fulfilled in practice.

[43] Such is also the official explanation of the novelty. See The Explanatory memorandum of the Slovenian Ministry of Justice to the draft amendment of the Civil procedure Act (2008), p. 136.

[44] Návrh legislatívneho zámeru rekodifikácie civilného práva procesného, Ministerstvo spravodlivosti Slovenskej republiky (2013), p. 32.

[45] Návrh legislatívneho zámeru rekodifikácie civilného práva procesného, Ministerstvo spravodlivosti Slovenskej republiky (2013), p. 32.

5.4 Reasons for Deficiencies in the Preparatory Stage of Litigation

5.4.1 The Preparatory Stage of Proceedings Without Restrictions for Putting Forward Facts and Evidence During the Main Hearing?

The above overview shows that there exist a variety of attempts to promote at least some features of a preparatory stage of proceedings in all three discussed jurisdictions. So, why have all these attempts failed to bring the expected results?

The undoubtedly unsuccessful fate of the instrument of a preparatory hearing in Slovenia (already from the era of the Yugoslav communist rule) and in the Czech Republic (introduced in 2005 and substantially reinforced in 2009) is telling. The Slovenian experience clearly shows that the question of efficient preparatory stage of proceedings is inherently linked to a proper system of procedural sanctions for the parties' failure to timely bring forward facts and evidence. As it has already been mentioned pursuant to the Yugoslav Civil Procedure Act of 1976 (in this regard the law of the then CSSR was the same), the parties were free to submit new facts and evidence until the end of the last session of the main hearing and—except in commercial cases—even during an appeal. Obviously, such system did not allow for the proper organisation of the preparatory stage of litigation, structuring of proceedings and early identifying of disputed and relevant issues of the case. It was also not able to prevent the common, however, from the aspect of the efficiency of proceedings, outright fatal practice that lawyers filed further preparatory briefs, adducing new facts and evidence, as late as during the main hearing. It is hence not surprising that in such system the institute of a preparatory hearing could not fulfil its goals.

Thus, the first lesson we can learn is that without a proper system of procedural sanctions for facts and evidence submitted late, there can be no genuine distinction between preparatory stage of proceedings and the main hearing.

5.4.2 The Incumbent Interdependence Between the Judge's Duty to Provide Clarifications and the Sanction of Disallowing Facts and Evidence, Submitted in Default

Introduction on the legislative level of the judge's power to disregard facts asserted and evidence adduced past the set time-limits is a necessary, but still not sufficient in order to ensure the efficiency of the preparatory stage of proceedings.[46] Firstly, it should be stressed that a rigid system of preclusions is not preferred. Rather, the system of sanctions should be flexible and should take into account that preclusions restrict parties' right to be heard and thus they should be applied carefully and with a proper balance between competing policies.[47] The courts should accept that "unexpected shifts" do sometimes occur in litigation, resulting in different facts appearing as legally relevant only at a later stage of proceedings.[48] Such an approach is justified not only from the viewpoint of effective exercise of the right to be heard, but also in order to avoid the negative consequences of a rigid "*Eventualmaxime*". If parties were to be rigidly required to put forward all facts and evidence already at a very early stage of proceedings, including those which might only eventually become relevant if the legal evaluation of the case shifts to a different direction, the pleadings of parties would become too complex and incomprehensible.[49] It seems that the Civil Procedure Acts in all three discussed countries acknowledge these concerns as they all enable the parties to put forward new facts and evidence even at later stages of litigation provided that the party was not culpable of default as regards the late submission (Art. 286 SiCPA, Art. 118a SkCPA, Art. 118b CzCPA), whereas the notion of "culpability for default" is interpreted with a degree of flexibility.[50]

The next problem that arises is how to ensure that a requirement that all facts and evidence be submitted already before the main hearing does not collide with the judge's duty to provide clarification, hints, and feedback. This duty—which has traditionally been one of the central features of the Austrian inspired procedural regimes—*materialno procesno vodstvo* in Slovenia (Art. 285 CPA), *poučovací povinnost soudu* in the Czech Republic (Art. 118a CPA) and in Slovakia (although

---

[46] As explained above, since the 2009 reform the instrument of a preparatory hearing in the Czech Republic is reinforced by sanctions—if a preparatory hearing takes place, this (or when the 30 days time-limit after the conclusion of the preparatory hearing elapses, if the judge allows further written submissions) is in principle the final opportunity for the parties to bring forward new facts and evidence (Art. 114c and 118b CPA). However, the instrument of a preparatory hearing still does not produce the expected results.

[47] E.g. the decision of the Supreme court of Slovenia No. II Ips 289/2010 of 26 July 2012, Judgment of the Supreme court of Slovenia No. II Ips 449/2008 of 10 July 2008, Judgment of the Supreme court of Slovenia No. II Ips 1083/2007 of 10 March 2011.

[48] Decision of the Supreme court of Slovenia No. III Ips 14/2010 of 20 December 2011. (Judgment of the Supreme court of Slovenia No. II Ips 197/2009 of 7 April 2011). A motion that the expert should supplement his expert opinion (within limits of the initial *thema probandum*) does not count as a fresh proposal for evidence (Judgment of the Supreme court of Slovenia No. II Ips 191/2007 of 16 December 2009). What is stressed is also the inherent link between the duty of the judge to pose adequate questions and promote clarification on the one hand and the effect of procedural preclusions on the other hand (Judgment of the Supreme court of Slovenia No. II Ips 449/2008 of 10 July 2008).

[49] This was the reason, why the so called "*Eventualmaxime*" was abolished in the past. On this topic see e.g. Juhart (1961), p. 75.

[50] See, e.g., Decision of the Supreme court of Slovenia No. II Ips 302/2011 of 26 April 2012.

at least pursuant to the letter of the law in a much more fragmented and restricted manner than in the Czech Republic; Art. 118/2 old CPA and Arts. 150 and, more importantly, 171 new CPA[51]) aims at encouraging parties to supplement their insufficient assertions of relevant facts and to designate adequate means of proof. The judge is bound by factual assertions and evidence, offered by parties, but has a right and a duty to stimulate parties (with questions, hints and observations) to amend and clarify their assertions of facts and to ensure that misunderstandings are avoided. The judge also needs to warn the parties if she or he considered the evidence they offered as insufficient and warn them on the distribution of the burden of proof.[52] The judge also needs to openly consult with parties the legal viewpoints that the parties have neglected. With this activity, the judge can ensure that proceedings quickly concentrate on the factual and legal points that are really relevant for the case, which is extremely important for the rationalization of the taking of evidence.

The judge's activity of giving hints and feedback and posing questions in order to encourage parties to supplement and clarify their submissions has traditionally been performed only during the oral hearing. But, of course, if the law imposed a strict sanction of preclusion already prior to the oral hearing and if, at the same time, the time frame during which the judge can exercise the aforementioned duty were not extended to the earlier (preparatory) stage of proceedings as well, such a system would make the performance of the mentioned role of judges impossible. In principle, the discussed procedural regimes acknowledge this problem. Both in the Czech Republic[53] (where judge can schedule a preparatory hearing) as well as in Slovenia[54] (where the judge can implement a kind of written preparatory proceedings) it is acknowledged that sanctions due to the non-compliance cannot be imposed against the parties unless the judge was properly active in the first place. If the judge does not pose sufficiently focused and precise questions and instructions and provides proper feedback and observations in the preparatory phase, the parties are still free to bring forward new facts and evidence during the first session of the main hearing. It can be assumed that the new Slovak CPA (which requires the judge

[51] Magurová (2013), p. 326, Chrapková (2010), p. 117 et seq. See also Števček (2008), p. 1008 et seq.

[52] Decision of the Supreme Court of Slovenia No. III Ips 2/2009 of 6 November 2009, Judgment of the Ljubljana Court of Appeals No. II Cp 942/2001 of 8 August 2001.

[53] Svoboda (2009), p. 38, Drapál and Bureš (2009), p. 839.

[54] The Slovenian Constitutional court stressed that if there is no proper activity (observations, hints, requests for clarifications and supplementations) from the side of the judge already in the written preparatory proceedings, sanctions of disallowing new facts and evidence before the first oral hearing cannot be allowed as well (decision No. Up-2443/08 of 7 October 2009). Following the same pattern, the Slovenian Supreme Court held that sanctions for belated submission of facts and means of evidence may not be imposed in cases where the court itself has delayed the proceedings because of insufficient judicial clarification and case management (Judgment No. II Ips 449/2008 of 10 July 2008).

to reveal her or his preliminary legal evaluation during the preparatory hearing; Art. 179 SkCPA) will be construed in the same manner.

The judge's active role in case management and judicial control of litigation, including the duty to promote clarifications and to give hints and observations, can undoubtedly not only save time and cost of litigation but can benefit the substantive quality of the judgment as well. These positive effects can, however, be attained only along with the appropriate activity of the parties. The described duties of the judge should not mean that the parties (their counsel) have no burden of diligently and actively preparing and participating in litigation.[55] Otherwise, the results in the practice will inevitably resemble those which were typical of the communist era where the accentuated paternalistic activity of the judge resulted in the passivisation of the legal counsel and the decrease of overall quality and efficiency of proceedings. For the effectiveness of civil justice, from the viewpoint of substantive justice as well, it is lethal if the perception prevails that the lawyer, although a legal professional, can remain confident that there will be no adverse consequences for her or his client's case even if she or he completely fails to exercise due diligence in preparing for the case, since the entire burden of the goal of achieving a just result to the process remains on the court.[56] The system must be properly balanced and the required active role of the judge should not result in the passivisation of the parties (their legal counsel). Such balance however does not seem to have been stricken in the Czech Republic.[57] The judge's duty to seek clarification and to offer feedback and observations (*poučovaci povinnost soudu*) is construed in almost absolute terms, which imposes very heavy burdens upon a judge (e.g. concerning the need that the judge instructs the parties about own legal evaluation), whereas relieving the parties almost of any obligation thoroughly to prepare their cases. Moreover, the expectation that the judge should warn the parties if she or he considers the adduced

[55] For a plea that not only the court but the parties as well should contribute to the concentration and quality of proceedings and for more emphasis to be put on a preliminary stage of proceedings in the Czech Republic see Juráš (2011), pp. 131 ff.

[56] For example, the rule that the judge has to forewarn parties about possible relevant legal aspects, which the parties haven't thought of, is certainly a necessary precondition for safeguarding effective right to be heard. This requirement is not problematic in a court culture, where lawyers engage in thorough legal analysis of their clients' cases in the first place. If however can dangerously distort the proportionate distribution of burdens between the court and the parties in an environment, where it is still quite common that lawyer do not engage in any legal research whatsoever. Sadly, in the three discussed countries there still are many lawyers who still perceive the rule of *iura novit curia* (the court knows the law) as if they are not expected to undertake a serious and in-depth legal analysis of the case by themselves in the first place Similar findings concerning inadequate perception of the rule of *iura novit curia* in the legal culture of post-communist states are given by Kühn *(although the author argues that this is primarily on account of authoritative judges, and the passivisation of lawyers seems to be perceived merely as a necessary consequence thereof)*, Kühn (2008), p. 26.

[57] Since the new Slovak CPA is (in the time of submitting of this paper) still not in force it is too early to assess how extensively the judge's obligations, imposed by Art. 171 (stating which facts are relevant for the dispute, which are undisputed between the parties and providing preliminary legal evaluation) shall be construed.

evidence insufficient, does not relate only to assessing the proposed means of evidence *in abstracto* (like it is assumed in Slovenia[58]) but also to the evaluation of evidence after it is already taken (which is during the main hearing). It is claimed that parties cannot be prevented from stating anything before the judge informs them, what they should state.[59] The consequence of the judge's failure to properly exercise its duties in the Czech Republic is, however, strikingly far reaching. Not only are the parties allowed to bring forward new facts and evidence concerning the particular issue, concerning which the judge failed to ensure proper clarifications and feedback; rather even in case of a minor failure of the judge to perform his or her duties of *poučovací povinnost soudu*, the system of preclusions ceases to apply in total and parties can bring forward any new facts and evidence at the main hearing. Therefore, as the Czech authors agree, the preparatory hearing can almost never fulfil the role of representing a cut-off date for adducing new evidence and asserting new facts.[60] Consequently, the distinction between the preparatory stage and the main hearing remains blurred.

5.4.3 The Habit of Having a "Serious Look" at the Case Only After the Main Hearing Commences

In Slovenia, the relationship between the judge's duties of active case management, on the one hand, and the requirement that the parties contribute to the effectiveness and efficiency of proceedings, on the other, seems to have been framed in more balanced terms than in the Czech Republic. For example, the Slovenian Constitutional Court holds that parties must diligently and thoroughly prepare their cases and confirms that a proper system of sanctions due to non-compliance is an essential part of this expectation. The judge's duty to seek clarification and to provide feedback (*materialno procesno vodstvo*) should not be perceived as a systematically built-in expectation that a lawyer's negligent and incompetent work will be remedied by the judge.[61]

The interplay between the judge's responsibility of *materialno procesno vodstvo*, on the one hand, and her or his power to disregard late facts and evidence, on the other, is sufficiently balanced in Slovenia. Nevertheless, instruments that were introduced by the 2008 reform and designed to enable a comprehensive (written) preparation for the trial are still insufficiently used in practice. It is undisputed that the introduction of a system of preclusions in fact imposes an

---

[58] For example, the judge should merely warn the parties e.g. that technical questions are concerned which calls for expert evidence and witness testimony, as proposed, is unlikely to be sufficient in such cases.

[59] Svoboda (2009), pp. 38–39.

[60] Svoboda (2013), pp. 394–397. See also Jurás (2011), pp. 131 ff.

[61] Decision of the Constitutional Court of Slovenia No. Up- 2443/08 of 7 October 2009.

additional burden of thorough preparation for both—the parties as well as the judge. It, therefore, might not come as a surprise that the system of preclusions is opposed not only by numerous lawyers but by certain judges as well. These tools require diligent preparation before the main hearing, thus good knowledge of the file and a serious preliminary legal analysis by the judge. However, such a preparation cannot be expected from a judge who cannot rid himself of the old habit of having "the first serious look" at the file only at the first hearing and only then truly starting to work on the case. Inevitably, such judge will neither be able to correctly apply the system of procedural sanctions for facts and evidence, adduced late, nor will the judge be able to exercise the duty to pose appropriate questions and promote clarification at the preparatory stage of proceedings. It is thus not surprising that the judges, who themselves do not prepare well for the case, are predominantly lenient toward sloppy preparation of the lawyers (just like the latter are predominantly lenient toward sloppy preparation of the former). It is still common that not only the parties' legal counsel but also judges appeared at hearings with little knowledge of the case and its factual and legal bases. When the habit of a lack of diligent preparation for the hearing prevails, numerous adjournments of hearings are actually preferred by all—lawyers and judges alike. Understandably, that is not a fertile ground for the idea of a thorough preparatory stage of proceedings to grow.

5.4.4 Time Limits for Bringing Forward New Facts and Evidence Perceived as a Formalisation of Proceedings

A large part of the legal community in all three discussed countries opposes the strengthening of procedural obligations, combined with the system of sanctions against belated submission of facts and evidence because it perceives such system to be incompatible with the goals of civil justice. The view is still very much present that such a system is an expression of formalization of proceedings and of an (assumed) trend that a goal of reaching a substantive justice is fading.[62] This perception is wrong. Extended and intensified procedural requirements for the timely submission of facts and means of evidence should primarily be understood as a clear message to the parties (their counsel) that a diligent and active preparation for their case is necessary. This can only be beneficial not merely for saving time and cost (i.e.: efficiency) but for the substantive quality of judicial process as well. Equally, for the substantive quality of justice it is essential that all relevant submissions are given on time, so the opponent (and the court as well) has sufficient time to reflect on them and that "ambush tactics" cannot succeed. Also the Constitutional court of Slovenia has already confirmed that a proper (though necessarily flexible) system of procedural sanctions, burdens and time limits in civil litigation is

[62] Jelačin (2008), p. 10.

not only admissible but actually welcome.[63] By expecting parties and their lawyers actively and diligently to prepare the case and participate in the course of litigation, the law strives to achieve not only acceleration of proceedings but better substantive quality of adjudication.[64] A system of sanctions must be attached to the imposed time limits, otherwise it would remain entirely without effect. In addition, the parties should be well aware of the fact that the judge will not too leniently relieve them from these sanctions. In such case it is not unrealistic to expect that in most cases time limits and court orders are respected and that the culture of compliance prevails. True, the procedural sanction of debarring late facts and evidence, if applied in the individual dispute that happens to be before the court, runs contrary to the goal of reaching adequate results on the merits. But the effect of such sanctions from the perspective of functioning of the justice system as a whole is predominantly preventive—thus resulting in better, more thorough and timely preparation by all participants in proceedings and it is, hence, beneficial exactly from the substantive aspect of adjudication (the effect of behaviour modification).

In the discussed three countries, however, few are willing to consider not only the effect of imposing sanctions for the case at hand, but also the question of the impact of a judicial decision for the functioning of the justice system and for the future behaviour of the addressees of the law. Neither has it been fully accepted yet that the legislature as well as the judge in every specific case must seek out the proper balance between the goal of reaching a substantively correct decision, on the one hand, and using the adequate resources and time that can be devoted to that goal, on the other hand, as well as the proper balance between the burdens of the judge and of the parties. Some authors in Slovenia go as far as suggesting that "imposing any legal obstacles, which prevent the court from finding the truth, is a 'step back in time' and 'far from being compatible with a contemporary idea of civil justice.'[65] In the Czech Republic, introduction of time-limits as to until when the parties may bring forward new facts and evidence is still often perceived as prevalence of the "formal" over the "material" truth.[66] Understandably, until a large part of the legal community has difficulties in understanding that a requirement of timely presentation of all relevant materials in the litigation can have very positive effects for the substantive quality of adjudication, the concept of a preparatory stage in civil proceedings cannot flourish.

5.4.5 Aversion Towards Judicial Discretion

As a prominent Czech author *Zdenek Kuhn* contends, there exists a deep continuity in the methods of legal reasoning employed by judges in the post-communist

[63] Decision of the Constitutional Court of Slovenia, No. Up- 2443/08 of 7 October 2009.

[64] Decision of the Constitutional Court of Slovenia, No. Up- 2443/08 of 7 October 2009.

[65] Varanelli (2012), p. 6.

[66] Hamuľáková (2010), p. 42, Svoboda (2008), p. 1, for a more critical view Juráš (2013), p. 288.

countries originating from the communist era.[67] Hence, in order to understand and analyse the pressing problems of the legal science and legal profession in these countries today, we have to understand their communist predecessors. Although there were significant differences between these "communist predecessors" in Slovenia, on the one hand, and in the Czech Republic and Slovakia, on the other, there are certain common elements that produce negative effects precisely concerning conduct of preliminary stage of litigation. Legal communities in these countries have difficulties in embracing the idea of judicial flexibility and judicial discretion. The majority of judges and lawyers still prefer a rigid procedural regime with detailed rules, frowns upon the use of open-ended terms in procedural legislation any rejects attempts to provide more room for the judge to adapt the unfolding of proceedings to the characteristics of each particular case. This, however, should be one of the main elements of modern approach to effectiveness of preparatory stage of civil proceedings. In addition, a preference to formalistic or downright bureaucratic approach to adjudication is still present, which in the same is inevitably linked to lack of appropriate skills and experience of case management, particularly in a complex litigation.[68] Furthermore, judges are insufficiently used of applying the principle of proportionality, for example, when it comes to striking a proper balance between the goal of reaching adequate results on the merits, on the one hand, and the need to control cost and time, on the other.

5.5 The Lack of Further Essential Instruments for Ensuring Effectiveness of Preparatory Stage of Proceedings

There are numerous further points where the reform is needed. Procedural systems of all three discussed countries still lack many preparatory tools, which could be implemented before the main hearing. For example (except to a certain extent in the new Slovak Act[69]), no instruments (such as: summary judgments) exist for a quick disposal of clearly unmeritorious claims or defences in an early stage of litigation—which, in turn, would enable the court resources to focus on cases with merits. Furthermore, since there is no clear formal distinction between the preparatory stage and the main hearing, there are also no particular procedural acts at the end of the preparatory stage; no summaries are made either by the judge or by the parties and neither are the parties expected to make closing statements at that stage. Tools aimed at proper presentation of evidence are inexistent. The lawyers' habit of adducing an excessive amount of documentary evidence "in a bundle", thus without

[67] Kühn (2011), pp. 165–166.

[68] Kühn (2011), p. XV and 165.

[69] Art. 138 (*zjavne nedôvodná žaloba*) pursuant to which *a* judge may recommend the claimant to withdraw the manifestly ill-founded claim.

indexation and without precise indication as to which factual allegations it refers and without proper references to its particular contents is still common. It is only since 2008 in Slovenia, the judge can require lawyers to prepare summaries and indexation of voluptuous documentary evidence,[70] but even this modest requirement has been fiercely opposed by the bar (whereas even such modest requirements are not imposed in the other two discussed countries). Written witness statements are unknown of in the Czech Republic, whereas they are admissible in Slovenia since 2008[71] and (to a certain extent) in the new Slovak CPA (Art. 196). But since parties are only entitled and encouraged and not required to present written witness statements, they are not pressed to present them in an early stage of proceedings. More usually, such written witness statements are only submitted once the main hearing has commenced, thus they cannot fulfil their role of a better preparation of the main hearing (or stimulating settlements in an early phase of proceedings). No proper system of disclosure of evidence has been introduced in any of the three discussed countries. The party's request for disclosure should always be specific and directed to individualised documents (which practically can only apply if the party has sufficient knowledge as to what is "in hands" of its opponent). There is no obligation that the parties should *sua sponte* disclose evidence, which adversely affects their case or which support their opponent's case. Even when disclosure orders are made (relating to individualised documents), in practice, this does not occur before the commencement of the main hearing.

A further weak point is that even the implemented instruments that put more emphasis to the preparatory stage of litigation (such as those, adopted with the 2008 amendment of the Slovenian CPA) still express a certain repressive approach. It is the judge who unilaterally determines binding time-limits. There is no requirement or even the expectation that the judge should co-operate with the parties' counsel in order to agree or at least get their opinion concerning the time frame for proceedings and the manner in which they shall unfold. Consequently, there are no instruments encouraging informal communication between the judge and the parties (their counsel), such as telephone conferences or informal in-camera meetings. Instruments such as a "provisional time-table" or a "procedural plan" (where issues such as the number of hearings, setting of the calendar for future actions in the proceedings at the outset of the case, the order of taking of evidence, etc.) are unknown of. This is regrettable. If the parties (their counsel) are invited to participate in the determination of time-limits and time-frames, and they voluntarily accept them, it can be expected to a greater extent that they will comply or at least in good faith try to comply with them.

With regard to costs, the principle of 'loser pays' applies in all three countries.[72] This covers the right to recovery of opponent's (necessarily occurred) lawyer fees up to the limit calculated pursuant to the state lawyers' tariff. As long as the lawyer

[70] Art. 226 SiCPA.

[71] Art. 236.a SiCPA.

[72] Art. 154 SiCPA, Art. 255 new SkCPA, Art. 142 CzCPA.

fees are calculated in accordance with the state's lawyers' tariff, the court has no authority to refuse to award costs that are disproportionate to the claim. The system of reimbursement of the lawyers' fees does not stimulate lawyers to strive for a focused trial or avoid a piecemeal manner of litigation. A typical feature of both the Slovenian as well as the Czech system of the reimbursement of lawyer fees is that an attorney at law was (pursuant to a scale, depending on the amount in controversy) entitled to reimbursement for every single procedural act performed (thus, the plaintiff for the claim, for every following written preparatory submission, for attendance of every single hearing separately...) and not (like, for example in German law) for a certain phase of proceedings as a whole, where these flat fees provide an incentive for lawyers to push for focused trial and for the settlement in early phases of litigation. The system, adopted in Slovenia and the Czech Republic, on the contrary, does not stimulate a lawyer to strive for a focused trial and for efficient progress of the proceedings and neither to vigorously oppose the dilatory tactics of the opponent's lawyer. However, the attempts to change the system are, at least in Slovenia, always faced with a stiff opposition from the Bar. In Slovenia, during the 2009 and 2015 the new lawyers' tariff abolished the system of reimbursement for each procedural step taken (each brief, each attended hearing) and introduced the aforementioned German system (one lump-sum fee for the written phase of proceedings—irrespective of the number of briefs filed and one lump-sum fee for the oral phase—irrespective of the number of hearings; the same again for the second and the third instance proceedings).[73] Nevertheless after the change of the government in 2011 and after a successful lobbying of the Bar, the new government re-introduced the old system, which started to be operable since early 2015. Hence, the lawyers' tariff once again adheres to the old system of calculation of the lawyers' fees where the lawyers are better paid if the procedure takes longer, more briefs are filed and more hearing are scheduled. In the Czech Republic the newly introduced system of lump-sum calculation of lawyers' fees was quashed by the Constitutional court[74] (supposedly, it inflated the costs of proceedings, which were often disproportionate) and the system of separate calculation of fee for every single procedural act is in place again.[75]

The existence of the lawyers' tariff does not mean that the fee cannot be freely negotiated in the lawyer-client contractual relationship. They can agree on a payment of an hourly rate on the basis of the time actually spent working on the case or a payment pursuant to rates, higher than those in the Lawyers' Tariff. The purpose of the lawyers' tariff is exclusively to bind the courts when they determine reimbursement of costs in the "loser pays" system (and hence to protect the losing party from having to reimburse exorbitant fees to the opponent). But in reality,

---

[73] *Zakon o odvetniški tarifi*, Official Gazette No. 67/2008.

[74] Nález Ústavního soudu ze dne 17. dubna 2013 sp. zn. Pl. ÚS 25/12 ve věci návrhu na zrušení vyhlášky č. 484/2000, č. 116/2013 Sb.

[75] Vyhláška Ministerstva spravedlnosti č. 177/1996 Sb. ze dne 4. června 1996 o odměnách advokátů a náhradách advokátů za poskytování právních služeb (advokátní tarif).

many lawyers do adhere to the tariff (so they can ensure their clients that full expenses will be reimbursed if they win the case). Therefore the system of the lawyers' tariff has significant effects as to whether it promotes a piece-meal or focused trial.

Concerning the relationship between the lawyers' fees and promotion of settlements and alternative dispute resolution (ADR), in general, there are incentives (extra fee) in all three countries for the lawyers to settle cases in court. In addition, in Slovenia, there exists an adverse cost sanction merely in a case when the court deems that the party has refused to participate in an ADR (e.g. mediation) proceeding without proper justification (see *infra*).

5.6 Court-Connected Mediation and Judicial Settlement Efforts

None of the three discussed legal systems provides for a mandatory pre-action mediation or for an obligation to formally communicate with the opponent (for example, via the pre-action protocols).[76] All three countries have adopted laws on mediation,[77] which were based on (as in Slovenia and in the Czech Republic) or subsequently adapted to (as in Slovakia, where the Mediation Act was adopted already in 2004 and later amended in 2010)[78] the EU Directive Number 52/2008 on certain aspects of mediation in civil and commercial matters. Thus, pre-action voluntary mediation is possible, but has not started to fully flourish yet although the level of awareness of and acceptance of ADR in legal and general community is gradually growing.[79]

Following the positive experience with certain pilot-projects of court-connected mediation, the Slovenian Civil Procedure Act was amended in 2002 in order, for the first time, to take account of court-connected and other mediation schemes. It provided that the court is empowered to stay civil proceedings for up to 3 months

---

[76] There exists merely a possibility for a party to ask the court to assist the parties in reaching settlement before bringing a lawsuit (so called: praetorian settlement attempt; *pretorična poravnava*, *prétorský smír*, see Kutlik (2012), p. 304. see e.g. Art. 309 of the SiCPA, Art. 67 of the CzCPA and Art. 67 of the (old) SkCPA. In the discussed countries, this instrument is almost never used in practice. Precisely for this reason the new Slovak Civil Procedure Act abolishes this instrument altogether. See Šínová (2014), p. 1. In addition, in the Czech Republic: the claimant is obliged, before filing the lawsuit, to call upon the defendant to fulfil her or his outstanding obligations; failure to do so may result in cost sanctions (Art. 142a CzCPA).

[77] Slovenia: Mediation in Civil and Commercial Matters Act (*Zakon o mediaciji v civilnih in gospodarskih zadevah*), The Czech Republic: The Act on Mediation and Amendment of Certain Other Acts, Coll. 2012/2012 (*Zákon o mediaci a o změně některých zákonů, zákon č. 202/2012*), Slovakia: The Act No. 420/2004 on Mediation and Amendment of Certain Other Acts (*Zákon č. 420/2004 Z.z. o mediácii a o doplnení niektorých zákonov*).

[78] Kutlik (2012), p. 304.

[79] Kutlik (2012), pp. 303 and 313 ff., Cholenský (2010), p. 1.

if parties voluntarily agree to try an ADR procedure, whether out of court or court-connected.[80] In this regard, the legislation in the Czech Republic goes one step forward. There the judge has not only a power to recommend mediation at any appropriate stage of proceedings but may, if practical and appropriate, order the parties to proceedings to hold an initial 3-h meeting with a mediator. The obligatory referral relates merely to an informative meeting with a mediator, and not mediation itself, in such cases, proceedings may be suspended for up to 3 months.[81] Practically identical rule was included in the old Slovak CPA, whereas the new CPA provides that where possible and appropriate, the court will try to resolve the dispute amicably, or recommend the parties to try to settle the dispute through mediation.[82]

Furthermore, in Slovenia, in order to reach an in-court settlement, but also to examine options for ADR, the court can call a settlement conference as a special stage in the civil procedure, following follows receipt of a reply to an action and prior to the trial.[83] In a settlement conference a judge (the same judge to whom the case is assigned for ordinary adjudication) has an active role and must openly discuss with the parties factual and legal issues and possible settlement options. In this regard the settlement conference also pursues a purpose of a preparatory meeting, aimed at better preparation of the trial even if the settlement is not reached. The scheduling of a settlement conference is quasi-obligatory; the court may omit it only if the parties have already (unsuccessfully) carried out a procedure of out-of-court ADR or if believes that that there is no possibility for a settlement. However a statement of parties that the settlement is not possible, even if given by both parties, does not per se mean that the court shall refrain from ordering a settlement conference. The experience shows that even in such cases of initial refusal, a settlement can often be reached. Furthermore, the court may skip the settlement conference if it evaluates that a settlement does not represent a suitable means to resolve a dispute (for example, essential actual inequality between the parties, violent disputes, precedents or pattern cases that dictate a decision on merits, an action in which the legal and factual situation is clear, evidently ill-founded claims, among other things).

In practice, settlement conferences do not play as important a role as it was expected. Court-connected mediation programmes are successful, but the court makes the proposal to the parties and (where they consent) refers them to mediation in an early stage of the proceedings before the settlement conference (usually the defendant is invited to give consent to the mediation upon service of the claim; if the consent is given, the court then invites the claimant to do the same). Thus, by the

[80] Art. 305.b SiCPA.

[81] Arts. 99 and 100 of the CzCPA (as amended through Art. 30 of the Mediation Act No. 202/2012). See in detail: Heyninck (2012), p. 61, De Palo and Trevor (2012), p. 11.

[82] Art. 99 of Act No 99/1963 Rules of Civil Procedure as amended in 2012. Art. 170 of the new SkCPA.

[83] Art. 305a–305c, SiCPA.

time a settlement conference is called, the parties have usually already been through an (unsuccessful) mediation or refused to participate in one. Equally, the settlement conference does not really fulfil its purpose of a preparatory hearing (*see supra*) either. Namely, if the main hearing is scheduled for the time immediately after the settlement conference (which, in practice, almost always is the case), this initiative cannot genuinely serve the purpose of a preparation of a trial. On the contrary, Art. 170 of the new Slovak CPA more adequately foresee that discussions concerning possible settlement in court or referral to ADR forms a part of a proper preparatory hearing.

On the other hand, and in line with traditional role of the judge in an Austrian-based type of civil procedure, a civil judge in all three discussed legal systems undertakes an active role in assisting parties to reach settlement (judicial settlement efforts) during the whole trial, not only in the settlement conference. It should be noted, however, that in the communist era—for ideological reasons—the instrument of settlement was perceived sceptically in (then) Yugoslavia and even downright suppressed in (then) Czechoslovakia. The instrument, based on party autonomy and hence individual freedom, just did not fit well into ideological concept of "quest for material truth", the (Czechoslovak) soviet-style omnipotence of the State and (Yugoslav) state paternalism. So, this accentuated promotion of judicial settlement efforts is a result of a post-transition era.[84] In Slovenia, especially the 2008 Amendment of the SiCPA, emphasises to a greater extent the obligation of the court throughout the whole course of proceeding to be more active at encouraging of settlements. The court must evaluate, whether there exists the possibility of dispute resolution and actively assist the parties in reaching such (Article 306c, SiCPA). This applies during the entire proceedings (a suitable time to try to reach a settlement could also be after evidence has been taken, particularly after the expert's opinion has been submitted). A judge may actively advise the parties on how to reach a settlement, and in practice, a judge does not hide his or her views as to what content of settlement would be appropriate for the case. The judge is expected to openly discuss the case with parties and gives preliminary evaluations, which, if done in appropriate manner, is not considered to be incompatible with the request of impartiality. The Czech CPA, in addition to explicitly stating that a consensual resolution is a primary goal of the judge's activity in litigation (Art. 100) even explicitly requires the court to inform the parties of the case-law of the Supreme Court and its own legal evaluation of the case as a method of judicial conciliation (Art. 99 CzCPA). A similar approach is adopted also in the Slovak law, which, in addition of stressing that the judge should, where appropriate, promote settlements (Arts. 148, 170 and 179 SkCPA) requires the judge to inform the parties

[84] This is clearly evident also in statistics. Whereas in the late eighties' only about 5 % of civil and commercial cases ended with settlement in court, the number has been constantly growing and in recent years, nearly 20 % of filed cases are settled—either by judicial conciliation or after being referred to court-connected mediation. See Ministrstvo za pravosodje, Sodna statistika za leto 2013, pp. 77 and 79.

(already in the preparatory hearing) of its preliminary legal evaluation.[85] In all three countries, settlements reached in court have an effect of *res iudicata* and an effect of direct enforceability.[86] Whereas settlements reached in mediation do not have such effect automatically, parties can require the court to confirm such settlements and thereby grant them such effects. The agreement reached in mediation is binding as a contract, however, it is not, in itself, an enforceable title, unless a party requests the court to endorse such agreement as an in-court settlement.[87]

There are practically no court-connected mediation programmes in the Czech Republic and in Slovakia.[88] On the contrary, Slovenia may well claim to be the pioneer among the former communist countries when it comes to implementation of court-connected ADR programmes. A pilot programme on voluntary court-connected mediation was initiated by the Ljubljana District Court as long ago as the late-1990s, and it proved to be quite successful. These pilot programmes were "institutionalised" in 2009 when Slovenia adopted the Court-Connected ADR Act (*Zakon o alternativnem reševanju sodnih sporov*).[89] The Act promotes a genuine "multi-door courthouse" approach by imposing all courts of first instance as well as appellate courts must offer mediation or another ADR method. In this regard, the Act relied closely on the positive experience of court-connected mediation programmes that existed in many Slovenian courts before enactment of this obligation. In an overwhelming majority of cases, the courts of first instance indeed offer the parties opportunity to try mediation. Any party can object, but such rejection can have adverse consequences when it comes to determination of costs of (subsequent) litigation. If the court considers that the party has unreasonably objected to mediation it can later order him/her to pay all or part of the other party's costs, regardless of the final outcome of the case. The programmes are administered by the court; in larger courts, separate ADR offices were established for that purpose. The court provides a roster of mediators and establishes criteria for inclusion on the roster, adopts rules regarding assigning neutrals to the case and guidelines for conducting the ADR sessions.[90] Mediation sessions are held in the court. When the programmes were first introduced, most mediators were judges (who of course cannot mediate cases that are assigned to them for adjudication), but over time lawyers and retired judges were included on the roster.[91] In practice, mediation is offered to parties automatically very early in the proceedings and the

[85] Art. 100 of the old and Arts. 170 and 171 of the new SkCPA.

[86] Art. 308 SiCPA, Art. 99 CzCPA, Art. 99 old SkCPA and Art. 148 new SkCPA.

[87] See for the Czech Republic De Palo and Trevor (2012), p. 112, for Slovakia Kutlik (2012), p. 304 and for Slovenia Ristin (2011), p. 145.

[88] Heyninck (2012), p. 60. Particularly for Slovakia, the EU Commission has found that alternative dispute resolution was not sufficiently used. See Final Recommendation for a Council Recommendation on Slovakia's 2013 national reform programme and delivering a Council opinion on Slovakia's stability programme for 2012–2016 (2013) at Par. 15.

[89] *Zakon o alternativnem reševanju sodnih sporov,* Official Gazette RS, No. 97/2009.

[90] Betetto (2007), p. 212.

[91] Ristin (2011), pp. 143–149.

invitation letter is a general one, not tailored for a particular case. Consent of both parties for the mediation procedure is reached in about 25 % of cases and about 40 % of mediations are successful, resulting in a settlement.[92] Equally importantly, it is observed that even in cases, where no settlement was reached in court-connected mediation, there are positive effects for the further course of litigation; namely the parties' arguments are clearer and more focused and not rarely, the parties settle the case once it is referred back to litigation.

The use of mediation and judicial settlement efforts can, thus, enhance efficiency of preparatory stage of civil proceedings. It should be noted, however, that it is also the other way around: putting more emphasis to the preparatory stage of civil proceedings and promoting the idea of "cards on the table" approach (requiring the parties to put forward relevant facts and evidence as early as possible and to articulate their legal positions already before the trial) has very positive effects from the viewpoint of promoting settlements. From such viewpoint, it is very useful if the parties can early enough realistically assess the strengths and weaknesses of their position—also in light of the arguments invoked and evidence disclosed by the opposing party. If a party cannot know before the main hearing what arguments and evidence are "in the hands" of the opponent, he or she cannot realistically assess its prospects of success. In such a case, settlement negotiations during the early stages of litigation can hardly be effective.

5.7 Conclusion

It would be unfair to claim that the legislatures of the three discussed countries have failed to realise the importance of a focused and thorough preparation of the main hearing. Particularly the Slovenian reform of 2008 and the new Slovak Civil Procedure Act are in line with the worldwide trend of putting more emphasis on the preparatory stage of proceedings, as well as giving the judge more discretion in determining the manner of unfolding of proceedings. However, the achieved results so far have clearly not been satisfactory. The reasons for this are manifold, ranging from insufficient legislative reforms and inadequate construction of these reforms in the case law to the court culture that does not favour thorough preparation before the main hearing. There are deficiencies concerning procedural sanctions for non-compliance with the requirement of timely presentation of relevant material, whereby certain tools for preparation of the main hearing are inexistent altogether. In addition, courts have difficulties in striking a proper balance between the required burdens of the court and those of the parties and their legal counsel, as

[92] Whereas court-annexed mediation schemes in Slovenia are undisputedly successful, a downside is that precisely the success of mediation in courts, which is almost free of charge for the parties, makes it more difficult for private ADR providers to establish their activities on a market oriented basis.

well as a proper balance between the system of preclusions and the need of flexibility. Furthermore, there is a persistent aversion towards judicial discretion, as well as the equally persistent perception that time limits for presentation of facts, evidence and legal arguments are necessarily incompatible with the goal of doing justice one merits. Changes in legislation are only one—and actually the easier part—of the necessary reform. A much more difficult task is to achieve a change in the court culture and judicial method. The existing one, regrettably, does not favour a timely and thorough preparation of the case and neither does it sufficiently embrace the expectation that the lawyers will provide a proper share in ensuring both the efficiency as well as the substantive quality of adjudication.

References

Assessment of the 2013 national reform programme and stability programme for Slovenia – Commission Staff Working Document, Brussels, 29.5.2013, SWD(2013) 374 final

Assessment of the 2013 national reform programme and stability programme for Slovakia -Commission Staff Working Document, Brussels, 29.5.2013 SWD(2013) 375 final

Betetto N (2007) Court-based mediation and its place in Slovenia. In: Uzelac A, Van Rhee CH (eds) Public and Private Justice. Intersentia, Antwerpen, pp 211–223

Bobek M (2009) Quantity or quality? Reassessing the role of supreme jurisdictions in central Europe. Am J Comp Law 57(1):33–58

Bohata P (2003) Justizreformen in der Tschechoslowakei und ihren Nachfolgestaaten, Forost Arbeitspapier Nr. 16, Forschungsverbund Ost- und Südosteuropa, München. http://www.forost.lmu.de/fo_library/forost_Arbeitspapier_16.pdf (accessed 10 August 2015)

Cappelletti M, Garth B (1987) Introduction – policies, trends and ideas in civil procedure. In: Cappelletti M (ed) International encyclopaedia of comparative law, vol XVI, pp 2–82

Cholenský R (2010) Mediation Country Report Czech Republic, JAMS International ADR Center Info Sheet. http://www.adrcenter.com/jamsinternational/civil-justice/Mediation_Country_Report_Czech_Republic.pdf (accessed 10 August 2015)

Chrapková L (2010) Dokazovanie v občianskom súdnom konani (Česko-slovensko-nemecká komparaciá, Dizertačná práca. Univerzita Karlova, Praha

De Palo G, Trevor M (2012) The Czech Republic Mediation Act: a work-in-progress. Alternatives 30(5):110–113, http://www.chinagoabroad.com/en/article/czech-republic-mediation-act-work-progress-potential (accessed 10 August 2015)

Drapál L, Bureš J (2009) Občanský soudní řád I., Komentář, 1. Vydání, C. H. Beck, Praha

Dvořák B (2012) Die Entwicklung des tschehischen Zivilprozessrechts seit dem Jahre 1989. In: Sutter-Somm T, Harsagy V (eds) Die Entwicklung des Zivilprozessrechts in Mitteleuropa um die Jahrtausendwende. Schulthess, Zurich, pp 123–136

Final Recommendation for a Council Recommendation on Slovakia's 2013 national reform programme and delivering a Council opinion on Slovakia's stability programme for 2012-2016 {SWD(2013) 375 final}, Brussels, 29.5.2013 COM(2013) 375. http://ec.europa.eu/europe2020/pdf/nd/csr2013_slovakia_en.pdf (accessed 10 August 2015)

Hamuľáková K (2010) Zásada koncentrace řízení a její uplatnění v civilním soudním řízení. Vyd. 1, Leges, Praha

Heyninck B (2012) The Czech Republic. In: De Palo G, Trevor M (eds) EU mediation law and practice. Oxford University Press, Oxford, pp 59–73

Jelačin M (2008) Novela ZPP-D, njene skrite pasti in pravne praznine. Pravna praksa 25:9–10

Juhart J (1961) Civilno procesno pravo FLRJ. Univerzitetna Založba, Ljubljana

Juráš M (2011) Odpovědnost účastníků civilního soudního řízení *za* spravedlivý proces - proces bez zbytečných průtahů. In: Kotásek J et al (eds) Dny práva 2011, Právo na spravedlivý proces, Acta Universitatis Brunensis – Iuridica; Spisy Právnické fakulty, vol 416. Masarykova Univerzita, Brno, pp 131–141

Juráš M (2013) Aktivní role soudu při zjišťování skutkového stavu v civilním sporu. Zborník z medzinárodnej vedeckej konferencie Bratislavské právnické fórum 2013:286–295

Kamhi S (1957) Građanski sudski postupak. Sarajevo

Kengyel M (2000) Die Zukunft des ungarischen Zivilprozessrechts nach der Zivilverfahrensnovelle 1999. Zeitschrift für Zivilprozess International 5:361–375

Kranjc J (1993) Probleme der Übernahme ausländischer Rechtssätze in nationale Rechtssysteme. WiRO (Wirtschaft und Recht in Osteuropa) 409–413

Kühn Z (2008) The authoritarian legal culture at work: the passivity of parties and the international statements of Supreme Courts. Croatian Yearb Eur Law Pol 2:19–26

Kühn Z (2011) The Judiciary in Central and Eastern Europe: mechanical jurisprudence in transformation. Martinus Nijhoff Publishers, Leiden

Kutlik F (2012) Slovakia. In: De Palo G, Trevor M (eds) EU mediation law and practice. Oxford University Press, Oxford, pp 301–316

Magurová H (2013) Ako kvalifikovat' neodržanie povinnosti, ktorú predsedovi senátu alebo samosudcovi ustanovuje §118 ODS. 2 O.S.P.? Zborník z medzinárodnej vedeckej konferencie Bratislavské právnické fórum 2013:326–330, http://www.lawconference.sk/archiv/bpf_2013/sprava/files/zborniky/Session%20of%20Civil%20Law.pdf (accessed 10 August 2015)

National Reform Programme of the Czech Republic (2014) Office of the Government of the Czech Republic. http://ec.europa.eu/europe2020/pdf/csr2014/nrp2014_czech_en.pdf (accessed 10 August 2015)

Návrh legislatívneho zámeru rekodifikácie civilného práva procesného, Ministerstvo spravodlivosti Slovenskej republiky, Bratislava, 2013

Nový Z (2009) Občanské právo procesní. In: Bobek M, Molek P, Šimíček V (eds) Komunistické právo v Československu. Kapitoly z dějin bezpráví (Communist Law in Czechoslovakia – Chapters from the History of Injustice), Mezinárodní politologický ústav, Masarykova univerzita, pp 513–552

Přibáň J (2002) Judicial power vs. democratic representation. In: Sadurski W (ed) Constitutional justice, east and west: democratic legitimacy and constitutional courts in post-communist Europe in a comparative perspective, law and philosophy library, vol 62. Kluwer Law International, The Hague, pp 373–394

Rechberger W (2008) Die Ideen Franz Kleins und ihre Bedeutung für die Entwicklung des Zivilprozessrechts in Europa. Ritsumeikan Law Rev 25:101–110

Ristin G (2011) New legislation on alternative dispute resolution in the Republic of Slovenia. Croatian Arbitr Yearb 18:143–149

Schelleová I, Schelle K (2005) Úvod do civilního řízení, 1 vyd. Eurolex Bohemia, Praha

Šínová R (2014) Srovnání změn v civilním procesu v ČR a SR, Pravni prostor, 04.09.2014, http://www.pravniprostor.cz/clanky/procesni-pravo/k-srovnani-zmen-v-civilnim-procesu-v-cr-a-sr (accessed 10 August 2015)

Števček M (2008) Poučovacia povinnosť súdu a koncentrácia civilného súdneho konania po ostatnej novele OSP v prospektívnej anticipácii vývoja civilného procesného práva. In: Dny práva - Days of Law. Masarykova Univerzita, Brno, pp 1008–1011

Study on Individual Access to Constitutional Justice - Adopted by the Venice Commission at its 85th Plenary Session in Venice, 17-18 December 2010, Strasbourg, 27 January 2011, Study No 538/2009. http://www.venice.coe.int/webforms/documents/default.aspx?pdffile=CDL-AD(2010)039rev-e (accessed 10 August 2015)

Svoboda K (2008) Další novela OSŘ – změny v režimech koncentrace, Právní zpravodaj [online] 10. 5. 2008

Svoboda K (2009) Pár poznámek k novému režimu koncentrace civilního sporu. Bulletin Advokacie [online] 11:37–40

Svoboda K (2013) Procesní vývoj povinnosti tvrdit a prokazovat, Zborník z medzinárodnej vedeckej konferencie Bratislavské právnické fórum, pp 394–397
The EU Justice Scoreboard, Communication from the Commission to the European Parliament, the Council, the European Central Bank, the European Economic and Social Committee and the Committee of the Regions COM(2015) 116 final. http://ec.europa.eu/justice/effective-justice/files/justice_scoreboard_2015_en.pdf (accessed 10 August 2015)
The functioning of judicial systems and the situation of the economy in the European Union Member States, Strasbourg, 15 January 2013; Report prepared for the European Commission (Directorate General Justice) http://ec.europa.eu/justice/effective-justice/files/cepej_study_justice_scoreboard_en.pdf (accessed 10 August 2015)
Ude L (1988) Civilni pravdni postopek. ČZ UL, Ljubljana
Uzelac A (2004) Accelerating civil proceedings in Croatia – a history of attempts to improve the efficiency of civil litigation. In: van Rhee CH (ed) History of delays in civil procedure. Intersentia, Maastricht, pp 283–313
Válová I (2014) Roman Fiala znovu v čele Komise pro rekodifikaci OSŘ, Česká justice, 13. 3. 2014. http://www.ceska-justice.cz/2014/03/roman-fiala-znovu-v-cele-komise-pro-rekodifikaci-osr/ (accessed 10 August 2015)
Varanelli L (2012) Sodišče in ocenjevanje dokazov v civilnem postopku. Pravna praksa 2:5–8
Winterová A, Macková A (2012) Civil procedure - Czech Republic, International Encyclopaedia of Law, Suppl. 66. Kluwer Law International, Alphen aan der Rijn

Chapter 6
Preparatory Stage in the Baltic States: Similarities and Differences

Vigita Vėbraitė

Abstract This chapter covers the preparatory stage in civil litigation in Lithuania, Latvia and Estonia. The main attention is devoted to the goals of preparatory stage and possible forms and stages of preparation of a civil case for the main hearing. The text also discusses judicial settlement efforts and court-connected mediation in the preparatory stage. The author concludes that there are differences in legal regulation of the preparatory stage in all three Baltic States, but still the challenges are quite similar. In some civil cases, there are too many preparatory hearings and the possibilities to take judicial settlement efforts are usually not completely exercised during the preparatory stage. Processes to modernise the preparatory stage in all Baltic States is still ongoing. A number of amendments are being done or under discussion for the codes of civil procedure in order to make this stage more flexible and clear.

6.1 Introduction

The history of civil procedure in Lithuania, Latvia and Estonia has had many similarities since the middle of eighteenth century, as all three countries became part of Russian Empire and Russian Statute of civil procedure in 1864 was adopted. Until this legal act, Lithuania had applied really well-known statutes, albeit Lithuania lost its independence in 1795. The first of them was adopted in 1529, the second one in 1566 and the last one in 1588. These three statutes had embedded rules of civil procedure influenced by canon law and Roman law.[1] Russian Statute of civil procedure was created according to French code of civil procedure from the year 1806. This means that the statute implemented ideas of a liberal model of civil procedure. Interestingly, after declaration of independence in 1918, Latvia, Lithuania and Estonia did not adopt new laws of civil procedure but still applied

[1] Driukas and Valančius (2007), p. 69.

V. Vėbraitė (✉)
Faculty of Law, Vilnius University, Saulėtekio al. 9 - I Rumai, LT-10222 Vilnius, Lithuania
e-mail: vigita.vebraite@tf.vu.lt

L. Ervo, A. Nylund (eds.), *Current Trends in Preparatory Proceedings*,
DOI 10.1007/978-3-319-29325-7_6

with some amendments the former Russian Stature of civil procedure. The quality of this legal act and its innovative adaptation to local conditions by the doctrine of law and case law was one of the reasons that the new codes of civil procedure were not prepared until 1940. For instance, in Lithuania, many lawyers raised the question of the preparation of Lithuania's own Code of Civil Procedure. But the Ministry of Justice and Council of State in 1938 decided to codify substantial law at the beginning – to prepare the Lithuanian Civil Code and, only after the adoption of the Civil Code, to start preparation of the Code of Civil Procedure. Unfortunately, this idea was not realised due to the events of 1940 and World War II.[2] As after the war all three countries were annexed by the Soviet Union, new codes of civil procedure were adopted according to the model law for civil procedure for Soviet Union States. These codes were absolutely different from latter ones. The court has absolute power; the courts had to ascertain objective truth; civil cases could be initiated without will of participants to the dispute but according to the statement of prosecutor, etc. These codes with huge amendments were applied after the restoration of independence in all three Baltic States, as it took quite a long time to prepare new laws of civil procedure.

Until the new codes of civil procedure[3] or huge amendments to the codes had been done, preparatory proceedings in Lithuania, Latvia and Estonia were quite similar and were understandably influenced by the tradition of soviet style civil procedure. The main idea of such preparatory proceedings was that only the judge was responsible for the preparation of the civil case for a main hearing; the parties and other participants to the proceedings were not obliged to be active during the preparatory stage. Also almost impossible terms for the preparatory proceedings had been set in the Soviet codes of civil procedure. In most of the civil cases, the judge had to prepare the case in seven days.[4] Naturally, the judges did not comply with such terms and overall the preparatory proceedings were not an important part of civil proceedings in the court; also commentaries for the codes of civil procedure stressed that main idea of preparatory proceedings is to inform the defendant about the claim and upcoming main hearing.[5] In the new codes of civil procedure, all stages of civil proceedings, including preparatory proceedings, were significantly modified. Still, as it will be shown later, all Baltic States introduced quite different systems of preparatory proceedings, albeit the systems of courts are quite similar in all three countries. For instance, all three countries have courts of general jurisdiction and administrative courts.

[2] Mikelėnas and Mikelėnienė (2014), p. 112.

[3] In Lithuania the Code of Civil Procedure was adopted on 28 February 2002 and came into force on January 2003; in Estonia the first Code of Civil Procedure was adopted 19 May 1993 and came into force on 15 September 1993, another new Code of Civil Procedure was adopted on 20 April 2005 and came into force on 1 January 2006; In Latvia the Code of Civil Procedure was adopted on 3 November 1998 and came into force on 1 March 1999.

[4] Laužikas et al. (2005), p. 73.

[5] Žeruolis et al. (1980), p. 128.

A court system of Lithuania is made up of courts of general jurisdiction and courts of special jurisdiction. Special jurisdiction is nowadays only administrative courts. Courts of general jurisdiction, which deal with civil and criminal matters, consist of the Supreme Court of Lithuania, the Court of Appeal, five regional courts and 49 district courts. Regional courts are first instance courts for civil cases assigned to its jurisdiction by law, and appeal instance for judgments, decisions of district courts. The Court of Appeal is the appeal of instance for cases heard by regional courts as courts of first instance. It also hears requests for the recognition of decisions of foreign or international courts and foreign or international arbitration awards and their enforcement in Lithuania. In most instances civil cases in the first instance are heard by one judge; however, there is the possibility that a chairperson of the court, considering the complexity of the civil case, can form a judicial board of three judges. Usually civil cases are heard and the judgments are passed quite quickly in Lithuania. According to statistics of the European Commission for the Efficiency and of Justice (CEPEJ)[6] and according to the Lithuanian National Courts Administration, about 95 % of judgments in civil cases in the first instance are finalised within six months after the filing the claim to the court. It is possible that such successful statistics are shown because judgments in all civil cases are included in it (including court orders, summary proceedings, documentary proceedings, etc). There is also the Constitutional Court in Lithuania, but private persons or entities until now do not have a right to initiate a case in the Constitutional Court.

Latvian court system consists of 34 district courts of general jurisdiction, five regional courts and the Supreme Court of Latvia. Some civil matters, according to the rules of jurisdiction, can be heard in a regional court, as in the court of first instance. In such civil matters, an appeal compliant must be filed to the Chamber of Civil Cases of Latvian Supreme Court and afterwards a cassation appeal can be filed to Department of Civil Cases of Latvian Supreme Court. All civil cases in first instance are heard by one judge. Usually it is said and the data of statistics show that in Latvia civil cases in the first instance are heard the longest in comparison with Lithuania or Estonia (approximately about ten months). There is also the Constitutional Court in Latvia, but the situation is the same as in Lithuania and private persons or entities are not able to start proceedings in this Court.

The court system in Estonia is perhaps the simplest of all three countries. There are four county courts that serve as the courts of first instance for civil and criminal matters. In the composition of county courts, there are also land registries and registry departments. One judge hears all civil cases in county courts. Circuit courts are the courts of appeal instance and review judgments of county courts on the basis of appeals against judgments and rulings. There are two circuit courts in Estonia: one in Tallinn and the other one in Tartu. The Supreme Court of Estonia performs simultaneously the functions of the highest court of general jurisdiction, of the

[6] CEPEJ Report on European judicial systems – Edition 2014 (2012 data): efficiency and quality of justice.

supreme administrative court as well as of the Constitutional Court. As Estonia is the smallest country of all Baltic States there are only about 250 judges in total in this country. In comparison, there are about 750 judges in Lithuania and, in Latvia, about 540 judges. Judgments in civil cases in the first instance are finalised in Estonia approximately within six months after the claim is initiated.

Comparing this statistics in Baltic States it should be noted that Estonia has the smallest population, about 1.2 million inhabitants, while the population in Latvia in 2014 was about 2 million. Lithuania has about 2.9 million inhabitants.[7] As it will be seen later, the declining number of inhabitants does not mean that the case load in courts is also diminishing.

6.2 Goals and Steps of Preparatory Stage

After the new codes of civil procedure have been adopted in all three Baltic States, the main hearing model of civil procedure has been introduced and the goals of preparatory stage have been set according to this model. The main idea is to organise preparation is such a manner that it would be possible to hear the civil case in a single oral main hearing. All three countries, while drafting codes of civil procedure, took into account the Recommendation No (84) 5 of Committee of Ministers of Council of Europe on the Principles of Civil Procedure designed to improve the functioning of justice. This legal act states that normally the proceedings should consist of not more than two hearings, the first of which might be a preliminary hearing of a preparatory nature and the second for taking evidence, hearing arguments and, if possible, giving judgment. The court should ensure that all steps necessary for the second hearing are taken in good time and, in principle, no adjournment should be allowed except when new facts appear or in other exceptional and important circumstances. However it can be said that such goals are not achieved in every civil case. It is still possible to find civil cases in all Baltic States where the preparatory stage lasts quite long and follows number of oral hearings until the final judgment is rendered.

The goals of preparatory stage are mainly defined in legal doctrine, case law, or in *travaux preparatoires* for codes of civil procedure, but not itself in the legal acts. Legislators mainly place emphasis on the speediness of procedure. For instance, Art. 147 (1) of Latvian Code of Civil Procedure states that in order to ensure timely adjudication of a civil matter, after the receipt of a statement of claim, the civil matter must be prepared for a trial. Legal literature usually says that the goals of preparatory stage are as follows[8]:

- to guarantee that the parties would indicate all their claims, arguments, evidence;

[7] Statistics according to official portals for statistics: http://www.stat.ee/; http://www.csb.gov.lv/; http://osp.stat.gov.lt/.

[8] Driukas and Valančius (2007), p. 193.

- to formulate finally the claims and counterclaims of the parties;
- to inform all the necessary participants to the proceedings about the civil matter;
- to try to reconcile the parties to the dispute;
- to ensure that the civil matter would be heard in one single hearing.

Pre-action stage is not really relevant in all three Baltic States. There is no obligation for parties to the dispute to disclose evidence or to go through mandatory mediation before filling a statement of claim to the court. There is only an obligation for some specific disputes to go through prior court obligatory extrajudicial dispute resolution. Such obligation is usually prescribed in special laws. Otherwise it is not possible to file a statement of claim to court for such civil claims. Such obligation has been established since the times of the Soviet Union for some labour disputes and for some specific civil disputes, such as defamation or refutation.

In Lithuanian, legal doctrine it is admitted and stressed that the preparatory stage, which begins after the receipt of statement of defence by the defendant and when the court decides how to prepare for the main hearing.[9] In Estonia and Latvia, there is no clear division when the preparatory stage begins. Moreover, all procedural actions after the receipt of the statement of claim until the main hearing are considered to be part of preparatory stage. The procedure of filing a claim to the court and the content of the statement of claim is quite similar in all three countries. Statement of the claim must include the following:

- claim of the plaintiff (object of action);
- the factual circumstances which constitute the basis of the action (cause of action);
- the evidence in proof of the circumstances which constitute the cause of the action;
- the value of the claim if it is pecuniary one;
- the opinion on the possibilities to pass default judgment; and
- whether or not the plaintiff will be represented by the attorney at law or other representative.

The peculiarity of requirements for the statement of the claim in Lithuania starts it is necessary to provide an opinion as to whether or not it is possible to achieve peaceful settlement in the dispute (Art. 135). In Estonia, it is necessary to provide the opinion of the plaintiff if the plaintiff agrees with the conduct of written proceedings in the matter or wishes the matter to be heard orally in a court hearing (Art.363). In Latvia, it is necessary to indicate the law on which the claim is based (Art.128).

The content of the statement of defence to the action is also quote similar in all three countries. It must include agreement or disagreement with the filed statement of claim; agreement or disagreement with the filed statement of claim; evidence on

[9] Nekrošius (2004), p. 77.

which the reasons for disagreement are based; opinion on the default judgment; and if the defendant will be represented by the attorney at law or other representative. In Lithuania and Estonia, it is necessary for the defendant to provide the opinion if it possible to settle the matter by way of compromise. In Estonia, it is also necessary to provide the opinion whether the defendant agrees to the conduct of a written proceeding or wishes the matter to be heard in a court hearing. In Latvia, it is not necessary to provide for the defendant the legal grounds for the objections to the claim.

It must be mentioned that in Estonia it is also possible to have an oral response of the defendant. According to Art. 395 of the Estonian Code of Civil Procedure, the court may permit the defendant to respond to an action orally in a court hearing if, in the court's opinion, this is in the interests of the expeditious adjudication of the matter. In such a case, the court obligates the defendant to thoroughly prepare the presentation of the defence to the action in the court hearing, schedules the hearing and explains the possible consequences of failure to respond and failure to use other legal remedies in the hearing to the defendant. This possibility can be used in really quite clear civil cases where usually court is quite ascertained that the defendant can bring all the evidence to the court hearing and the adjudication will not be delayed because of such response to the claim.

Usually it is not regulated in the law how long the preparatory stage should last. The length of proceedings depends on the difficulty and complexity of the civil matter and the actions of the court and participants to proceedings. Still, there are some categories of civil cases that have time limits how long preparation must last. For instance, in Lithuania in labour disputes preparation for hearing the case in court must be ended no later than within thirty days of the day the statement of claim was accepted. The same rules are applied for the cases concerning infringement of possession of a thing or in cases concerning public procurement disputes. In Latvia, preparatory stage in labour disputes must last no longer than 10 days. It is not really clear if these time limits are taken into account while adjudicating mentioned civil disputes, but it can be assumed that there are certainly cases where these time limits are violated.[10]

6.3 Oral or Written Preparation

Considering the aim of the laws, case law and legal doctrine, usually the preparatory stage in all three countries is obligatory. The judge has to decide if according to the exact circumstances of the civil case it is better to prepare case in written form

[10] According to unofficial statistics from Lithuanian national courts administration, for instance in year 2013, in 80 proc. of labour cases 30 days term for preparatory stage is observed. Some interviewed judges and officials in Latvia told that 10 days term for preparatory stage in Latvia is not wise and usually infringed.

or it is necessary to have an oral preparatory hearing. On the other hand, it is still possible for the judge to decide not to organise preparatory stage and instantly after the receipt of the response from the defendant the judge can decide that more procedural actions for preparation of the case are not necessary and the ruling to hear the case in main hearing can be passed.

Such possibility after the amendments of Lithuanian Code of Civil Procedure, in 2011, is highly criticized in legal doctrine. It is believed that such novelty makes it possible for courts to abandon the preparatory stage of civil proceedings, which can lead to favourable conditions for the parties to delay proceedings, whenever it is necessary.[11] Also, it is argued that it is an unfavourable practice not to have objective criteria when it is possible to waive preparation stage. Fortunately, it looks like that there are only few civil cases where it has been decided that preparatory stage is not needed.[12] From discussions with judges in other Baltic States, it looks like similar situation is also in their countries. It can be mentioned that in Lithuania in so-called small claims civil disputes (disputes not exceeding EUR 1,500), the court can decide not to organise preparatory stage or to hear the case in written form. Also, the preparatory stage is not applied in civil cases regarding issuing payment order in all three Baltic countries.

Preparatory stage can be written or oral in all Baltic countries. It is not possible to mix it and to arrange the written and oral preparation stage in the same civil case in Lithuania if we consider that a statement of claim and a statement of defence is not part of preparation stage. In Latvia and Estonia, it would be possible to have written explanations from the parties to the dispute and organise a preparatory hearing after that. In all three countries, the judge, who presides over the case, is responsible for deciding the form of the preparatory stage.

It can be concluded that, when comparing all Baltic States, in Lithuania, the forms of preparation of the case and the conditions when each form can be used are the most comprehensive regulated by law. That is the reason why the forms of preparatory stage in Lithuania will be presented more detailed.

In Lithuania, according to Art. 227 of the Code of Civil Procedure, preparation of the case in the form of preliminary documents takes place if both parties are represented by attorneys at law or assistants of attorneys at law; or parties are legal entities that have legal counsellors or simply it is obvious for the court that both parties understand the legal side of the dispute well and are able to express themselves in the form of documents (for instance, both parties to the dispute have university degrees in law). Also, for instance, such written form of preparation is applied in disputes regarding public procurement. The court cannot allow preparation of a case in written if there are possibilities to reach settlement in the dispute, as there is obligation to take judicial settlement efforts in the civil dispute.

---

[11] Nekrošius and Vėbraitė (2011), p. 181.

[12] It is very difficult to find exact examples of such civil cases in the system. Only some judges from district courts say that they can remember several such civil cases in their courts. Usually such civil cases happened in smaller district courts.

If the civil case is prepared in written in Lithuania, the plaintiff must submit a *duplicatio* (plaintiff's replication to the plea submitted by the defendant) and the defendant must submit a *triplicatio* (defendant's replication to the *duplicatio*). A term not exceeding fourteen days may be fixed for submission of preliminary documents that starts running from the day of handing the preliminary documents. During such preparation for a court hearing, a judge can carry out other procedural actions necessary for proper preparation of the case for the court hearing (for example, recover evidence that may not be obtained by the participants in the proceedings, collect evidence *ex officio* when it is needed, etc.).

In Lithuania, oral preparation of the case in a form of preparatory court hearing takes place if the court believes the case may be closed in a peaceful settlement or when the law obligates the court to take measures to take judicial settlement efforts or when this is a way for better and more comprehensive preparation for the hearing in the court. Normally, under the Law, one preparatory court session should be enough to prepare the case hearing in court, but, in exceptional instances or believing that the case may be ended in a peaceful settlement, the court is entitled to assign the date of the second preparatory court session that may not be later than thirty days afterwards. There cannot be more than two preparatory court sessions, but unfortunately in practice this rule is quite often infringed. The court is obliged to assign preparatory court session in all family and labour cases. According to statistics, usually in Lithuania preparation of the case for the main hearing takes from three to four months; very seldom preparation continues less than two months.[13]

6.4 Collection of Evidence

The preparatory stage is designed to collect all necessary evidence for the civil case in order to hear later the case in one court hearing and to pass a judgment in reasonable time. Therefore, it is useful to present some rules and problems concerning evidence in civil procedure while discussing preparatory stage. For example, in Lithuanian Code of Civil Procedure in Art. 181 (2), it is stressed that a court is entitled to disallow acceptance of evidence if it could have been presented earlier and later presentation thereof will delay the proceedings. Interestingly, Latvia Art. 93 (3) of the Code of Civil Procedure states that evidence must be submitted to the court not later than 14 days before a court sitting, unless the judge has set another time period within which evidence is to be submitted. Still it is later said that during adjudicating of the matter evidence may be submitted upon reasoned request of the party or other participants in the matter if it does not impede the adjudication of the matter or the court finds the reasons for untimely submission

[13] Statistics provided by Lithuanian National courts administration for the Commission to reform Lithuanian Code of Civil Procedure in 2014.

of evidence justified, or the evidence concerns facts that have become known during the adjudication of the matter. In all three countries a decision by the court to refuse acceptance of evidence may not be appealed, but objections regarding such may be expressed in an appellate complaint. Notwithstanding such legal regulation there are many cases where the parties to the dispute are allowed to present evidence later as the preparatory stage of civil case. Usually courts do not agree to examine witnesses if such request is made by the party after the preparatory stage or to issue an expert opinion,[14] but there are many cases where written evidences are accepted later after the preparatory stage is over.

For instance, some Estonian scholars stress that there is no clear understanding in practice as to what the duty of the parties and the judge in a proceeding should be. Without understanding what is important when hearing a case and what should be proven, the parties either fail to present the court with facts needed to adjudicate the case or, on the contrary, flood the court with information. All these problems arise from the poor organisation of preparatory proceedings.[15]

In all three Baltic States there is no real discovery institute in civil procedure. Usually all evidence should be collected only after a statement of a claim is filled to the court and accepted by the court. It is only possible to take evidence before the trial for safeguarding the necessary evidence. In Estonia, such procedure is regulated most detailed. Chapter 26 of the Code of Civil Procedure says that pre-trial taking of evidence may be organised by a court ruling if the opposing party agrees to this or if it can be presumed that evidence could be lost or using the evidence afterwards could involve difficulties. The court also initiates pre-trial taking of evidence in order to safeguard evidence if a person substantiates that the copyright and related rights, or industrial property rights thereof have been infringed, or that a danger of infringement exists. So, such procedure is possible in Estonia only for some specific civil cases. The court sets a term, by a ruling, within which the person must file the action. The term cannot be longer than one month. If an action is not filed on time, the court cancels the acts performed in the course of pre-trial taking of evidence. The court does not initiate pre-trial taking of evidence if the applicant fails to provide the court with a good reason why the applicant cannot specify the opposing party in such proceedings. If the opposing party did not participate in the court session of the pre-trial taking of evidence or in the performance of another procedural act, relying on the outcome of pre-trial taking of evidence is not permitted if the opposing party had not been summoned to the court session or the performance of such other procedural act in a timely manner or the rights of the opposing party were materially violated in the pre-trial taking of evidence due to another reason and the opposing party contests the evidence on such grounds.

In Lithuania on the contrary safeguarding of evidence is possible in all civil cases and not much attention is paid for protection of rights of opposing party. Art.

[14] For instance, Decisions by Lithuanian Supreme Court No. 3 K-3-563/2014, No. 3 K-3-348/2013.

[15] Kove (2013), p. 7.

221 of Code of Civil Procedure states that persons who may be reasonably afraid of later inability or difficulty to present required evidence are entitled to apply to a court, whether before filing of a claim or afterwards, for safeguarding of the aforementioned evidence. Persons must indicate in the application: evidence to be safeguarded; circumstances to be proved by the evidence; reasons of applying for evidence safeguarding. When a person requests for evidence safeguarding before a statement of claim is filed, a court may concurrently fix a period not exceeding fourteen days to file the claim. In case of failure to file the claim by the fixed time-limit, the court passes a ruling to cancel measures of evidence safeguarding. When safeguarding evidences, the court may ask for a bail to be provided by a person requesting to safeguard evidence. If the statement of claim is not filed by the fixed time-limit and a person who sustained loss for safeguarding of evidence fails to lodge a claim for damages in thirty days, the bail is refunded.

The main rule in all three countries is that the parties to the dispute have to prove the circumstances used as a basis to substantiate their claims and objections or counterclaims. On the other hand, for instance, in Lithuania, it is allowed according to the Code of Civil Procedure quite broadly for the court itself to collect the evidence. Art. 179 (2) states that the court can collect evidence *ex officio* in the civil cases where there is public interest whenever there is reason to defend rights and lawful interests of an individual, society and the state. In legal doctrine, such amendments to the Code of Civil Procedure are criticized and are called as a danger for the autonomy of the parties and the essence of civil procedure.[16] In other civil cases court in all Baltic States can help parties to require evidence if the parties to the dispute ask it because they cannot get the evidence themselves. For example, in Latvia, Art. 93 (2) of the Code of Civil Procedure says that if the parties or other participants in the matter are unable to submit evidence, the court can, at their reasoned request, require such evidence.

It can be also mentioned that in Lithuania there is not finite tools of evidence in civil proceedings. In Latvia, as evidence are allowed explanations by parties and third persons, testimony of witnesses, documentary evidence, real evidence, expert opinion, and opinion of authorities. In Estonia the rules on possible evidence are quite flexible as Art. 229 (2) states that evidence may be the testimony of a witness, statements of participants in a proceeding given under oath, documentary evidence, real evidence, inspection or an expert opinion. In a proceeding on petition the court may also deem other means of proof, including a statement of a participant in the proceeding which is not given under oath, to be sufficient in order to prove the facts.

---

[16] Nekrošius and Vėbraitė (2011), p. 180.

6.5 Possibilities of Information Technologies

Lithuania and Estonia offer the best possibilities to use modern information technologies during the preparatory stage of civil proceedings, and overall for civil proceedings. In Latvia, this area has not been really developed, to date. Electronic civil case is used quite successfully in Lithuania and Estonia. For instance, in Estonia, Art. 60^1 of Code of Civil Procedure states that electronic case proceedings information system is maintained for processing proceedings information and personal data in civil proceedings and the purpose of which is to do the following:

1) provide an overview of civil matters in which proceedings are conducted by the courts;
2) reflect information concerning the acts made in the course of civil proceedings;
3) enable the organisation of work of the courts;
4) ensure the collection of court statistics necessary for making legal policy decisions; and
5) enable the electronic sending of information and documents.

This means that in Lithuania and Estonia it is possible for participants in the proceedings to submit all documents in electronic form. Furthermore, in Lithuania, all state and municipal institutions and organisations, attorneys at law and their assistants, bailiffs and their assistants, notaries, financial and insurance companies have an obligation to receive and send all procedural documents by electronic technologies. In order to promote service of documents via electronic means both countries set rules that lower state fee is paid by the parties if claim is sent electronically.

Also in both countries it is possible civil case hearings, including preparatory hearing, to organise in the form of video or telephone conference. Such possibility is aimed for civil cases where witnesses or participants to proceedings are in another place or country and it is difficult for them to attend personally court hearing. Taken into account that Estonia and Lithuania are not huge countries and, it is quite easy to reach courts for persons, such possibility so far has not been used often. In some civil cases it has been used where one of the parties of dispute has emigrated to live in other country. Also in both of these countries minutes during preparatory hearing or main hearing are made by audio recording.

There are intentions by the legislator and court administrations in both countries to expand the use of modern technologies in civil proceedings, but financing of courts delay such wishes. In Lithuania, to help to fasten modernisation of courts, including the readjustment of courts' information system, Norwegian financial support programme *Efficiency, Quality and Transparency in Lithuanian Courts* is used.[17]

[17] More information on this programme can be found here: http://www.teismai.lt/en/national-courts-administration/projects/norway-grants/691.

6.6 Rules on Costs of Proceedings

There are no special cost rules for the preparatory stage. Common rules on costs are applied. Generally, a rule that the costs of the party who wins the civil cases are covered by another party is applied in all Baltic States. If a claim has been satisfied in part, the recovery of amounts is adjudged in proportion to the extent of the claims accepted by the court. Also the party who initiates the civil claim must, in most cases, pays a state (court) fee. It can be fixed or proportionate according to the sum of the claim.

Also, there are claims that are released from the state fee and a plaintiff is regarded as a weaker party to a dispute (for instance, claims by employees in labour disputes; claims arising from personal injuries that result in mutilation or other damage to health or the death of a person; prosecutors, state or local government institutions and persons who are defending public interest; claims concerning compensation of property or non-property damages created by criminal activity, etc.). Also, the court can, at the request of the party, taking into consideration the person's material situation, release him or her in part from the payment of the state fee or postpone the payment. The institute of legal aid is applied in all three countries for the persons whose monthly income does not reach a certain set level. While comparing state fees for civil claims, it can be probably concluded that the state fees are the highest in Latvia. In Lithuania and Estonia, the state fees are quite the same and the basic rule is that 3 proc. of the claim value must be paid for monetary claims as the state fee. In Latvia such fee can be up to 15 % of the value of a claim. It is important that in Lithuania 75 % of the state fee and in Estonia 50 % of the state fee is refunded if parties to the dispute reach a settlement in the civil case.

Division of the litigation costs is done by the court *ex officio*. Reimbursement of costs for representation during civil proceedings is also regulated in all three countries and limits of reimbursement are set. In Lithuania, there is a special rule that expenses on representation by the attorney at law cannot be awarded if the request to award them and the proof confirming the size of the expenses is not submitted by the end of the hearing of the case on the merits. Also, it can be mentioned that in Lithuania a rule in 2011 was introduced that the court, while dividing the litigation expenses, can deviate from the set rules and take into account the procedural conduct of the parties. It means that if one party did not use its procedural rights fair and, for instance, delayed the proceedings or purposely did not agree to the settlement of the dispute, the court can decide not to reimburse some costs for that party.

6.7 Possibilities of Judicial Settlement and Mediation

It is obvious that one of the aims of preparatory stage in civil proceedings is to settle the dispute between the parties to the dispute. That is the reason why codes of civil procedure in all three Baltic countries, legal doctrine and some case law speak about judicial settlement efforts in civil disputes. This was not always the case. The fifty-year Socialist regime of the Soviet Union provided for the formation of a particular mentality in society. Such mentality was oriented towards obedience and full conformity to the rules and policy established by those in power and there were many restrictions in all fields of life. Creativity, pragmatism and personal interests were not the priority in those times. After the restoration of independence in Latvia, Lithuania and Estonia it was difficult to change the mentality of people, including lawyers, and to promote peaceful settlement in judicial proceedings. It has been especially complicated to introduce alternative methods of settlement in civil proceedings, for instance, such as mediation.

Nowadays in all Baltic States it is tried to encourage peaceful settlements in civil proceedings and to devote preparatory stage on some level for judicial settlement or mediation. It could be said that on legal base Lithuania regulates judicial settlement efforts during preparation most detailed. In Estonia Art. 398 (1) only stresses that preliminary hearing may be organised if this is in the interests of preparation or if the possibility to end the proceedings by way of compromise is higher. In Latvia, Art.149 (2) emphasises that in preparing a matter for main hearing a judge must strive to take judicial settlement efforts in order to reconcile the parties. There are no special rules on judicial settlement efforts while speaking about possibility to organise preparatory sitting and what should be done during such sitting.

In Lithuania, it is stressed that obligatory part of preparatory hearing is proceedings to take judicial settlement efforts. According to Art. 231 (1) of Code of Civil Procedure, after the essence of the dispute is identified in a preliminary session, the court must offer both parties to come to a mutually acceptable compromise agreement and to close the case in a peaceful settlement. Judicial settlement efforts may be applied to the entire dispute or any part thereof. Also, with consent of the parties or by their request court-connected mediation can take place. After amendments of code of civil procedure in 2011, it is allowed to organise closed hearing of the case for the purpose to try to reconcile the parties.

Also it is important that in Lithuania and Estonia there are some financial incentives to promote settlements in civil proceedings. Art. 87 (2) of Lithuanian Code of Civil Procedure says that 75 % of the amount of paid official state fee is refunded if parties conclude a settlement in a civil case. In Estonia, according to Art. 150 (2) of Code of Civil Procedure, 50 % of the state fee is refunded if a compromise between the parties to the dispute is reached.

In legal doctrine in Lithuania it is acknowledged that judicial settlement efforts should depend on category of the civil case; on the nature of relationships between the parties to the dispute; on the value of the claim; on the preliminary evaluation of the attitude of the parties towards the conflict; on the difficulty to prove the arguments of the parties.[18] It is also believed that it is wise not to regulate proceedings on judicial settlement efforts precisely in the law. In such way, a judge and participants of civil proceedings have more freedom and flexibility to take judicial settlement efforts in a manner suitable for an exact dispute. On the other hand, such legal regulation allows the possibility that there will be no steps taken to reconcile the parties in some civil cases.[19] Also, training of judges on techniques of judicial settlement efforts must be constantly ongoing.

Notwithstanding the legal regulation on judicial settlement efforts during preparatory stage, the statistics of reached settlements is quite similar in all Baltic States and, unfortunately, the rate of settlements is not really high. Usually only around 4–5 % of all civil cases are ended by peaceful settlements. Overall, for instance, in Latvia there were about 61,000 civil cases in the first instance courts in 2014[20]; in Estonia, there were approximately 30,000 civil cases (excluding payment order cases) in the first instance in 2014[21]; in Lithuania, there were about 200,000 civil cases (including payment order and other summary proceedings cases) in the first instance in 2014.[22]

There are possibilities of court-connected mediation during preparatory stage in all Baltic countries. Out-of-court mediation usually should be used before filing a claim to the court. It must be mentioned that the discussions about mediation and its advantages started only with the introduction of court-connected mediation and first projects to try such procedure to settle civil disputes in courts.[23] It can be also said that EU Directive 2008/52/EC on certain aspects of mediation in civil and commercial matters was really huge stimulus to promote mediation, to adopt laws on mediation. Now all three countries have laws on mediation.[24] It is interesting that in Lithuania and Estonia the word "mediation" in law is not used and this procedure is called conciliation (in Lithuania—'*Taikinamasis tarpininkavim*as'; in Estonia—'*Lepitusseadus*'). In practice, everyone uses the word 'mediation' in both countries.

Also, the Codes of Civil Procedure mention possibilities of court-connected mediation during civil proceedings in all three countries. For instance, Art. 4 (4) of Estonian Code stresses that if, in the opinion of the court, it is necessary in the interests of adjudication of the matter, considering the circumstances of the case and the process of the proceedings, it may order the parties to participate in the mediation proceeding provided for in the Conciliation Act (Act dedicated to mediation in Estonia). In Lithuania, there are also rules of court-connected

[18] Simaitis (2004), p. 22.

[19] Vėbraitė (2013), p. 271.

[20] http://www.ta.gov.lv/lv/statistikas_dati_58.

[21] http://www.kohus.ee/et/eesti-kohtud/kohtute-statistika.

[22] http://www.teismai.lt/lt/visuomenei-ir-ziniasklaidai/statistika/106.

[23] Kaminskienė et al. (2013)), p. 248.

[24] Lithuania and Estonia have Laws on Mediation from year 2010. In Latvia Law on Mediation was finally adopted on 22nd of May 2014.

mediation, which have been amended several times since 2005. These rules are adopted and amended by the Lithuanian Judicial Council.

Until today mediation proceedings in all three Baltic States are voluntary and the consent of the parties to the dispute is necessary notwithstanding the fact if mediation will take place before filling a claim to the court or already during the preliminary stage of civil proceedings. It can be also concluded that court-connected mediation is much more regulated in Lithuania and Latvia in comparison with Estonia. It is important that the Act on Conciliation in Estonia does not distinguish court-connected mediation and out-of-court mediation. It is interesting that only in Estonia in the Conciliation Act it is said that a mediator may, on the basis of the facts of mediation and the progress of proceedings, propose to the parties his or her own solutions to the dispute. Such legal regulation shows that possibilities of evaluative mediation are emphasised in Estonia.

Latvian Law on mediation states that court-connected mediation is mediation conducted by a mediator, if during court proceedings while adjudication of a matter on the merits has not been completed, the parties have expressed a willingness to settle the dispute using mediation upon recommendation of a court or a judge. A judge or a court than invites the parties to select a mediator from the list of certified mediators. As the certified mediator may be natural persons who has reached 25 years of age; has impeccable reputation; has acquired an education document attesting a state-recognised higher education; is fluent in the official language at the highest level; has attended a mediator's training course; has obtained a mediator's certificate. A certification examination of a mediator and an attestation examination of a certified mediator is organised by the Council of Certified Mediators.

In Lithuania, details of court-connected mediation are regulated in the already mentioned rules adopted by Judicial Council.[25] Court-connected mediation can be initiated by a judge hearing a civil case or by any person participating in the civil case. A dispute is assigned to mediation procedure by a ruling of the court. The written consent of the parties is also necessary. If parties agree on court-connected mediation in a court session, such consent can be recorded in the minutes of the court session. The hearing of the case is adjourned by the same court ruling. It is also possible to assign only part of the case to the procedure of court-connected mediation. Mediators in court-connected mediation can be persons included in the lists of court mediators. Currently on the list there are more than 100 court mediators and most of them have a law degree. Most of them are judges or assistants to judges, while some are lawyers or social workers in the sphere of child protection.[26] Until now not all district courts have at least one court mediator. There is Commission of court-connected mediation, which is responsible for allowing persons to be included into the list of court mediators. Persons who wish to be included into the

[25] The rules can be found here: http://www.teismai.lt/lt/visuomenei-ir-ziniasklaidai/teismine-mediacija/teises-aktai-reglamentuojantys-teismine-mediacija/1677.

[26] The list can be found here: http://www.teismai.lt/lt/visuomenei-ir-ziniasklaidai/teismine-mediacija/teismo-mediatoriu-sarasas/283.

list of court mediators must have at least 32 hours academic hour's courses on mediation; if a person is a judge he or she could have participated in the courses on mediation according to the training programme provided for judges. According to the most recent amendments, court-connected mediation rules the judge who hears the civil dispute and is on the list of court mediators is able to mediate the case personally if the parties agree. Several court mediators can be also assigned. If mediation procedure is not successful, later such judge cannot continue to hear that civil case and pass a judgment. A settlement reached during court-connected mediation must be approved by the judge who was hearing the case, but was not a mediator in the proceedings. According to the rules, if the same judge was the presiding judge and the court mediator, it is possible for that judge to approve the settlement.

Settlements approved by the court can be enforced under coercion in all three countries. Regardless of some differences in regulation of mediation, the similarity of all three Baltic States is that mediation is nonetheless not popular and there is a lack of awareness in society about such existing possibility to reach an agreement. It is difficult to get exact statistics about court-connected mediation, but, for instance, in Lithuania, unofficially National Courts Administration states that in 2014 there were 53 court-connected mediation cases in all Lithuanian courts. In 2013, there were 37 such cases. It must be signified that from 53 court-connected mediation cases in 2014 only in 12 cases settlement were reached and signed; in 2013 only two settlements were reached. Such statistics may mean that there are civil cases where court-connected mediation is perhaps only used to delay civil proceedings in some way. We believe that most of court-connected mediations took place during preparatory stage of civil proceedings.

In Latvia, unofficially it is said that in 2014 there were overall about 400 court-connected mediation cases (including civil, criminal and administrative cases) and success rate was about 60–70 %.[27] This shows that it is likely that court-connected mediation proceedings are more popular and more successful in Latvia than in Lithuania.

It is said in Estonia that one of the reasons for the under-usage of mediation could be the lack of awareness of how to negotiate based on interests. Most legal counsels in Estonia have been trained towards enhancing their active skillset (arguing, persuading) and not their passive skillset (listening, managing emotions of self and others). As a result, parties get torn up in emotions but professionals at their side are not equipped to calm them down.[28] We believe such situation exists also in other Baltic States. More education about alternative methods of dispute resolution is really needed. Other possible obstacles to popularity of mediation could be litigious culture, lack of finances devoted to promoting mediation, and the still quite small number of mediation professionals.

[27] For example, some statistics can be found here: http://www.mediacija.lv/?Aktualit%C4%81tes&id=190.

[28] Nurmela and Poldvere (2014), p. 40.

On the other hand, it must be mentioned that, for example, in Lithuania, the discussions and even actions to promote mediation have intensified in the last years. The Ministry of Justice, Judicial Council and other institutions began to prepare and adopt conception how to popularise mediation, how to increase the number of mediators in Lithuania, to decide in which cases mediation procedure could be mandatory. Now it is believed that in family cases one session of mediation could be mandatory before filing a statement of claim to the court. This session would be probably free of charge.

6.8 The Closing of Preparatory Stage

The closing of the preparatory stage and the effects of such closing is not clearly regulated in Latvia and Estonia. In Lithuania, the situation is quite different because in most civil cases it is necessary for the court to pass a ruling to hear a case in main court session. Such ruling must state evidence required by the court on its own initiative (*ex officio*), when this right of the court is provided for in the code of civil procedure; venue and time of the court hearing; commission to send summons for participants in the proceeding; commission to call to the session witnesses, experts, translators and interpreters and other persons listed in the ruling; if necessary, a ruling to involve state or municipal authorities in the proceeding for giving their findings; other commissions safeguarding proper hearing of the case. This ruling in Lithuania has a function to consolidate all the actions performed in preparatory stage and in theory it should be quite difficult to change something regarding the essence of the civil case after passing this ruling.[29] After such ruling it should be possible only in exceptional cases allowed to change the grounds or subject of the claim, increase or diminish claim requirements, to submit a counterclaim or to present more evidence. In practice, there are unfortunately quite many cases where a plaintiff or defendant is allowed to change his or her legal position quite easily during main hearing and, in such way, delay the proceedings.

It is allowed in Lithuania not to pass discussed ruling in cases when during the preparatory hearing it turns out that additional actions of preparation for court main hearing are not necessary, the court is entitled to start oral hearing and resolve the case on the merits right after the preparatory court session.

[29] Laužikas et al. (2005), p. 71.

6.9 Current Problems and Future Visions

It can be seen that legal regulation of the preparatory stage has seen many changes in the last decade in all three Baltic States. It is obvious that to change legal regulation and to change aims and role of preparatory proceedings is much easier than to change mentality and culture of judges, lawyers or participants of civil proceedings. One of the best examples is the admissibility of new evidence after the end of preparatory stage. Even if possibility of preclusions is set in the laws, there are civil cases where this rule is not applied and principles of concentration and cooperation in civil proceedings are breached. Another example is still very seldom used judicial settlement efforts. There are all appropriate conditions for judges to take judicial settlement efforts or to advice the parties to the dispute to try court-connected mediation. Still, the number of settlements is quite low in all three countries and the governments, judicial institutions, academic and non-governmental organisations must put more energy, invest more money in order to promote advantages of settlements and best features of court-connected mediation.

Certainly some parts of legal regulation of preparatory stage will be amended in the near future in Latvia and Lithuania, perhaps also in Estonia. For instance, there are attempts to regulate preparatory stage more detailed in Latvia; in Lithuania, the laws are being drafted at the moment to include mandatory mediation for some civil cases, first of all, for family disputes. Also there are attempts being made in Lithuania to raise the court fees. Similarly it is believed that new technologies will change the face of preparatory proceedings in the future. This tendency can be felt a bit so far in Lithuania and Estonia, but it is obvious that Latvia will be no exception in near future.

References

Driukas A, Valančius V (2007) Civilinis procesas: teorija ir praktika. TIC, Vilnius

CEPEJ Report on European judicial systems – Edition 2014 (2012 data): efficiency and quality of justice

Kaminskienė N, Mienkowska-Norkienė R, Tvarijonavičienė A, Uscila R (2013) Mediacija. Mykolo Romerio Universitetas, Vilnius

Kove V (2013) The main problems of civil proceedings from the point of view of a justice of supreme court and lecturer. Yearbook of Estonian Courts, Tallinn, pp 7–18

Laužikas E, Mikelėnas V, Nekrošius V (2005) Civilinio proceso teisės, II tomas. Justitia, Vilnius

Mikelėnas V, Mikelėnienė D (2014) Reception of the Russian Statute of Civil Procedure of 1864 in Lithuania during 1918–40. Russian Law J 2(4):104–113

Nekrošius V (2004) Pasirengimas teisminiam nagrinėjimui civiliniame procese: teoriniai ir praktiniai aspektai. Justitia 49(1):75–82

Nekrošius V, Vėbraitė V (2011) Reform of Lithuanian civil justice in 2011. ZZPInt 16:169–182

Nurmela I, Poldvere P (2014) Efficiency of mediation in commercial disputes with Emphasis on Estonia. Slovenska Arbitražna Praksa 6:35–41

Simaitis R (2004) Teisminis sutaikymas. Justitia 5:19–25
Vėbraitė V (2013) Teismo vaidmuo įgyvendint šalių sutaikymo tikslą šeimos bylose. Šeimos bylų nagrinėjimo ypatumai. Mykolo Romerio Universitetas, Vilnius, pp 266–276
Žeruolis J, Radzevičius J, Vėlyvis S, Vitkevičius P (1980) Lietuvos TSR civilinio proceso komentaras. Mintis, Vilnius

Chapter 7
Polish Civil Proceedings: Expanding the Floor for Preparatory Stage

Anna Piszcz

Abstract Polish civil procedural law has become highly regulated over the last half-century since the adoption of the 1964 Civil Procedure Code, which has been amended almost two hundred times, so far (piecemeal amendments). In this chapter, readers will find information about the preparatory proceedings (preparatory stage of proceedings) in the Polish civil justice system. The system of Polish procedural law and its history are briefly reviewed before the focus of the chapter is turned to the preparatory proceedings. Separate subchapters present the review of provisions on the activities preceding the hearing (trial), structural issues and deficiencies endorsed in practice. A considerable part of this chapter is intended to point out peculiarities that characterise the activities of court "actors" during this stage, including conciliatory activities. Special emphasis is given to the amendments to the Polish civil procedural law made during last few years that influenced (or rather were supposed to influence) the preparatory proceedings. This chapter also analyses whether the judiciary utilises the powers given to them by the legislation.

7.1 Brief Review of Polish Civil Procedure

The overall budget of the Polish justice system measured as the percentage of general government expenditure is approximately twice as high as the European Union average. Moreover, Poland has half as much full-time professional judges per 100,000 inhabitants as the EU, on average. In Poland, there exist a few systems and hierarchies of state courts (as well as the Constitutional Tribunal and the State Tribunal) with hugely varied procedures and differentiated structures. The Polish justice system consists of the Supreme Court, courts of general jurisdiction, administrative courts and military courts. The *Supreme Court* (Sąd Najwyższy), among others, hears cassation complaints and adopts resolutions to clarify legal issues.

A. Piszcz (✉)
Faculty of Law, University of Białystok, Białystok, Poland
e-mail: piszcz@uwb.edu.pl

L. Ervo, A. Nylund (eds.), *Current Trends in Preparatory Proceedings*,
DOI 10.1007/978-3-319-29325-7_7

Courts of general jurisdiction include 321 *district courts* (sądy rejonowe), 45 *regional courts* (sądy okręgowe) and 11 *courts of appeal* (sądy apelacyjne). They are organised into divisions, first and foremost criminal divisions and civil divisions. Judges are usually specialised in certain fields of law.

The Polish Constitution of 1997 provides for *at least two-instance proceedings*. Decisions of district courts can be appealed to a competent regional court and decisions adopted by regional courts as courts of first instance to a competent court of appeal.

The main body of legal rules that regard Polish civil procedure is *Civil Procedure Code* (Kodeks postępowania cywilnego, hereinafter CPC).[1] It was adopted in 1964 and entered into force on 1 January 1965. Provisions of CPC, in particular in conjunction with its provisions on labour and social insurance cases, as well as commercial cases embedded into the competence of courts of general jurisdiction in the 1980s, were viewed as embracing the whole civil court procedure (except for provisions on bankruptcy and composition proceedings that, in practice, were not applied in Poland's centrally-planned state economy).

The predecessor of CPC and the first modern Polish act on civil procedure was *Civil Procedure Code* of 1930, which entered into force on 1 January 1933. It came at a moment in history when different sets of civil procedural rules (Russian, German, Austrian and Hungarian rules) had been applied in respective parts of reborn Poland (1918).[2] It was regarded not only as an "inheritor" of civil procedural laws of the former occupants but also as a highly ingenious and well-constructed piece of legislation taking into consideration the experiences of other European countries.[3] It included, among others, principles, such as party autonomy, equality of arms between the parties, orality and directness, procedural formalism, three-instance proceedings. It contained provisions on contentious proceedings (but in contrast with CPC, not non-contentious proceedings), proceedings to secure claims and execution proceedings (adopted later, in 1932).

After World War II, the interwar procedural provisions were first interpreted and then amended so as to be drawn upon the Soviet communist model. In particular, the Supreme Court, insofar as it was competent to adopt guidelines for judiciary, used to fuse old rules with socialist content (often contrary to their linguistic interpretation) and even to declare some of them null and void because of their nature inconsistent with socialism.

Civil Procedure Code of 1964 (CPC) fully reflected the principles of socialism. Although it adopted provisions of the 1930 Code to a considerable extent, most of the interwar developments were eaten away by political and economic change. At the time of the adoption of CPC, neither party autonomy nor procedural formalism were fundamental procedural principles but rather (*inter alia*) substantive truth,

[1] Consolidated text Official Journal of 2014, item 101, as amended. Even unofficial English translations of the whole text are not available.

[2] Rylski and Weitz (2014), pp. 78 ff.

[3] Ereciński (2007), p. 111.

protection of public (collective) property (connected with the growing importance of the role of the public prosecutor), cooperation of participants, lay participation in the administration of justice (involvement of lay judges in the civil justice system), and two-instance proceedings.[4] An important implication of the socialist legal perspective was that, although CPC contained provisions on "*arbitration court*" (sąd arbitrażowy) *i.e.* arbitration "tribunals", arbitration embedded in the matrix of centrally-planned state economy was applied only to disputes between state-owned undertakings resolved by the so-called arbitration commissions, as CPC termed it (quasi-judicial and quasi-administrative form of state economic arbitration). Until1989 disputes between (state-owned) undertakings could not have been filed with and resolved by courts of general jurisdiction.

After the communist collapse in 1989, the principle of protection of public (collective) property was removed by the amendment of 1990, and the principle of equality of arms between the parties was brought back to Poland. In the wake of the Soviet collapse and marketization (privatization) of socialist economies, in Poland the competition (antimonopoly) court was established (1990). In this changed historical circumstance, courts of appeal were established and the Supreme Court ceased to be a court of second instance for appeals in some cases. Furthermore, in early 1990s, the European Convention of Human Rights was incorporated into Polish law.

It is true, however, that it was not until 1996 that lawmakers removed considerable socialist features of CPC (*e.g.* the lay participation was reduced) and transformed civil procedure so as to provide for principles and concepts that have served, so far, Western countries well, including party autonomy and adversariality. Furthermore, the appeal system was reformed. The most important innovation was the abolition of the extraordinary "revision" and the introduction of "appeal" by way of *cassation* from the Supreme Court (*cassation complaint*).

Since then, CPC has been amended even a dozen or so times a year. To mention but a few examples, the position of court clerk was created in 1997 (a counterpart of German and Austrian Rechtspfleger). New types of proceedings appeared, including small claims proceedings (of up to PLN 5,000, about EUR 1,250, originally, and of up to PLN 10,000, about 2,500 EUR, from 2005) introduced by the amendment of 2000. The rule of preclusion was articulated in CPC. The scope for review in cassation by the Supreme Court was limited, making it an extraordinary measure. With the amendment of 2004 provisions on the new extraordinary measure in the form of a complaint for declaring a final judgment contrary to law were adopted. There was also a shift of focus from the still-strong principle of substantive truth to somewhat greater scope for formal truth (la vérité judiciare in French).[5] It was extended additionally by the amendment of 2011, which came into effect on 3 May 2012. Rules on mediation were adopted in 2005. At the same time, revised provisions on arbitration were reintroduced.

[4] Siedlecki (1977), pp. 51–83.

[5] Lapierre (2014), pp. 124–127.

With the amendments of 2006 and 2011 the principle of concentration was strengthened. It is worth emphasising that, in general, there is no rule that the hearing should be conducted as a single hearing. It is only declared in Article 6 para 1 CPC that the court should prevent delays in the proceedings and aim to ensure that the resolution of the case occurred *at the first sitting* if this is possible without detriment to the clarification of the case. However, it is symptomatic that, in many instances, CPC uses an originally coined phrase "first sitting". The practice leads to regard Article 6 para 1 as of little practical value.

The backward-looking perspective of these studies should be considered a guide to understanding status quo and consulting on proposals for the future development of Polish civil procedure. Insofar as it seems that the stage (phase) preceding the hearing is somewhat neglected in practice, the purpose of this chapter is to explore and clarify the current legal framework on this stage. The aim in doing so is not just to support status quo. To the contrary, it is to posit a criticism thereof and to sketch the modernising tendencies generated recently by Polish lawmakers.

7.2 Stage Preceding the Hearing: After the Arrival of the Statement of Claim at the Court

CPC does not recognize specific stages preceding the hearing in the form of pleadings stage (initial stage) and preparatory stage (preparatory proceedings).[6] The stage preceding the hearing (preparatory stage *largo sensu*) is, as a rule, structurally "open" and, thus, somewhat vague. Only in some *specific types of proceedings* there are clear-cut preparatory stages distinguished from the remainder of the stage preceding the hearing.[7]

As a rule the stage preceding the hearing involves all the activities which precede the prospective hearing, including those aimed specifically at the preparation of the hearing (preparation *stricto sensu*). The stage preceding the hearing includes the very first activities of the court related to *pleadings*, *i.e.* activities which precede the service of the statement of claim to the defendant and consist mainly of the examination whether the statement of claim meet the formal requirements.

Firstly, the competence of the court to hear the case is examined. If the court is not competent to hear the case, it shall forward the case to the competent court; the decision thereon can be issued in chambers (Article 200 para 1 CPC).

---

[6] Łazarska (2012), p. 61; Karolczyk (2013), p. 156.

[7] Firstly, in labour and social insurance cases there is a stage of proceedings that consists of the initial examination of the case (Article 467 CPC). It includes: (1) the examination whether the statement of claim initiating the proceedings fulfils the legal requirements that allow proceeding with it, (2) the conduct of activities that allow resolution of the dispute at the first sitting. Secondly, in group proceedings, after group statement of claim arrives at the court and is examined in formal terms, there is a stage where the court decides on admissibility of the group proceedings.

If the court is competent to hear the case, the court examines whether the very content of the statement of claim shows that it will be dismissed on formal grounds, in other words, *rejected* (*e.g.* Article 199 CPC). If so, the court sitting in chambers shall dismiss the case.

If there are no formal grounds for the dismissal, the court examines whether the court registration fee has been paid. Article 126^2 para 2 CPC states that an applicant cannot be required to pay the court registration fee if the very content of the application shows that it will be dismissed (on formal grounds). At this stage, the court sitting in chambers may check the accuracy of the claimant's determination of a value of the case (Article 25 CPC).

The court also examines whether the statement of claim meets the formal requirements as to the contents and attachments, lawyer's power of attorney, etc. Article 130 CPC is the legal basis under which *the presiding judge* requires the claimant to correct the statement of claim within a specified period of time (one week) and, after the lapse of this time, returns the statement of claim to the claimant.

The court dismisses the statement of claim on formal grounds, if—according to the law—the defects of the statement of claim cannot be corrected (*irremediable defects*) or appropriate provisions provide so (*e.g.* in cases mentioned in Article 199 para 1 point 3 CPC—regarding problems with capacity to be a party to court proceedings or capacity to act as a claimant—the statement of claim will be rejected if a defect is not corrected).[8]

If there are no formal grounds to return or dismiss the statement of claim (irrespective of whether they did not exist at all or they ceased to exist due to timely correction of defects in the statement of claim), the court will perform activities provided for in Article 206 para 1 CPC, which states that the *date for the hearing* is set by the presiding judge. Altogether with setting the first sitting the presiding judge will *order the service of the statement of claim* and, if needed, appoint the reporting judge. As the CPC requires this at the same time, the statement of claim is served to the defendant by registered mail together with an order setting the date for the first sitting of the hearing. Courts set this date without even seeing the defendant's statement of defence.[9]

[8] Issues of these capacities on the side of the defendant are taken into account by the court at any possible stage of proceedings—see Article 202 sentence 3 CPC.

[9] Karolczyk (2013), p. 158.

7.3 Stage Preceding the Hearing: After the Order to Serve the Statement of Claim to the Defendant

7.3.1 The Types and the Course of Preparatory Activities

Although it is not clear-cut under Polish civil procedural law, the *preparatory stage* (*stricto sensu*) should be considered to have begun when the order to serve the statement of claim to the defendant is issued (as a rule, together with setting the date for the first sitting). The length of this stage is not limited in Poland.

This stage involves, first of all, some *"technical" activities of the presiding judge*. Article 206 para 2 CPC states that, together with the service of the statement of claim and the convening order, the defendant will be *served with the instructions* on the following: (1) procedural activities that may or should be undertaken by the defendant if the claim is not partially or fully admitted, in particular, on the possibility or obligation to deliver the statement of defence, including the applicable requirements in respect of the deadline and the form, and/or to present the claims, arguments/defences and evidence orally in a hearing; (2) the implications of failing to undertake such activities, in particular, on the possibility for the court to issue a default judgment as well as on conditions of its execution and the costs of the proceedings that will have to be paid by the defendant; (3) the possibility to grant a procedural power of attorney and the lack of obligation to be represented by a professional lawyer (advocate or legal advisor).

The defendant has the *right to provide a statement of defence* before the first sitting of the hearing (Article 207 para 1 CPC). However, from 3 May 2012, the amended Article 207 para 2 CPC stipulates that the defendant may be *ordered* by the presiding judge to provide a statement of defence within a specified period of time not shorter than two weeks (before 3 May 2012 the possibility to issue such order was limited to complex cases and cases involving calculations). The statement of defence provided in violation of Article 207 para 2 CPC, *e.g.* after a specified period of time, must be returned to the defendant.[10] The view espoused by the author is that Article 207 para 1 CPC allows the defendant to provide the statement of defence also where the court does not require so.[11]

Furthermore, in proceedings initiated after 3 May 2012, the *presiding judge* may also, before the first sitting of the hearing, order the parties to provide further submissions (preparatory submissions, written statements), giving to them directions on the sequence of submissions, deadlines and facts that have to be explained/clarified to the court (Article 207 para 3 sentence 1 CPC). This may be seen as a *surrogate for the plan for the preparatory proceedings*. The order in this respect may be issued in chambers. The *presiding judge or the panel* may also hear the

[10] There is no discretionary power of the judge here; judgment of the Court of Appeal in Warsaw of 29 September 2014, Case I ACa 370/14.

[11] Draniewicz (2012), p. 893.

parties in chambers (Article 207 para 4 CPC), which seems to be a kind of preparatory hearing.

In case law it is accepted that the parties, on their own initiative, can only file the statement of claim and the statement of defence; these are submissions in which the parties should include all their legal and factual arguments.[12] The presiding judge has the discretion to admit further submissions. At the same time, it does not matter whether there was a hearing in chambers or not. The order to provide further submissions may be issued from the effective filing of the statement of claim until (before) the first sitting of the hearing.

In the light of para 3 sentence 2, as a rule, the parties are not allowed to provide any submissions other than the statement of claim, the statement of defence and submissions required by the court; exceptionally CPC allows for *submissions that only adduce evidence*. Any submission provided in violation of para 3 will be returned to the defendant (para 7). In case law, these provisions were interpreted as allowing a party to provide a submission adducing evidence without any appropriate authorization of the court at any time; whether this evidence will be taken into consideration by the court depends on the occurrence of the grounds referred to in Article 207 para 6 CPC.[13] According to para 6, as a rule the court shall ignore any late arguments and/or evidence (*preclusion*, in Polish prekluzja).

In proceedings initiated before 3 May 2012 the presiding judge was allowed to order a party to provide a submission on pain of preclusion only if the party was represented by a professional lawyer (*judicial preclusion, discretionary power of the judge*). On the other hand, there was a distinction kept between the above and the *statutory (CPC-based) preclusion* applicable to disputes between undertakings (resolved in commercial proceedings).[14]

Further, prior to the hearing, the presiding judge issues, if needed, orders aimed at the *preparation of hearing*, based on the statement of claim and other submissions. In particular, the presiding judge may: (1) order the parties to appear at the hearing personally or through an attorney (unless it is ordered otherwise, in Poland, there is no duty to attend the hearing; however, under some circumstances a default judgment will be issued); (2) order that evidence in possession of state authorities or local authorities be delivered to the hearing, if the party may not obtain such evidence; (3) convene witnesses called by the parties; (4) convene expert witnesses the parties have jointly called; and/or (5) order that documents, items to be inspected, books, plans, etc. be presented. Moreover, the presiding judge may *inspect a piece of evidence prior to the hearing*, if necessary (Article 208 CPC).

---

[12] Decision of the Supreme Court of 14 January 2015, Case III CSK 317/14.

[13] Judgment of the Court of Appeal in Szczecin of 11 June 2014, Case I ACa 269/14.

[14] Cieślak (2007), pp. 171–173; Flaga-Wieruszyńska (2007), pp. 200 ff. On 3 May 2012, provisions on commercial proceedings were abolished.

Provided that preparatory procedures comprise activities of the presiding judge listed in Articles 206, 207 and 208 CPC, one can perceive that some of them are *mandatory* whereas others are *voluntary*.

First of all, none of them will take place if the order for payment is going to be issued. Then, the court will proceed in chambers (Article 201 para 1 CPC). Order for payment, if issued, will be served to the defendant together with the statement of claim. If the defendant does not file an objection to an order for payment, proceedings are considered closed without any hearing (trial). No preparatory stage *stricto sensu* is incorporated in such proceedings. On the other hand, if an objection is filed following the formal examination (and positive verification) the date for the first sitting will be set by the court. Although started as proceedings regarding order for payment, since then the proceedings become "normal" proceedings with "normal" preparatory activities.

Second, some preparatory activities are subject to the discretion of the presiding judge. Certainly, these are not activities contained in Article 206 CPC (setting the date for the first sitting, the order to serve the statement of claim, the instructions). If a reporting judge is not needed, the appointment can be omitted (*e.g.* there is a one-person panel). Activities listed in Articles 207 and 208 CPC are of a different kind. They are "optional". The presiding judge may: (1) order the defendant to file a statement of defence; (2) require the parties to file further submissions (*preparatory submissions*); (3) proceed to the hearing of the parties in chambers; (4) issue orders aimed at the preparation of hearing; (5) inspect a piece of evidence prior to hearing, if necessary.

However, these activities are not mandatory and many of them may be omitted or rather postponed and done after the first sitting, *e.g.* activities listed in Article 208 para 1 CPC. Even the Supreme Court in its judgment[15] of 14 March 2001 observed that Article 208 para 1 CPC does not place any specific duties on the presiding judge.

It is up to the presiding judge whether to transform preparatory "empty" stage into a series of activities that make the court appropriately prepared for the hearing and quick resolution of the dispute. It seems that recently Article 207 CPC is not the (almost) meaningless provision it used to be before 3 May 2012. But how is it used currently? One may fall under the impression that, frequently, the statement of claim is served to the defendant together with the order to file a statement of defence within two weeks and the information on the sufficiently distant date for the first sitting of the hearing. If filed by the defendant, the statement of defence is served to the claimant together with the order to file a further submission within a prescribed time limit (*e.g.* one week). Sometimes, a party tries to circumvent Article 207 para 3 sentence 2 CPC and file further submissions that do not adduce evidence (just contain legal or factual arguments etc.). Such submissions should be returned to the party; however, it happens that the court serves them to the other party. One of possible defences is that such submission should have been returned. Parties and

[15] Case II UKN 269/00.

their lawyers use this defence especially that they become more aware of the idea of "preclusion" resulting from Article 207 para 6 CPC. It is worth adding that under the new approach it is possible that the presiding judge will not permit the parties to file any submissions other than the statement of claim and the statement of defence by the defendant (except for submissions that only adduce evidence).[16]

Moreover, CPC provisions do not mention literally the notion of *summary*. It seems that Article 207 para 3 sentence 1 CPC allows the presiding judge to order parties to provide preparatory submissions in the form of summaries. However, it is doubtful whether this provision has been so applied even a few times so far. Any practical examples thereof have not been publicly known so far. On the other hand, a kind of summary may be contained in the minutes of the first sitting. According to Article 158 para 1^1 CPC the minutes taken in writing may contain requests and arguments of the parties, an outline of the results of the evidentiary proceedings and other circumstances essential to the course of the sitting. If the course of the sitting is not recorded by means of the audio recording or the audio and visual recording, the minutes taken in writing do contain requests and arguments of the parties, the instructions given by the court, the results of the evidentiary proceedings and other circumstances essential to the course of the sitting (para 2). In both cases, instead of requests and arguments the *preparatory submissions* may be referred to in the minutes.

In any event, except for proceedings regarding order for payment, *the court cannot decide on merits without the hearing*.[17] Even if the defendant admitted the claim, the case cannot be decided on merits without the hearing. The only extraordinary effect of such admission is the "reversed" rule for division of litigation costs. The losing defendant will be entitled to a reimbursement by the claimant, provided that the defendant did not provide a reason for filing a case and admitted the claim when performing the first activity in the proceedings (usually in the statement of defence but where it was not filed, the first activity may be the participation in the first sitting of the hearing).

Preparatory activities do not seem to influence the case to a considerable extent in practice; at the end of the stage preceding, the hearing the case does not look very different than it did before (when it was originally filed). The status of the case at the beginning of the hearing will be the result of the acuteness and activity of the presiding judge.

It is worth noting that the claimant is free to *withdraw the case* without the defendant's consent until the beginning of hearing or—if the defendant, at the same time, waives the claim—until issuing a judgment by the court (Article 203 para 1 CPC). However, in the case of withdrawal after the statement of claim has been served, the defendant can request that claimant must reimburse costs (para 2). If the

[16] Kosiński (2012), p. 29.

[17] However, in small claims proceedings the judgment of the court of second instance may be issued in chamber without trial unless the party requested the hearing in the appeal or the statement of defence (Article 505^{10} para 2 CPC).

withdrawal takes place outside the hearing, the presiding judge will cancel the hearing and inform the defendant about the withdrawal; within two weeks, the defendant may apply to the court for reimbursement by the claimant (para 3). In the case of withdrawal after the statement of claim has been sent to the other parties but before the beginning of the sitting, the claimant will get half of the paid court registration fee back. Furthermore, in the case of withdrawal before the statement of claim has been sent to the other parties, the claimant will get the whole paid court registration fee back.[18] These cost rules are applied by the court *ex officio*.

Last but not least, for many years, Polish provisions did not provide for a plan for the hearing consulted with the parties and made in the preparatory stage. This problem was solved, at least in principle, a few months ago. As of 8 July 2015, the Regulation of the Minister of Justice of 25 June 2015 relating to the rules of procedure in courts of general jurisdiction[19] came into force. The new Regulation provides for important procedural measures that could not be achieved through the previous Regulation, which referred to the preparation of hearing in just four paragraphs regarding only sittings outside the court building, convening lay judges, open sittings with audience participation and the way of setting the hour of the beginning of the sitting. The new Regulation contains one completely new paragraph. The most important measure provided for in the new Regulation, which might facilitate the preparation of the hearing and increase its efficiency is the *plan for the hearing* (paragraph 53(2)). One of the principal weaknesses of the construction of Polish civil proceedings has been the unpredictability of the schedule of piecemeal proceedings, which might last many years. The new provision states that if the examination of the case requires more than one sitting to be held, the presiding judge—if possible—will set dates of all sittings for consecutive days (if there are no obstacles to this end). Paragraph 53(1) provides for the so-called organisational sitting. It is convened, if necessary, in order to determine the dates of sittings with the parties and their lawyers. Where the organisational sitting has been convened, the plan for the hearing should be agreed upon, if possible, during this meeting. The precondition of the organisational sitting is the necessity for such a meeting.

The presiding judge and not the parties can be identified as a key influence in shaping the preparation of the hearing. The parties' involvement in the preparatory stage is restricted. Parties can have little impact on the course, form, content and length of the stage preceding the hearing. Actually, such impact can be seen only in Article 187 para 2 CPC, which stipulates mandatory formal requirements for a statement of claim. It states that the statement of claim may contain *requests aimed at the preparation of the hearing*, in particular, requests for the following: (1) convening witnesses and expert witnesses called by the claimant to the hearing;

[18] This rule will be applied also in unilateral (non-contentious) proceedings where the applicant withdraws the application before the information on the date of the sitting is sent to her or him by the court.

[19] Official Journal of 2015, item 925.

(2) conducting inspection; (3) ordering that the defendant delivers an item to be inspected or a document possessed by her or him and necessary to be presented as evidence; (4) ordering that evidence that is in possession of courts, authorities or third parties be brought to the hearing.

This can fairly be described, however, as non-binding on the court, in particular, with regard to the time when the court will perform such activities. The court may perform them later than before the first sitting of the hearing as well if it decides so.

7.3.2 Form of Preparatory Activities

As a rule, preparatory procedures are *written*. Article 127 CPC clarifies what should be the content of preparatory submissions of the parties. It stipulates that in submissions aimed at the preparation of the hearing (*preparatory submissions*) parties should describe concisely the status quo of the case, comment on the arguments and the evidence of the opposing party, and finally indicate pieces of evidence to be presented at the hearing or attach them. In the preparatory submissions parties may indicate the legal bases of their claims and/or requests. However, the listed contents of preparatory submissions do not include the party's own arguments which should be considered an obvious mistake of Polish lawmakers.[20]

Written activities *may be combined with oral activities* as well because the opportunity to proceed to the hearing of the parties in chambers is offered in Article 207 para 4 CPC. It is subject to the *discretion* of the presiding judge or the court; even if the parties applied for such sitting, their application would not be binding upon the presiding judge and the court. Such hearing seems something different than the newly introduced *organisational sitting* as the goal of the first one is the preparation of the case and not establishing the plan for the hearing. The practice will show whether judges are eager to join those two goals in single sitting participated by the parties. It would be efficient; two different kinds of outcomes might be expected from such a single sitting.

Has there been a shift in preparatory stage toward preparatory hearings in chambers after 3 May 2012? It should be emphasised that the general legal basis for proceeding to sittings (open, closed-door or in chambers), if needed, has already been in Article 149 para 1 CPC. In practice, it has not been used to conduct preparatory hearings in chambers. In spite of repeating the possibility in Article 207 para 4 CPC, a similar trend is expected in the future. Scholars have feared that the amendment might not influence the preparation of the hearing at all.[21] And it seems they have been right so far. The prevailing thinking is that judges doubt whether such preparatory hearing are to contribute much of practical importance to the case resolution. The message of lawmakers and the response of judiciary seem

---

[20] Strus-Wołos (2013), p. 192.

[21] Karolczyk (2013), p. 162.

akin to a dialogue of the deaf. Yet it may be believed that although currently all court "actors" prepare by themselves, the preparatory hearing may be used to prepare the case together to some extent.

Another important issue associated with the form of preparatory activities is the use of *technologies* in the preparatory proceedings.[22] Regrettably, at this stage of Polish civil proceedings, the potential of information technology is not fully harnessed. Neither preparatory hearings nor organisational sittings may be attended by the parties or their lawyers by means of audio (telephone conference) or audio and video (videoconference). Article 235 CPC allows only taking evidence this way, which takes place at the hearing. Documents can be sent electronically to the court only with a secure electronic signature or through a special user account. In general procedure, there are not any *flexible ways of convening* participants such as by telephone, fax, email or telegram.[23] The legal formalism of proceedings tells against technical possibilities that have been successful in other legal and cultural context, such as those of Norway. The absence of the use of information technology affects the preparatory stage; undeniably, as a result, proceedings are longer.

7.3.3 Goals of Preparatory Activities

Goals of these activities (perhaps except for those listed in Article 208 CPC) and the whole stage of proceedings is not clearly defined in CPC provisions related thereto. However, it is important what goals were mentioned by the explanatory notes to the Act of 16 September 2011 amending the Civil Procedure Code and some other acts[24] as of 3 May 2012. First, the amendments aimed at the transformation of the system of rules on evidence (Article 207 CPC) were expected to have a positive impact on the structure of contentious proceedings. Lawmakers aimed at its *simplification* and, therefore, *inter alia* abolished all specific elements of legal framework for commercial proceedings, including the statutory preclusion of evidence and claims. After amendments there is no difference made between undertakings and other parties to the proceedings. Second, lawmakers wanted to affect the course

[22] By contrast, electronic proceedings regarding order for payment and electronic registries kept by court (*e.g.* the registry of entrepreneurs or the land registry) proved successful.

[23] In labour and social insurance cases as well as, *mutatis mutandis*, in small claims proceedings the court may convene the parties, witnesses, expert witnesses and other persons in a manner considered the most purposeful, even when it disregards the general rules in this respect, if only the court considers this necessary to speed up the resolution of the dispute. It relates also to the service and orders aimed at the preparation of the hearing, in particular, requests for delivery of personal files and other documents necessary to the resolution of the dispute. Convening and service performed by other means than in writing have effects provided for by general rules if there is no doubt that the addressee has been reached. However, it is not possible to hear the parties, witnesses and/or expert witnesses by telephone. This can be done only in an oral hearing.

[24] Journal of Laws No. 233, item 1381.

of proceedings. The goals of the lawmakers were the improvement and the acceleration of proceedings. Amendments were aimed to enable efficient dispute resolution and remove defects of the previous legal framework, in particular, with regard to *the concentration of proceedings based on the discretionary power of the judge* (Articles 207 and 217 CPC).

In addition, goals of Article 207 CPC are explained in the most recent case law. First, in the decision[25] of 13 December 2012, the Supreme Court clarifies that the goal of Article 207 para 3 CPC is *to provide the proper meaning to the oral hearing* and—thus—*to strengthen the principle of orality*, which, in practice, has been frequently depreciated through the multiplication of superfluous similar submissions full of unproductive arguments not related to the merits of the case etc. Therefore, it is also about *more effective concentration of proceedings, good preparation of the hearing and its efficient course*, and in particular efficiency of the evidentiary proceedings. In literature the new Article 207 para 3 CPC is considered similar to Article 468 para 1 CPC regarding labour and social insurance cases.[26]

Second, in the decision[27] of 14 January 2015, the Supreme Court's position is that the objective of Article 207 CPC is the *concentration of evidence* and *enabling the court to set pace* (and course) of the provision of submissions by the parties, which, among others, can be used against abuses of procedural laws.

Article 207 CPC has been assessed also from the perspective of equality of arms between the parties as the emanation of the constitutional right to access to justice. It needs to be remembered here that although as a rule the parties collect evidence, Article 232 sentence 2 CPC allows the court to collect evidence *ex officio*. Polish case law provides that it is considered necessary to avoid recourse to this competence as far as possible and in any case to apply it only exceptionally.[28] The abuse of this competence could be contrary to the principle of equality of arms. However, the court should not only passively oversee the collection of evidence by the parties but if it has doubts concerning the meaning of facts or arguments presented by the parties, the court has a duty to use the instruments referred to in Article 207 para 3 CPC (the order to provide *preparatory submissions*) or Article 212 para 1 CPC which is going to be referred to later.

[25] Case III CSK 300/12.

[26] Sorysz (2012), p. 437. According to Article 468 para 1 CPC, as a rule, if the results of the initial examination of the case support this, the court will undertake explanatory activities, unless they do not accelerate proceedings or are obviously aimless for other reasons.

[27] Case III CSK 317/14.

[28] Judgment of the Court of Appeal in Szczecin of 25 June 2014, Case I ACa 352/14.

7.4 Evidentiary Proceedings

The issue of evidence in the stage preceding the hearing has already been discussed in certain passages of this chapter. It has been shown that, in practice, the burden of evidentiary proceedings can be entirely moved to the hearing. Worth mentioning here are some general observations regarding preclusion and evidentiary proceedings.

In Poland, for a dozen years we have had a traditional embrace of *evidence preclusion* and *argument preclusion*, in particular, in commercial cases (statutory preclusion) and/or with regard to parties represented by professional lawyers (judicial preclusion, subject to the discretion of the court). Before 3 May 2012, there was the statutory principle of preclusion applicable to disputes between undertakings resolved in commercial proceedings. According to this principle, evidence could be filed by the parties to commercial proceedings only within the dates specified by the provisions of Article 479^{12} para 1 and Article 479^{14} para 1-2 CPC (all of them now repealed). The claimant had to include all arguments in the statement of claim, as well as indicate all pieces of evidence to support these arguments. The court would ignore late arguments and/or evidence not filed within the deadlines laid out by CPC. They could be admitted only exceptionally if the claimant proved that it had been impossible to include them in the statement of claim or the need thereof had not occurred before (in such cases a two week deadline was given). On the other hand, defendants were precluded from making arguments/presenting corresponding evidence if they failed to include them in the statement of defence to the statement of claim and failed to prove the applicability of one of aforementioned exceptions. The statutory principle of preclusion was introduced in order to speed up, facilitate and shorten commercial proceedings and in order to overcome the most pressing problems of increasing workload of courts. However, widely criticised was the fact that what counted was production of the formal truth by commercial divisions of courts rather than to be as close as possible to the substantive truth of the case (and achieve justice).[29] Apparently, under the old rules the preclusion principle was applied eagerly and accurately by courts in commercial proceedings.

Currently, the principle of preclusion is contained in the above-mentioned Article 207 para 6 CPC. This provision says that the court "shall ignore" late arguments and/or evidence and not "may" or "might ignore" them, which means the preponderance of the timeliness over the truth.[30] It also seems not to give too much discretion to the courts. Exceptionally, however, late arguments and/or evidence will be taken into account by the court if the party presents plausible reasons in support of the conjecture that: (1) the delay is no fault of their own, (2) investigating late arguments and evidence will not lead to a delay in the resolution of the case, or (3) there are other exceptional circumstances.

---

[29] Szanciło (2012), p. 125; Piszcz (2012), pp. 71–72.

[30] Arkuszewska and Kościółek (2012), p. 13.

The language of these exceptions is "blurred", which, in fact, may provide discretion to the courts. In literature, it is believed that these provisions may prove non-compliant with the Constitution.[31] When ordering the service of the statement of claim, the statement of defence or further submissions, the presiding judge or the panel will inform the parties of the content of para 6.

This *statutory preclusion* refers to all cases (not only to commercial cases). In literature, it is called "the new face of procedural preclusion".[32] At the first glance, the new rules on preclusion may seem difficult to interpret if one is aware of Article 217 CPC. Article 217 para 1 says that arguments and evidence to prove the disputed facts and to refute and rebut any arguments and evidence of the other party must be made *before the closing of the hearing* (para 1). The court ignores late arguments and evidence, unless the party presents plausible reasons in support of the conjecture that the delay is no fault of their own or investigating late arguments and evidence will not lead to a delay in the resolution of the case or there are other exceptional circumstances. The court ignores also arguments and/or evidence if they are invoked only for the purpose of delaying proceedings or if disputed issues of the case have already been sufficiently clarified. Therefore, a conflict among Article 217 para 1 and Article 207 CPC seems to exist. However, in legal literature the prevailing view has been so far that Article 207 CPC takes precedence over Article 217 CPC.[33]

The court ignores late arguments and evidence. And, in fact, the court if applies Article 207 para 3 sentence 1 CPC decides the meaning of the word "late"; thus, courts are now much more free to decide on the boundaries of the application of the principle of preclusion. What was given to courts in this provision is perhaps not their total autonomy in respect of preclusion; but provided that they require the parties to file further submissions or—on the contrary—not, they shape the parties' strategies, expectations and behaviour to a considerable extent. Any published studies on how Article 207 para 3 sentence 1 CPC is being applied are not known but reports of practising lawyers in the region of the author (north-eastern Poland) show that the manner in which courts apply this provision is frequently not much different from the application of the "old" preclusion in commercial proceedings. Parties have to move in the restrictive model of proceedings, perhaps slightly more irregular because of the fact that the schedule is dictated not only by CPC but also by the court. The previous solution was considered inflexible, but, at the same time, transparent and the new approach seems to reduce legal certainty for parties.[34] The way of the application of the new provisions is diversified across Poland.

In the stage preceding the hearing, evidentiary issues do not play any essential role. General provisions on preparatory activities contain neither rules on disclosure

[31] Cieślak (2012), p. 26.

[32] Karolczyk (2012), p. 516.

[33] Strus-Wołos (2013), p. 194; Mucha (2012), p. 3D.

[34] Piszcz (2012), pp. 72–73; Mucha (2012), p. 6D.

of evidence[35] nor solutions similar to the ones regarding only labour and social insurance cases; the court is not obliged to conduct explanatory activities aimed at the determination of which pieces of evidence should be admitted in order to clarify issues disputed between the parties. The court is not obliged to adopt decisions that specify pieces of evidence and the verified facts. Furthermore, currently, even if the presiding judge proceeded to the hearing in chambers in order to discuss the preliminary matters, the court would not be allowed to rule on evidentiary requests. The court cannot rule on evidence outside the hearing, except for rulings on expert witnesses.[36] Such decisions shall be made at the first sitting of the hearing. Exceptionally, the presiding judge may inspect a piece of evidence prior to hearing, if necessary (Article 208 para 2 CPC). The presiding judge may also issue orders necessary to prepare the evidentiary proceedings, according to Article 208 para 1 CPC.

Furthermore, the initial questioning of the parties takes place as late as the hearing (preferably the first sitting). Pursuant to Article 212 para 1 CPC, the court at the hearing asks the parties questions in order to make parties to present, complete their arguments, and/or provide evidence to support these arguments and give explanations necessary to determine the true factual basis for claims and/or rights pursued by them. In the same manner, the court aims at clarification of important disputed issues of the case. When needed, the presiding judge may provide necessary guidance to the parties and advise them that it would be useful to grant a procedural power of attorney.

Some scholars are afraid that the aim of these provisions ("in order to make parties to present or complete their arguments or evidence to support these arguments") may lead to situations where the judge becomes a helper of one of the parties (instead of neutral observer)[37] or intends to confirm the judge's anticipations rather than to discover substantive truth.[38]

The initial questioning of the parties is not the same as taking the evidence (testimony). Parties may be questioned by the court with regard to arguments and evidence, but this is done in order to get general understating of the case.[39]

As a result, the first sitting of the hearing is frequently used to prepare the next one and not the entire hearing (*piecemeal preparation, deconcentrated proceedings, the lack of main hearing in the proper sense*).[40] So there is, undoubtedly, an imbalance between the preparatory stage and hearing stage.

This inevitably impacts on the length of proceedings. Still, there were some attempts to offer a partial solution to protracted proceedings, at least a

[35] Except for disclosure regime introduced into the industrial property law due to implementation of the 2004/48/EC Directive; Rejdak (2012), pp. 96 ff.

[36] Rylski (2010), p. 314.

[37] Fik and Włosek (2012), p. 42.

[38] Gapska (2013), p. 38.

[39] Karolczyk (2013), p. 158.

[40] Ibid.

half-measure. Before the regulation relating to the rules of procedure in courts of general jurisdiction was adopted, one of versions of the draft regulation (of 30 March 2015)[41] provided for the judge's task of setting the calendar for hearings in a way that would allow for breaks between sittings not longer, as a rule, than 3 months. The adopted regulation, however, lacks a satisfactory account for the problem of long breaks between sittings.

In the course of the stage preceding the hearing, the court cannot admit or dismiss evidence. As a rule, evidence cannot be evaluated by the court. Parties can add or exclude evidence from the case within the boundaries of the preclusion. As has already been stated, Article 232 sentence 2 CPC allows the court to collect evidence *ex officio*. But decision thereon can be made at the hearing.

7.5 Conciliation and Mediation

Article 10 CPC, present in the Code from its very beginning, imposes an obligation of judicial settlement efforts on courts. They are obliged to promote settlement—where settlement is permissible—that is, to aim at *amicable resolution* of disputes at each stage of the proceedings. The parties may reach a *settlement* before the mediator as well. *Mediation* was developed in 2005 as a new form of amicable resolution of civil disputes.[42]

As to *conciliation* (promoting settlement by the judge), Article 184 et seq. CPC allow to apply for convening to a *conciliation hearing*. However, this can take place only before filing the statement of claim; therefore, such conciliation hearing cannot be considered the preparatory (preliminary) stage of given proceedings (these are separate proceedings, a kind of pre-action stage).

Second, Article 223 para 1 CPC stipulates that the presiding judge will *encourage the parties to reconciliation* (settlement) at the right moment, particularly at the first sitting, after the initial clarification of the positions of the parties. The *in-court settlement* will be entered into the minutes of the sitting or contained in a separate document that is a part of the minutes. This conciliatory tool could be used *during the preparatory stage* if courts made use of Article 207 para 4 CPC that allows convening of the parties to the hearing in chambers before the hearing. However, in practice, courts do not order hearings in chambers in order to discuss the preliminary matters with the parties.[43] They usually "sit" in chambers during the stage preceding the hearing, but they do not invite parties thereto. Therefore, Article 223 para 1 CPC is not applied during the preparatory stage but only during the

[41] Paragraph 66(1). In Polish at: http://legislacja.rcl.gov.pl/projekt/12271203/katalog/12283173#12283173 (accessed on 19 August 2015).

[42] Ereciński (2007), pp. 116–118.

[43] Karolczyk (2013), p. 162.

hearing. In 2013–2014, 1.8 % of all civil contentious cases were concluded with in-court settlements.[44]

Third, we take on the topic of mediation. Under Article 183^{1} paras 1–2 CPC the *mediation procedure* is voluntary[45] and is undertaken either on the basis of agreement concluded by the parties or on the basis of a court decision (court-connected mediation). The mediation procedure is conducted: (1) before initiating the court proceedings or (2) upon the parties' consent—within the course of court proceedings.

Had parties to the dispute signed a prior mediation agreement, the court will order parties to engage in mediation in response to an argument by the defendant filed prior to the initiation of any dispute as to the merits (Article 202^{1}CPC).

As to the second possibility, the court may—only once—*refer the parties to mediation till the closing of the first sitting of the hearing*; afterwards, this can be done only upon both parties' request (Article 183^{8} para 1 CPC).[46] The order in this respect may be issued in chambers (para 3 sentence 1). The case cannot be mediated without consent of the parties; the court-connected mediation procedure will not be initiated if the party does not give her or his consent thereto within one week as of the publication of the order at the sitting or the delivery of the order issued in chambers (para 3 sentence 2).

The time limit for court-connected mediation procedure stipulated by the court will not exceed 1 month, unless both parties applied to the court for longer time limit (before or after its determination by the court). According to Article 183^{2} para 2 CPC, the task of mediating cannot be performed by a judge. Furthermore, court-connected mediation is not a part of the court hearings. Mediation is confidential and the mediator must be impartial. The mediator may not testify what they learned in mediation, unless all parties agree otherwise (Article 259^{1} CPC). In proceedings before the court or in arbitration tribunals, the parties cannot use information of the settlement offer or other statements made in mediation.

If the negotiated conflict is resolved and the parties reach the settlement before the mediator, it will be approved by the court. In order to be approved, the settlement cannot be against the law or *bonos mores*, be aimed to circumvent the law, be incomprehensible (unclear) or contain discrepancies (Article 183^{14} para 3). The court, upon the party's request, immediately undertakes the procedure aimed to approve the settlement concluded before a mediator. The approved settlement is binding as an in-court settlement.

The possibility of court-connected mediation does not relate to proceedings regarding an order for payment and proceedings regarding a writ of payment that

[44] More at: http://isws.ms.gov.pl/pl/baza-statystyczna/opracowania-wieloletnie/ (accessed on 27 August 2015).

[45] Skrodzka (2014), p. 172.

[46] However, Article 7 of the *Act of 17 December 2009 on Pursuit of Claims in Group Proceedings* (Official Journal 2010, No. 7, item 44) states that at each stage of the group proceedings the court may refer the parties to mediation.

are simplified to some extent. Until 2010 also cases resolved in small claims proceedings could not be mediated.

It is unlikely that mediation has been used to a considerable extent so far either during the stage preceding the hearing or afterwards. The statistics of the Ministry of Justice show that in 2013–2014, 6523 civil cases of over 1.5 million contentious civil cases[47] filed to the courts in 2013–2014, that is 0.43 % of cases, were referred by district and regional courts to mediation; only 556 (8.5 %) of them were resolved with settlement.[48] From the above it follows that amicable dispute resolution has not been priority for both courts and parties to the proceedings.

As the mediation order may be issued in chambers, it is more probable that mediation is used during the preparatory stage than that conciliation does. The potential effect of mediation on efficiency of dispute resolution is recognised by the author but, at the same time, judicial settlement efforts are considered a bit diffident, tentative and unsatisfactory. Perhaps, judicial settlement efforts might succeed to a larger extent if they were made at the preparatory hearing. Indeed, for the parties it might be much more difficult to refuse to have the case referred to mediation standing in front of the judge or judges; parties should be more open to mediation in such circumstances than being offered the same in writing.

According to the opinion of one of the Supreme Court's judges, the underlying cause of the dysfunctional amicable dispute resolution in Poland is generally low level of legal and political culture in the society aimed at multiplying conflicts and limiting social dialogue.[49] Such society has a culturally very different sense of justice than "conciliatory" societies do. Neither conciliation nor mediation is a successful feature of the Polish preparatory proceedings. But it is not proving easy to come up with exactly the right legislation to facilitate amicable dispute resolution in Poland if the problem lies in the culture (cultural barriers) of court "actors" themselves.

However, some attempts have been made to improve the legal framework for mediation. Legislative works aimed to bring Polish laws into alignment with the Directive 2013/11/EU of the European Parliament and of the Council of 21 May 2013 on alternative dispute resolution for consumer disputes and amending Regulation (EC) No 2006/2004 and Directive 2009/22/EC (Directive on consumer ADR)[50] are conducted in parallel with works on the draft Act amending CPC and some other acts with regard to the promotion of alternative dispute resolution (ADR) methods. The draft prepared by the government is now "travelling" back to the lower chamber of the parliament (Sejm) from the higher chamber of the

---

[47] For the purposes of statistics, civil cases do not include family cases, labour cases and commercial cases (cases between undertakings).

[48] Learn more at: http://isws.ms.gov.pl/pl/baza-statystyczna/opracowania-wieloletnie/ (accessed on 27 August 2015).

[49] Ereciński (2013), p. 129.

[50] Official Journal L of 18.06.2013, 165/63.

parliament (Senat) where some minor revisions have been proposed.[51] Some important amendments have been offered in the draft amendment act regarding the promotion of ADR methods. Its authors have sought ways to make mediation friendlier to the needs of the parties it exists to serve. They have contrived *inter alia* the following new solutions:

- possibility to refer the parties to mediation at each stage of the proceedings;
- possibility to conduct the information meeting regarding ADR methods, in particular, mediation;
- possibility to hear parties in chambers before the first sitting of hearing in order to decide on the need for referring the parties to mediation;
- moderated deadline for mediation (up to 3 months);
- mandatory content of the statement of claim in the form of information on whether the parties tried to amicable resolution of the dispute and, if not, what were the reasons thereof;
- mediator will be obliged to use various methods aimed at amicable resolution of disputes, including the support for the parties determining their settlement offers and—if required by all parties—the presentation of ways to resolve the dispute that are not binding on the parties;
- Article 10 CPC will state that the court should aim at amicable resolution of disputes at each stage of the proceedings, in particular, through the promotion of mediation.

If adopted, the amendment act would come into force from 2016.

As one looks in the future what can be expected is increasing litigation due to the fact that legal consciousness arises in the society, old opinions on judiciary are being revised (for example, it is not frequent nowadays to think of judges as corrupted), lawyers' assistance becomes cheaper because of growing competition in legal services and the height of court fees (5 % of claim as a rule) cannot be deemed to make access to justice difficult. Therefore, issues related to ADR should be as vital as ever. There should be strong interest of judiciary, lawyers and lawmakers in how ADR can be used more efficiently and come up with new techniques of dispute resolution.

Worth mentioning here is also that the *amicable resolution of the dispute is treated in a special way from the costs perspective*, but irrespective of whether it takes place during the preparatory stage or later. There are the following rules (applied by the court *ex officio*) in this respect:

1) Article 79(1)(2)(a) of *the Act of 28 July 2005 on Court Costs in Civil Proceedings*[52] (hereinafter CCA)—in proceedings before the court of first instance the claimant will receive 75 % of the paid court registration fee back, if there is a

[51] In Polish at: http://www.sejm.gov.pl/sejm7.nsf/PrzebiegProc.xsp?nr=3432 (accessed on 27 August 2015).

[52] Official Journal of 2014, item 1025, as amended.

settlement agreement reached by the parties before a mediator (this does not refer to conciliation, only to mediation)[53];

2) Article 79(1)(3)(c) CCA—the party will receive half of the paid court registration fee back, if in a given instance there is a settlement agreement reached by the parties;
3) Article 79(2) CCA—in proceedings before the court of first instance in cases regarding divorce or separation of a married couple, the party will receive the paid court registration fee back, if the application is withdrawn as a result of conciliation, and only half thereof if it takes place in proceedings before the court of second instance); the word "conciliation" is used here in a broad meaning that includes also mediation.

7.6 Concluding Remarks

An array of factors contributes to a continuing general feeling of inefficiency of Polish court proceedings. For several years, while lawmakers have been proceeding to develop some new procedural standards and, as a result, have been revising CPC through piecemeal amendments, divergent conceptions of the reform have been produced (including on whether the new Code should be adopted or CPC should be further amended insofar as there is no possibility of a single reform of CPC that could work as a panacea for its shortcomings). CPC has been amended quite slowly and in parts so far. The reform is desirable and indispensable, at least insofar as it is true, from experience, that civil proceedings are quite long-lasting. The civil or commercial case disposition time has been reported to be as long as 180 days in 2012.[54] It is "so short" *inter alia* because of the fact that the average is forced down by some typically short disposition times of non-contentious civil and commercial cases (e.g. handled within around one week in registration proceedings). In fact, especially in certain regions, in many litigious civil and commercial cases, the court efficiency is not adequate. However, taking into account that the Polish system is not uniform, transparent, technologically advanced or conciliatory, the average is not very much above the most representative countries having a developed preparatory stage (*e.g.* Norway).

Some scholars are afraid that the discretionary power of judges may lead to unequal treatment of the parties[55] or judges' arbitrariness that is subject to control only by the court of upper instance and—in case of appeals/complaints—may result in overall longer proceedings.[56] However, Article 207 para 3 CPC can still be perceived as an opportunity to use preparatory procedures for efficiency reasons. This opportunity has not been missed yet. It is still possible that the discretionary power of the

[53] Bieliński (2014), p. 42.

[54] Dubois et al. (2013), p. 417.

[55] Gapska (2013) p. 38.

[56] Pecyna (2012), pp. 812–813; Szczurowski (2013), pp. 875–876; Kwaśnicki and Bokina (2012), pp. 614–616; Piebiak (2012), p. 619.

judge (Article 207 para 3 CPC) might appear as the feature of Polish preparatory stage of civil proceedings capable of contributing to its efficiency, in particular, together with the new regulation provisions on the preparation of the hearing.

However, if their potential is to be fulfilled, particularly with regard to speediness of proceedings, not only discrepancies of the current legal framework should be removed (Article 207 and Article 217), but also judges need to place a strong focus on the development of new ways of managing cases and be more amenable to collaboration with the parties at the preparatory stage. It seems that the real difficulties with this are two fears of judges that must be overcome to this end. First, it is a fear of costs. It seems that judges do not want to conduct an expensive and time-consuming mini-main-hearing at the preparatory stage, thus, they limit this stage to few activities in writing. The second fear is that collaboration with the parties may be detrimental for the impartiality of the judge. It is the reason why judges build “Chinese walls” so effectively that they contact parties only in the hearing. Perhaps the new regulation will contribute to a shift of focus from isolation to balanced collaboration with all the parties aimed at the preparation of efficient hearing. On the other hand, this analysis shows that the Polish piecemeal process, which is a (historical) fact, is not going to be overcome as a result of the new regulation. The efficiency of the stage preceding the hearing may also be increased as a result of the proposed amendments of the legal framework on mediation. However, the key to success of preparatory proceedings through the proposed solutions would naturally depend on the approach of the judges. This may be the question of their education and training.

References

Arkuszewska AM, Kościółek A (2012) Nowelizacja Kodeksu postępowania cywilnego – wybrane zagadnienia. Cz. 1. Przegląd Sądowy 5:5–21

Bieliński A (2014) Costs of the proceedings in the civil judicial procedures and alternative dispute resolution on the example of mediation – selected problems. In: Etel M, Kraśnicka I, Piszcz A (eds) Court culture. Conciliation culture or litigation culture. Temida 2, Białystok, pp 38–47

Cieślak S (2007) The latest trends in Polish civil procedure. In: The recent tendencies of development in civil procedure law – between East and West. International Conference to celebrate 100th anniversary of the birth of Professor Jonas Žeruolis. Justitia, Vilnius, pp 170–176

Cieślak S (2012) Koncentracja materiału procesowego po nowelizacji Kodeksu postępowania cywilnego z 16 września 2011 r. Palestra 9–10:17–26

Draniewicz B (2012) Nowelizacja KPC – wybrane wątpliwości praktyczne. Monitor Prawniczy 16:891–896

Dubois E, Schurrer Ch, Velicogna M (2013) The functioning of judicial systems and the situation of the economy in the European Union Member States. Report prepared for the European Commission (Directorate General Justice), Strasbourg

Ereciński T (2007) Recent developments in civil procedure in Poland. In: The recent tendencies of development in civil procedure law – between East and West. International Conference to celebrate 100th anniversary of the birth of Professor Jonas Žeruolis. Justitia, Vilnius, pp 111–122

Ereciński T (2013) Kilka uwag o mediacji w sprawach cywilnych. In: Szczepanowska-Kozłowska K (ed) Oblicza prawa cywilnego. Księga Jubileuszowa dedykowana Profesorowi Janowi Błeszyńskiemu. Wolters Kluwer, Warszawa, pp 122–131

Fik P, Włosek M (2012) Wybrane zagadnienia w świetle nowelizacji Kodeksu postępowania cywilnego. Studia Prawno-Ekonomiczne 86:31–47
Flaga-Wieruszyńska K (2007) Tendencies in the Polish separate procedure in economic cases – chosen aspects. In: The recent tendencies of development in civil procedure law – between East and West. International Conference to celebrate 100th anniversary of the birth of Professor Jonas Žeruolis. Justitia, Vilnius, pp 197–205
Gapska E (2013) Realizacja zasady prawdy w świetle ostatnich nowelizacji kodeksu postępowania cywilnego. Rejent 5:23–41
Karolczyk B (2012) Odpowiedź na pozew w postępowaniu zwyczajnym – wybrane zagadnienia w świetle nowelizacji KPC. Monitor Prawniczy 10:509–517
Karolczyk B (2013) Pretrial as a part of judicial case management in Poland in comparative perspective. Comp Law Rev 15:151–188
Kosiński P (2012) Prekluzja dla wszystkich. Radca Prawny 124:28–29
Kwaśnicki RL, Bokina W (2012) Nowelizacja Kodeksu postępowania cywilnego – skutki uchylenia art. 479^{17} KPC. Monitor Prawniczy 11:614–616
Lapierre J (2014) Zasada prawdy materialnej i zakres jej funkcjonowania w polskim procesie cywilnym. In: Jodłowski J, Resich Z, Lapierre J, Misiuk-Jodłowska T, Weitz K (eds) Postępowanie cywilne. LexisNexis, Warszawa, pp 124–127
Łazarska A (2012) Sędziowskie kierownictwo postępowaniem. Przegląd Sądowy 5
Mucha J (2012) Ciężar wspierania postępowania i granice dyskrecjonalnej władzy sędziego w świetle znowelizowanych przepisów Kodeksu postępowania cywilnego. Radca Prawny 126:2D–6D
Pecyna M (2012) Postępowanie "dwóch prędkości" w nowelizacji Kodeksu postępowania cywilnego. In: Pisuliński J, Tereszkiewicz P, Zoll F (eds) Rozprawy z prawa cywilnego, własności intelektualnej i prawa prywatnego międzynarodowego. Księga pamiątkowa dedykowana Profesorowi Bogusławowi Gawlikowi. LexisNexis, Warszawa, pp 801–813
Piebiak Ł (2012) Nowelizacja Kodeksu postępowania cywilnego – uwagi praktyczne. Cz. 1. Monitor Prawniczy 12:677–690
Piszcz A (2012) Still-unpopular sanctions: the private antitrust enforcement developments in Poland after the 2008 white paper. Yearb Antitrust Regul Stud 6(7):55–77
Rejdak M (2012) Wydobycie dowodów od pozwanego w postępowaniu cywilnym o naruszenie praw własności przemysłowej (w świetle art. 6 dyrektywy 2004/48/WE i prawa polskiego). Zeszyty Naukowe Uniwersytetu Jagiellońskiego Prace z Prawa Własności Intelektualnej 4(118):96–159
Rylski P (2010) Dopuszczenie dowodu na wniosek. In: Błaszczak Ł, Markiewicz K, Rudkowska-Ząbczyk E (eds) Dowody w postępowaniu cywilnym. C.H. Beck, Warszawa, pp 308–315
Rylski P, Weitz K (2014) The impact of the Russian Civil Judicial Proceedings Act of 1864 on the Polish Civil Proceedings. Russ Law J II(4):78–90
Siedlecki W (1977) Postępowanie cywilne. Zarys wykładu. Państwowe Wydawnictwo Naukowe, Warszawa
Skrodzka MJ (2014) Civil law mediation and the culture of pre-trial litigation: a mediator's perspective. In: Piszcz A (ed) Court culture: Contemporary problems. Temida 2, Białystok, pp 170–181
Sorysz M (2012) Koncentracja materiału procesowego w sprawach z zakresu prawa pracy na tle zmiany ustawy Kodeks postępowania cywilnego z 16.09.2011 roku – zagadnienia wybrane. Studia z Zakresu Prawa Pracy i Polityki Społecznej:435–440
Strus-Wołos M (2013) Możliwości składania wniosków dowodowych przez pełnomocników poza pierwszym pismem. In: Giezek J, Malicki A (eds) Adwokatura a modele procedur sądowych. Wolters Kluwer, Warszawa, pp 189–196
Szanciło T (2012) Pozycja procesowa przedsiębiorcy po zmianach Kodeksu postępowania cywilnego. Radca Prawny 125:9D–14D
Szczurowski T (2013) Dyskrecjonalna władza sądu gospodarczego po nowelizacji KPC. Monitor Prawniczy 16:870–877

Chapter 8
Hungary: Towards More Efficient Preparatory Proceedings

Adél Köblös

Abstract The Hungarian rules of civil procedure developed in the streamline of German and Austrian models at the beginning of the twentieth century and were influenced by the Soviet solutions in the second half of the century. Since the change of the regime in 1989, the legislator has made several attempts to concentrate the procedure and hear cases within a reasonable time, the results of which have been partly successfully. Hungarian civil procedure, in first instance, may not be divided into an efficient preparatory stage and a concentrated main hearing. Written preparation—apart from the formal examination of the statement of claim—is optional. It is shaped by the judge's attitude and the types of the cases whether the court calls the parties upon to prepare the case through correspondence. The success of a written preparation is dependent on the parties' willingness to actively participate therein. No real preclusion is attached to this stage of the procedure. Due to the lack of written preparation, the first hearing functions as a preparatory hearing and, as a result, a great proportion of the cases are adjourned. One of the aims of the pre-action negotiations prescribed by the law would be also to prepare the case for hearing in case amicable settlement fails; nevertheless, in practice, it falls short of the expectations of the legislator. The concept of the new code of civil procedure urges a caesura between the preparatory and the main hearing stage.

8.1 Historical Background

In order to understand the resent structure of the civil litigation in Hungary, it is necessary to throw a light on how we got to this state of affairs.[1]

Going back to the nineteenth century, during the revolution and the war of independence in 1848–1849, there was no occasion to pass a modern Hungarian law on civil procedure. After the Habsburg monarchy had repressed the Hungarian

[1] See a similar summary on historical development: Varga (2008), pp. 276–280.

A. Köblös (✉)
National University of Public Service, 2 Ludovika sqr, 1083 Budapest, Hungary
e-mail: koblos@mkab.hu

L. Ervo, A. Nylund (eds.), *Current Trends in Preparatory Proceedings*,
DOI 10.1007/978-3-319-29325-7_8

war of independence, the Austrian code of civil procedure[2] was introduced in Hungary. There was a deep repugnance against this code; therefore, in 1861, the old Hungarian rules of civil procedure were temporarily restored. After the compromise between the Hungarian political elite and the Habsburg emperor in 1867, a new law was passed (Act LIV of 1868). The legislator thereupon adopted a code, unfortunately based on written procedures, a model of passive judge, secrecy, eventuality and formalistic evidence. This law still mainly followed the Austrian temporary code of 1852[3] and it was planned to be temporal, since it was clear that further reforms would have been necessary to catch up with the European trends. By Act XVIII of 1893 on summary proceedings[4] the legislator introduced a set of rules based on an oral and immediate civil procedure and the free weighing of evidence. The latter principle was extended to the whole civil justice system. This was an attempt to establish a procedure with a new philosophy. The test was successful, and it was clear that the results would be extended to all kinds of civil procedures. There were two main patterns to follow: the French and German one. Both systems were deeply studied[5] and finally the latter won: the new code of civil procedure (Act I of 1911) was based on the German ZPO, and, at the same time, the results of the new Austrian code of civil procedure of 1895 were also taken into consideration.[6] Until the 1950s there was no codified private law,[7] but despite this fact the code of civil procedure of 1911 reflected the principles of the contemporary codes of civil litigation.

The code of 1911 required rather only the individualisation of the claim at the commencement of the procedure, the statement of claim was deemed a request of the claimant addressed to the court to summon the parties in order to establish the action.[8] The court first examined whether the statement of claim satisfied the formal requirements and contained all the data necessary for the court to notice circumstances *ex officio* (e.g. jurisdiction, etc.). If the statement of claim did not have to be rejected, the court set a day for hearing establishing the action (*perfelvételi tárgyalás*), this was a sort of preparatory hearing. The statement of claim had to be attached to the citation addressed to the defendant. The parties were called upon to appear before the court in the time and at the place indicated in the summons, they were noticed of the consequences of absence. In procedures before the district

---

[2] Provisorische Civilprozessordung (1852).

[3] Fodor (1916), p. 235.

[4] This act regulated litigation of claims of miner subject matter value.

[5] Two academics were delegated to study the foreign codes. Kornél Emmer prepared a proposal based on the French system, while Sándor Plósz prepared a proposal following the German model.

[6] See Rechberger (2012), pp. 1–13.

[7] The process of codification started in this field of law, too, but enacting the code of private law failed, therefore, judges followed the bill filed with the Parliament in 1928. The first code of civil law was passed in 1959 (came into force on 1 May 1960), so already under the soviet regime. It was modified several times, especially after the change to the regime. The code in force now was passed in 2013 (Act V of 2013).

[8] Magyary (1939), p. 343.

courts, the parties were also cited to the hearing on the merits at the same time and were called upon to bring along the original documents and other evidence relevant to the case (e.g. witnesses).

The hearing thus was divided into two parts: a preparatory hearing and a main hearing (hearing on the merits), between them there was a *caesura*. This means that once the defendant entered an appearance, the claimant was not allowed to modify or drop the claim without the defendant's consent, thus it was a kind of preclusion. The claimant was bound in the litigation and even contrary to his or her will had to bear the adjudication of the case on the merits. The preparatory hearing aimed at clarifying what the dispute was about exactly (claim and defence), terminating lawsuits where a procedural bar emerged and disposing of the dispute on the merits in obvious cases. The most important effect of the preparatory hearing was the appearance of the defendant.[9] The hearing on the merits consisted of the parties' arguments on the merits, taking evidence and the delivery of the judgment.[10]

At the beginning of the preparatory hearing, the claimant presented the claim. There was a wide freedom to deviate from the original one that had been presented in the statement of claim. The defendant could allege the inadmissibility of the claim that had to be examined and adjudicated before turning on the merits of the case. If the procedure did not have to be terminated the defendant could enter appearance, in other words: present the statement of defence on the merits. In lawsuits before the district courts, the court usually had to continue with the hearing on the merits on the same day, but on the parties' mutual request the court had to set a new day, so the parties could also influence the course of the proceeding. In lawsuits before the regional courts, the court usually had to set a new day for the hearing on the merits, securing at least thirty days interval. With the parties' mutual consent or in urgent cases on the motion of either of the parties this interval could be shortened or the hearing on the merits could be held on the same day as the preparatory one. This interval was necessary to prepare the main hearing: the parties had to present in writing their allegations as to the facts and the evidence, the parties' advocates had to send these papers to each other. The written preparation of the hearing on the merits was not applicable in the procedures before the district courts where legal representation was not mandatory. The court could prepare the hearing on the merits by citing witnesses, calling up the parties to produce documents and smaller objects of inspection at the hearing, requiring documents from officials or notaries public.

Once the defendant entered an appearance (defence on the merits), the claimant could not drop or modify the claim without the defendant's consent. In the latter case, the consent could be given tacitly by dealing with the substance of modification. The defendant was not limited to submit his counterclaim or setoff at the preparatory hearing, a counterclaim or a setoff could be presented at the hearing on the merits, too.

---

[9] Beck and Névai (eds) (1959), p. 229.

[10] Magyary (1939), p. 377.

At the preparatory hearing the court could dispose of the claim only in obvious situations, such as the claimant dropped the claim or waived the right, the defendant admitted the claim, failed to appear before the court at the preparatory hearing or the parties settled the dispute.

Preparatory hearing could not be skipped or replaced with a written procedure. The caesura clearly marked out the line between the preparatory stage and the main hearing. The preparatory hearing focused on establishing the case by the presentation of the claim and the defence. Facts supporting the parties' cases could be asserted and evidence could be moved for at the preparatory hearing, as well. Nevertheless it was also possible to state new facts and to adduce further evidence later in the procedure. Delaying tactics could be sanctioned by ignorance of those new facts and evidence and by ordering the procrastinator to bear the extra costs. Written preparation came to the front in procedures before the regional courts where the hearing interval after the preparatory hearing served the written preparation of the hearing on the merits by the parties' advocates. The parties—with their consent or common request—could influence the course of the procedure to some extent.

At the end of World War II Hungary came under the influence of the Soviet regime. This effect was reflected in the new rules of civil procedure (Act III of 1952, *polgári perrendtartás,* hereinafter: HCCP.), too.[11] The HCCP. declared the principle of party control and free disposition,[12] nevertheless in fact there were so many exceptions thereto that they consumed the original meaning and function of this principle. Free disposition suffered from a lot of restrictions, including a general authorisation of the prosecutor to institute any kind of civil action.[13] Inquisitorial solutions played an important role, and the rules of civil actions were approximated to the criminal procedure regulation. Notwithstanding this direction of the development, the Hungarian legal system did not adopt the soviet inquisitorial model in a subservient way, instead the production of evidence was based on rules under which taking evidence *ex officio* and the parties' responsibility for gathering the material of the case was much more balanced.[14] The court not only had to decide a legal dispute, but, at the same time, strike a proper balance between the parties' and the public interests, while searching the material or objective truth became the core of the lawsuits.[15] As Varga put it: 'the principle of free disposition had been limited and the responsibility and managerial elbowroom of the court had correspondingly been increased'.[16]The *caesura* between the preparatory hearing and the hearing on the merits was abolished, the single hearing system was preferred.[17] The claim could be modified till the closing of the first instance

[11] Varga (2008), pp. 278–280, Kengyel (2014), pp. 61–63.

[12] Section 2(1) of the HCCP.

[13] Kengyel (2014), p. 62.

[14] Kengyel (2014), p. 63.

[15] Kengyel (2014), p. 62.

[16] Varga (2008), p. 279.

[17] Varga (2008), p. 279.

hearing. New facts could be presented and evidence adduced even on appeal without real restrictions. Therefore parties typically withheld their fact allegations and evidence until the appeal phase, the first instance procedure became of no weight.

Since the change to the regime in 1989 the code of civil procedure of 1952 has been amended several times in order to restore the proper role of the principle of party control, to cope with the challenge of timely administration of justice and to gear the procedural rules to the new structure of the judiciary. This Act is still in force; nevertheless the re-codification of the civil procedural rules has been launched by the government in 2013.[18]

8.2 General Course of Hungarian Civil Litigation

The HCCP. is based on the principle of free disposition. Civil action may never be instituted *ex officio* but only on the request (statement of claim) of the claimant. The parties are responsible for alleging their rights, the facts to underpin their claims and defence and to produce evidence proving those facts. The court is allowed to take evidence *ex officio* only where the law specifically authorizes to do so (e.g. in status actions generally or in judicial review of state administrative decisions in certain questions). The court is bound by the claim and the defence, it may not exceed the claim (may not adjudge more than the sum claimed).[19] Nevertheless, the court is not bound by the legal qualification of the facts given by the parties.[20]

The principle of oral proceeding is not regulated in the HCCP., nevertheless, it plays a very important, although not an exclusive role. Most of the requests, arguments, statements, etc. can be presented orally by a party not represented by an advocate. The most important place of oral communication is the hearing, while written submissions come to the front in the preparation of the first and the adjourned hearings.[21]

In general, legal representation in first instance is not mandatory, but there are exceptions in cases before the regional courts. Legal representation is obligatory before the regional courts of appeal and the Curia for the party filing an appeal or a petition for revision in law.

A civil action is commenced with filing a statement of claim with the competent court. If there is a legal dispute derived between legal person economic operators

[18] Decision of the Government of 1267/2013 (V. 17).

[19] *Bírósági Határozatok* (BH, Judicial Decisions) 2012.169.

[20] *Bírósági Döntések Tára* (BDT, Collection of Court Decisions) 2013.2866; BDT 2008.1823; BDT 2007.1543; BH 2000.20; So called surprise judgments are very much criticised in legal practice. The Concept of the new Code of Civil Procedure suggests a similar system to the German ZPO in order to prevent surprise decisions (p 9), that is 'substantive or material case management' where the judge seeks clarification and provide feedback for the parties as to the essence of the dispute.

[21] Kengyel (2014), p. 83, Kiss (2014), pp. 104–105.

(*gazdálkodó szervezet*) it is obligatory for the parties to negotiate before instituting a lawsuit. This issue is deliberated in details below, under Sect. 8.3.

The minimum elements of the statement of claim are the following: the domicile and the contentious position of the parties and those of their representatives, the right to be claimed, the facts with the evidence underpinning the claim, a determined and expressed request (prayer for relief) to the court concerning the final judgment (*petitum*), the competent court and the data establishing the court's jurisdiction. If mediation took place between the parties beforehand, this fact shall be indicated, as well. If the claimant has a telephone number, fax number or e-mail address, these shall be included in the in the statement of claim. The documentary evidence shall be attached to the statement of claim.

Although there is not a unanimous agreement on this question, some say that the HCCP. tends to require the claimant to substantiate the claim in the statement of claim,[22] so the claimant should present detailed facts founding the claim already at the commencement of the lawsuit. Claimants are not required to present their rights by referring to a certain legal provision, it is enough that the right (to be) claimed can be identified on the basis of the facts and the *petitum*. Legal qualification of the facts is the duty of the judge (*jura novit curia*). It is not a base for rejecting a statement of claim if references to the means of evidence are not complete, since this default can be made up later at the hearings.

A statement of claim filed with the competent court is registered in the court record and the president of the court appoints the judge (or council) hearing the case. The judge shall examine the statement of claim immediately but within thirty days at the latest and prepare the case for hearing. The preparatory stage is deliberated in details under Sect. 8.4.

An oral hearing is required in the first instance, apart from the judicial review of state administrative decisions. The first hearing shall be within 4 months of the arrival of the statement of claim at the court or after the completion of it.

The recent Hungarian civil litigation is based on a single hearing[23] that is not divided into two stages, namely a hearing founding the lawsuit (*'perfelvételi tárgyalás'* or preparatory hearing) and a hearing on the merits (*'érdemleges tárgyalás'*). The hearing stage may nevertheless consist of several sessions. Neither the code of civil procedure, nor the legal literature mentions the term of 'main hearing'. Instead the HCCP. uses the concept of 'substantive hearing' (*'érdemi tárgyalás'*), which starts when the defendant presents the defence on the merits of the case.[24]

At the beginning of the first hearing the claimant or the judge presents the statement of claim. Then, the claimant may maintain the claim or present a modified claim. The claimant is entirely free to deviate from the original claim.

---

[22] Kengyel (2014), p. 248.

[23] This was the effect of the soviet ideology on the Hungarian civil procedure. In the socialist legal literature the general and firm belief was that the hearing aimed at founding the lawsuit is superfluous and makes the procedure longer and more complicated than a single hearing system. [Éless (2013), pp. 26–27, Kengyel (2014), p. 245] Nevertheless, now there is an opinion that the recent system is a single-divided one. [Éless and Ébner (2014), p. 383].

[24] Kengyel (2014), p. 239.

Next, the defendant presents the defence that may be formal or on the merits.[25] Formal defence aims at terminating the lawsuit, while in defence on the merits the defendant asks the court to dismiss the claim. The defendant may present a counterclaim or a setoff, as well. During the first hearing, the frame of the dispute is designated as to law and facts, as well. However, contrary to the structure of the code of civil procedure of 1911, the rule at present is that the claimant is not prevented from modifying the claim until the closure of the first instance hearing.

If the proceeding is not terminated at the first hearing, the court deals with the case on the merits. If the facts can be established at the first hearing, the court adjudicates the dispute.

If a case could not be finished on one hearing day, at one session, the judge adjourns the hearing appointing a new day and, at the same time, citing the parties present orally. In practice, adjournment and piecemeal hearings are quite common. It is usually necessary to take evidence (e.g. to summon witnesses, appoint an expert, etc.) or because the parties need time to present further facts or statements, arguments. The day of the next hearing usually follows several months later and not on consecutive days. In order to prepare the next hearing, the judge can call the parties to submit their remarks, replies and requests in writing. Then the judge forwards the copies of these documents to the opposing party who can submit remarks and replies in writing. Furthermore, the judge may order the party to send submissions both to the court and the opposing party. The law does not restrict the number of adjournments; it depends on the circumstances of the cases, the parties' conducts and the judge's attitude.

Once the court finds the case matured for decision, it closes the hearing and in closed session forms its judgment. It is possible to adjourn the open announcement of the judgment for fifteen days at the longest; otherwise, right after the closing of the hearing the court will put the operative part of the judgment in writing. It will then announce the judgement in open court.

8.3 Pre-Action Procedures in the Hungarian Code of Civil Procedure

Mandatory pre-action negotiation, conciliation or other process as a general model is not preferred by the Hungarian legislator. Obligatory pre-action proceedings feature rather the lawsuits between undertakings.[26]

In 1972 (came into force in 1973) the legislator introduced a particular procedure applicable to actions between economic operators including rules on mandatory

---

[25] As to legal consequences of the defence on the merits see: Kengyel (2014), p. 260, Kiss (2014), pp. 545–546, Szabó (2013), pp. 266–267.

[26] In other particular procedures or matters special pre-action processes may also occur, either obligatory or optional, such as in divorce matters or labour disputes, etc. This study, however, does not concern these special provisions, neither in legal history, nor the rules in effect now.

pre-action negotiation. The aim of the negotiation was to settle the case without litigation. This pre-action negotiation was limited to the exchange of the parties' standpoints in writing. The particular rules on actions between economic operators were repealed in 1992.

From January 2009[27] to July 2010 pre-action negotiation reappeared in a form resembling to a rather restricted common law disclosure. This new disclosure-type of pre-action procedure was introduced in disputes between legal person economic operators. The former provision of Section 121/A prescribed that the parties had to negotiate before instituting a lawsuit in order to settle a dispute.

The prospective claimant had to draw up a document containing detailed arguments as to facts and law and references to the relevant evidence. This document together with the necessary documentary evidence had to be communicated to all other parties affected by the dispute. Within fifteen days, the prospective opposing parties had to file a written reply setting out in details their standpoints as to facts and law, references to the relevant evidence and the necessary documentary evidence had to be attached to the reply. Pre-action negotiation and document-exchange had double functions. On the one hand, pre-action process aimed at settling the dispute without instituting a lawsuit. It was obligatory for the parties to make attempts to reach an amicable resolution of the case. The other goal was to prepare the future hearing in case the settlement failed and litigation could not be avoided. By the end of the pre-action process the parties could have been well aware of each other's arguments as to law and facts in the light of the documentary evidence, in other words: what facts and what legal allegations or arguments were disputed between them.

In 2009, the legislator passed an act[28] in order to introduce a particular procedure in disputes between undertakings. These rules would have come into force in January 2011. The provisions on pre-action negotiation would have been transferred to this particular procedure and an additional set of rules would have been applicable to the disclosure of documentary evidence.

On request either of the parties should have given documents (the original ones or the copies thereof) to the other party. The requested party would have been exempted from this obligation if the contents of the documents were not in relation with the facts or the disclosure would have revealed disproportionally its trade secrets. In case the requested party failed to complete its statutory obligation, the other party could have moved to the court for ordering the party to hand the requested documents over. Such a motion could have been submitted before the commencement of the lawsuit as a request for interim measure or during the procedure in a written submission or it could have been made orally at a hearing. The parties could have been sanctioned (with fine) for non-compliance with the court order.

[27] Act XXX of 2008, came into force on 1 January 2009.

[28] Act LXVIII of 2009.

Finally, the rules applicable to disputes between undertakings never came into force and the disclosure-type of pre-action procedure was abolished.[29] In my opinion, this special procedure was entirely alien from the Hungarian civil procedure traditions both as to the structure of the procedure and the role of the advocates in a lawsuit.[30] In practice, it was too difficult to obey the provisions and rendered the relationship between the parties more complicated.[31]

In March 2011, a moderated form of mandatory pre-action negotiation was introduced. These rules are still in effect and resemble the solution adopted in 1972. The parties (economic operators that are legal persons) shall attempt to settle the dispute out of court. It can be substituted by drawing up common minutes of the conflicting views. The claimant shall attach documents verifying the attempt to settle the case (such as the common minutes or the correspondence between the parties, or when the prospect defendant was not willing to participate in the negotiation, a document verifying the prospect claimant's attempt to settle the dispute out of court) to the statement of claim. These documents shall contain the data of the different standpoints of the parties, the result of a preliminary accounting, and if a court ruling or other decision was delivered in the dispute, the reference number thereof.

The defendant is motivated to participate actively in the negotiation through the cost rules. The court may order the defendant to bear all the costs of the procedure or a part of the costs otherwise to be borne by the claimant if the defendant without a good reason did not perform its obligation to negotiate. The sanction of the claimant's failure to negotiate is that the court rejects the statement of claim. Negotiation is not obligatory if time limit open for filing a statement of claim is no longer than 60 days, in cases where an order for payment procedure has transformed to a litigation, in particular procedures and in high priority procedures.[32]

8.4 Preparatory Stage of Civil Procedures

8.4.1 The Concept of Preparation

According to some commentators, the preparatory stage covers the stage of the civil procedure from filing the statement of claim to the beginning of the first hearing. The preparation of the first hearing is mainly a written procedure

[29] Act LIX of 2010.

[30] As to critics see: Szalai (2010), pp. 235–245.

[31] See the reasons for the bill of Act LIX of 2010 (http://www.parlament.hu/irom39/00351/00351-0006.pdf. Accessed 7 Aug 2015).

[32] A set of special rules are applicable to actions where the sum in dispute exceeds HUF 400 million (cc. EUR 1.3 million). These cases are called actions with 'outstanding significance' (Sections 386/A-386/U).

consisting of the following phases: examination of the statement of claim, preparatory measures (in details see below) and setting a day for hearing (including issuing summons).[33] Its aim[34] is to filter cases not capable of being tried and make statements of claim complete enough to set a day for hearing. If one takes the division of civil procedures into three stages (pleadings—preparation—main hearing) as a model, preparation under this approach qualifies rather the pleading stage.

Under another approach the concept of the 'preparation of the hearing' is used in a narrower sense: it is the stage of the civil procedure following the examination of the statement of claim.[35] In this view, the preparation of the hearing covers only the preparatory measures regulated in Section 124 (3)–(6), thus the appointment of the hearing day and the service of the summons on the parties do not form part of the preparation.

There is a third understanding of the preparatory stage distinguishing between the preparation of the action and the preparation of the hearing.[36]

It is generally admitted that the careful preparation of the hearing promotes to finish cases within a reasonable time.[37]

The code of civil procedure does not use the terminology of 'preparation of the hearing' for indicating or identifying a separate stage of the procedure. It uses the concept of 'preparation of the hearing' in relation with the preparation of the first hearing[38] and contains rules on preparatory written submissions in connection with the adjourned hearings, as well.[39]

If one looks at the Hungarian system from the main hearing model perspective, one might say that civil litigation lacks the clear separation of hearing preparation and main hearing. In some cases written preparation contributes to finishing the case at the first hearing. In other cases, the first hearing may fulfil the purposes of (pleadings and) hearing preparation, provided that questions of law and facts are clarified and the relevant evidence is identified there, but taking evidence and deciding the case is shifted to the adjourned hearings. Otherwise, the first hearing is rather a part of the pleading stage of the procedure (and the preparatory function is narrowed to the examination of the formal bars of the litigation) and further preparation takes place before the next hearing in writing, if at all.

---

[33] Kengyel (2014), p. 246.

[34] Nagy (2008), p. 306.

[35] Kiss (2014), p. 515; Oszovits (2013), p. 229.

[36] Imregh (2008), pp. 785–794.

[37] Kengyel (2014), p. 246, Nagy (2008), p. 329.

[38] Section 124 (3)–(4).

[39] Section 141 (3)–(5) In Section 141 (2)—maybe a little bit surprisingly—the HCCP uses the expression 'further preparation of the litigation".

8.4.2 Ways of Preparation

Preparation takes place out of a public hearing, and it is basically a written procedure. The judge is, however, allowed by the law to hear the parties in the preparatory stage in the presence of each other.[40] This hearing is not a public hearing (trial); this is rather a possibility for the judge to communicate with the parties orally if it seems more efficient than written preparation. The object or role of such an *in camera* hearing is not determined by the law and no procedural legal consequences are connected to such a hearing. In theory, it could be flexibly used by the courts, in practice, it hardly ever occurs.

Information technology is not specifically regulated in the preparatory stage. At present it is a possibility for the parties with some exceptions[41] to choose electronic communication with the court. This choice is however covers the whole procedure, including extraordinary remedy procedures, as well. A party hot having a legal representative is allowed to switch back to paper based procedure only once after undertaking electronic communication. Where only one of the parties chooses electronic communication, the court serves paper copies on the opposing party. From 2016, it will be mandatory for economic operators and legal representatives to file submissions and other documents by way of electronic means, and they are served with electronic copies of the documents. For other parties the present system is maintained. Telephone and videoconference are unknown in general civil procedures.[42]

Less formal ways of communication (fax, e-mail, telephone) were planned to be introduced in certain questions in disputes between undertakings, and there would have been a preparatory case management conference to bring forward evidence and other motions and to make a timetable for the procedure. Finally, these rules did not come to force.[43]

8.4.3 Elements of Preparation

Taking the concept of preparation in the wide sense, the first phase thereof is the examination of the statement of claim. It means that the judge checks whether there are any formal bars to the procedure, so whether the statement of claim is inadmissible. These bars shall be examined *ex officio* by the court, for example, excluded

---

[40] Section 124 (4) point (e).

[41] In some cases it is excluded (e.g. if an order for payment procedure has transformed to a civil action), while in others it is mandatory (in a special type of high priority cases).

[42] There was a short period of time when videoconference was planned to be introduced [see Section 1(4) of Act LXVIII of 2009], but finally it did not come realty (probably because of financial reasons).

[43] See Act LXVIII of 2009 and Act LIX of 2010.

international jurisdiction, lack of subject-matter or territorial jurisdiction, failure of the time limit for filing a statement of claim (except for limitation), *lis pendens*, *res judicata*, incomplete statement of claim, lack of legal capacity of either of the parties, etc.[44] This part of the procedure proceeds without the participation of the defendant and any official knowledge of the lawsuit on the defendant's side. Finding the statement of claim inadmissible, the court rejects it without issuing summons. Later in the procedure the defendant can base the formal defence on most of these procedural bars at the first hearing or in a written statement of defence. Some of these bars shall be taken into account during the whole procedure *ex officio,* while some of them may not be taken into account after the summons are issued or the defendant presented the statement of defence on the merits. The examination of the statement of claim may entail a completion procedure (where the statement of claim is defective) or the transfer of the statement of claim to the competent court in lack of subject-matter or territorial jurisdiction.

If the statement of claim did not have to be rejected, the judge may take preparatory measures, such as acquiring documents from authorities or other organisations, ordering preliminary evidence, taking temporary measures or hearing the parties *in camera* in the presence of each other (see above). Since collecting evidence *ex officio* is only allowed in limited cases, preliminary evidence requires a request from the parties in general civil cases. The preparatory measures may be ordered either before appointing the first hearing and issuing of the summons or later, on request as a rule, or exceptionally ex officio.

Once the court appointed the hearing day, it cites the parties. A copy of the statement of claim shall be attached to the summons addressed to the defendant. The notification of the claim to the defendant is a very important moment because the procedure becomes two-sided at this point, and several important legal consequences are attached thereto.[45] Such as the action is deemed pending from this time (*lis pendence*), the statement of claim may not be rejected any more, instead the procedure shall be terminated almost on the same grounds, the interval before the first hearing ensuring enough time for the defendant for preparation starts at this time. This interval may not be shorter than fifteen days.

Under the general rules of citation the court shall warn the defendant in the summons to present the defence at the first hearing at the latest. The summons contains a warning that the facts underpinning the defence shall be alleged, evidence proving those facts shall be adduced and documents concerning the case shall be produced at the first hearing, as well. The court may also call the defendant upon to submit written statement of defence securing him or her enough time, but at least fifteen days, for the preparation. Defence can be presented orally before the court, as well, where the party does not have a legal representative. Even if the submission of a written statement of defence is not ordered, the defendant is informed of such a possibility. If a statement of defence is filed and there is enough

---

[44] The list of the bars can be found in Section 130 (1) of the HCCP.

[45] Kiss (2014), p. 527, Kengyel (2014), p. 254.

time before the first hearing, the court can forward it to the opposing party calling up the claimant to submit remarks within fifteen days. The efficiency of the preparation and therefore the hearing is strengthened by calling upon the claimant to produce documents at the first hearing, as well, if they have not been attached to the statement of claim yet.[46]

This exchange of statements (submissions) in essence is a sort of facultative written preparation. Therefore, if the judge and the parties use this means, the hearing can be prepared quite well, so at the first hearing the judge can go deeply in the substance of the case and take evidence.

The flexible rules mentioned above would open the possibility for the judge to choose between the amp ways of communication with the parties, such as written and oral preparation. In the latter case, the first hearing plays a preparatory role. Nevertheless, as far as I see, on the one hand, to some extent judges are under a pressure to perform their obligations to hold hearings and they do not always have enough time to prepare cases properly out of the courtroom.[47] On the other hand, choice between written preparation and scheduling immediately a hearing might depend not only on the particularities of the cases but on the judges' attitude and preferences. Some tendencies, however, might be discovered. For example, in small claims procedures written preparation works well in practice.[48] Written preparation is especially preferred by courts seated in Budapest and the central region, where the number and the complexity of the cases results in a larger workload and parties are usually represented by advocates.

The success of a written preparation depends on the parties' and especially the defendant's willingness to co-operate, since the defendant faces no real sanctions for failing to submit a statement of defence in writing despite of a court order. Adjournment of the first hearing often roots in the insufficient knowledge of what the dispute is about both on the judge's side, and on the parties' or their representatives' side. The exchange of statements and the preliminary production of documentary evidence would open the way for the judge to study thoroughly the case for the first hearing. The same is true to the parties.

8.5 Identifying the Essence of the Dispute, Rules of Preclusion

The substantiated claim in the statement of claim may serve to identify the object of the action. However, the claimant is free to modify the claim until the closure of the first instance hearing. Modification is only restricted in cases where legal

---

[46] See Section 126 of the HCCP.

[47] This is one of the reasons why dispensing with an oral hearing in judicial review cases is not a successful resolution, either.

[48] Part Six of the HCCP (Sections 387–394/A).

representation is obligatory [except for lawsuits where the sum in dispute exceeds HUF 200 million (cc. EUR 670,000)] and in small claim procedures. Where legal representation is mandatory, the claimant is allowed to modify the claim within thirty days of the defence on the merits. However, the claimant may present new facts or rectify the original facts if the right claimed is not altered, claim another thing because of changes to the circumstances; or reduce the sum claimed or to extend the claim to incidentals not claimed before; or require performance instead of declaration or reverse, since under the provisions of the HCCP. these changes are not qualified as a modification of the claim.[49] In small claims procedures, once the defendant has entered an appearance, the claimant is allowed to modify the claim only once and exclusively at the first hearing. After this time, the claim can be modified during the first instance procedure and with the defendant's consent. There are some exceptions to this rule.[50]

The defendant is free to make a counterclaim until the closure of the first instance hearing, unless making a counterclaim is clearly a delaying tactics of the defendant. In the latter case, the court may reject the counterclaim without deliberating it on the merits. In cases where legal representation is obligatory—with certain exceptions—counterclaim can be made within thirty days of the first hearing.[51] In small claims proceedings, a counterclaim can be made at the first hearing without restrictions. After the first hearing, the defendant can introduce a counterclaim only with the claimant's consent or when the claimant has modified the claim. In the latter case, a counterclaim may be made at the same hearing or if the claim was modified in the hearing interval, the next hearing. On request, the defendant can be allowed to present the counterclaim in writing after the first hearing within a short period of time. In small claims proceedings, a counterclaim submitted clearly to delay the procedure shall be rejected.[52]

The parties are quite free to present new facts or bring forward further evidence. Serious restrictions derive mainly from Section 141 (2) and (6) of the HCCP. Section 141 (2) requires the parties to put forward statements as to the facts, motions that the court take evidence or other petitions and allegations in a time which facilitates finishing the case by the court within a reasonable time. This is a general obligation deriving from the statutory provision. Disregarding this obligation however does not entail automatically a sanction. Negative legal consequences follow from non-compliance with a court order. Under Section 141 (6) if a party—despite of the general obligation under Section 141 (2)—fails to allege facts, make statements or assert evidence without a good reason, the judge calls this party to make up for those statements, motions setting a proper time limit. If the party culpably fails to meet this court order and waiting for the statements and motions would delay the end of the case, in other words, the hearing does not need to be

[49] Section 146 of the HCCP.

[50] Section 391/A of the HCCP.

[51] Sections 147-147/A of the HCCP.

[52] Section 391/B of the HCCP.

adjourned for other reasons, the judge gives a judgment without waiting for the statements and motions. The facts, evidence that a party failed to put forward in due course of the procedure in spite of a court order, may not be adduced on appeal or in a reopening of the case.

Another important rule can be found in Section 3 (3) and (4) of the HCCP. Under the first provision the court shall give a notice to the parties of what facts need to be proved in order to adjudicate the dispute, the burden of proof and the consequences of unsuccessful taking of evidence. The latter provision says that, the court shall disregard new evidence if the party on his or her own fault asserted it too late or in a way that is not in accordance with the principle of good faith, unless the law provides otherwise. The relationship between Section 141 (6) and Section 3 (4) cannot be easily identified and clarified.[53] Section 141 (6) provides a solution when a statement or assertion is missing, while Section 3 (4) regulates a situation where evidence is produced late and therefore it is disregarded. The first rule applies both to facts and evidence, while the latter is limited to evidence. In case law the two rules are strictly linked to each other. However, neither of the two rules are applied in the preparatory stage (i.e. preparation of the first hearing), especially because the facts to be proved can be determined only after the defendant has presented the defence on the merits and notice can be typically given by the court at the first hearing. In small claims proceedings parties are allowed to bring forward new evidence at the first hearing at the latest. There are several exceptions to this rule.[54]

Preclusion thus is not linked to a certain stage or point of the procedure, although there are some exceptions. The general rule of preclusion is not rigid. It may be used flexibly depending on the certain state of affairs in the procedure and the notices and warnings of the court.[55] It might be called dynamic preclusion which takes into account that the material of the case is a 'living texture'.[56]

As one can see, there are rules in the HCCP. restricting the possibility of modifying the claim, making counterclaims, stating new facts or adduce new evidence, especially in small claims procedures or where legal representation is mandatory. Thus, judges have some tools to concentrate the hearing on the merits. Nevertheless, some provisions are still too permissive: e.g. the right to modify the claim or make a counterclaim or setoff until the closure of the first instance hearing. Therefore preparation of the main hearing remains illusory. Apart from insufficient statutory rules, another possible reason why Hungarian civil procedures may drag for years is that in practice dynamic preclusion raises numerous difficulties.[57]

[53] See e.g.: A bizonyításra vonatkozó tájékoztatási kötelezettség a polgári perben , 1/2009. (VI.24.) PK vélemény a Polgári perrendtartás tájékoztatási kötelezettségre vonatkozó szabályainak alkalmazásával kapcsolatos egyes kérdésekről. 1/2014. (VI. 30.) PK vélemény az ítélet hatályon kívül helyezésével kapcsolatos egyes kérdésekről

[54] Section 389 of the HCCP.

[55] Slovenia has a similar system, see Sect. 5.4.2.

[56] This expression is borrowed from Éless (2013).

[57] BDT 2010.2246; BDT 2008.1895; BDT 2007.1694; BDT 2004.952; BDT 2001.386; BDT 2000.177; BDT 2000.176; BDT 2000.135; BDT 1999.69; BH 2010.125; BH 2003.509; BH 2003.204; BH 2002.149; BH 2002.79; BH 2001.328, etc.

Preclusion applied contrary to the law often leads to setting aside the first instance judgment on appeal and the repetition of the first instance procedure.[58] This practice of the appellate courts has been criticised on the ground that it may arise from the vestige of the philosophy to search the material truth. A third probable cause of protracting procedures may be that some judges are not willing to apply Section 3(4) and 141 (6) properly or to control the parties' delaying tactics, or limit superfluous evidence. The reason may be that the object of the action is often not correctly and precisely defined or it is altered. Determined and well-prepared judges can usually keep the litigation in due course: they recognise at an early stage of the procedure the essence of the case, identify properly the factual and legal issues in dispute, deliver amp instructions to the parties concerning what facts to be proved and which party should prove those facts and prevent and sanction the parties' delaying conducts.

8.6 Judicial Settlement Efforts and Court-Connected Mediation

Since in Hungarian civil procedure the strict separation of the main hearing and the preparation thereof does not exist and the latter in practice typically focuses on formal prerequisites and conducted in writing, judicial settlement efforts and mediation has no special relevance in the preparatory stage. The legislator does not encourage parties with special rules to mediate in this stage. The provisions in the HCCP. concerning judicial settlement efforts and court-connected mediation are therefore basically linked to the hearing stage. It does not mean that the parties are prevented from using alternative ways of dispute resolution earlier, but there is no outstanding emphasis on those ways in the preparatory stage under the general rules.

The law on mediation was passed in 2002,[59] it was amended several times.[60] Court-connected mediation was introduced in 2012,[61] while in 2013[62] the legislator established the provisions on mandatory mediation (came to effect in March 2014).

[58] See Összefoglaló vélemény—A perorvoslati bíróságok hatályon kívül helyezési gyakorlata. (A másodfokú és felülvizsgálati bíróság kasszációs jogköre).

[59] Act LV of 2002. On mediation in Hungary see: 'Rebooting' the Mediation Directive: Assessing the Limited Impact of its Implementation and Proposing Measures to Increase the Number of Mediations in the EU.

[60] As Hungary is an EU member, the domestic law must implement the Directive 2008/52/EC of the European Parliament and of the Council of 21 May 2008 on certain aspects of mediation in civil and commercial matters.

[61] Act CXVII of 2012.

[62] Act CCLII of 2013.

It is generally accepted that the parties are free to choose between court-connected mediation and out-of-court mediation.[63]

Court-connected mediation is a type of mediation where court secretaries, judges or senior judges—after certifying that they have obtained the 3-year training[64]—appointed as mediators by the president of the National Office for the Judiciary act as mediators. Court-connected mediation can take place only when there is a civil procedure pending before a court. The parties with their common request may turn to any court providing mediation services. If a party requires so the court-connected mediator and the court make efforts to get the other party's consent to mediation. The list of the court-connected mediators' names and phone numbers is accessible on the Internet. Mediators may be contacted directly on phone or by e-mail, a party may also ask for a date for personal consultation on reception days. The court petitioned for mediation—after consulting with the parties—informs the parties of the person of the mediator, the date of the information meeting and the right to authorise a representative. Mediation and civil procedure are strictly separated. The judge conducting the litigation may not be a mediator in the same dispute, and the judge or the court secretary having participated in the mediation may not act as a judge in the lawsuit. Information gained in mediation may not be used in the action, unless the parties decide otherwise. Court-connected mediation is free of court fees.

The HCCP. motivates the parties through cost rules to perform their agreement reached in mediation. The party instituting a lawsuit despite of an agreement concluded in court-connected or out-of-court mediation may be ordered to bear the opposing party's costs emerged in the mediation and in the litigation, notwithstanding the party's success at the end of the procedure. One of the incentives to settle a case is a partial exemption from the court fees of litigation.[65]

In the course of a civil procedure the judge informs the parties—if there is a chance for its success, particularly if it is requested by a party—of the main features of mediation, the possibility of participating in mediation and the rules on intermission of the court procedure. If the parties have decided to turn to a mediator and for this reason agreed on the intermission of the litigation, they have to notify the court of this fact. Within 3 months either of the parties may ask the court to continue the procedure. If the parties settled in mediation, they may ask the court to approve their agreement. Approval by the court may be denied only if the agreement is contrary to the law. In such a case or when the parties could not settle the case in mediation, the court proceeds with the action under the general rules.

From 2014, the court can order mandatory mediation in certain family law disputes, such as child custody cases. Participation in mediation is not mandatory.

[63] This requirement flows from EU law, especially that ordinary mediation may not be less advantageous than court-connected mediation.

[64] See Decree 63 of 2009 (XII.17) of the Minister of Justice and Law Enforcement.

[65] Ninety per cent, 70 % or 50 % of the fees is remitted depending on not only when settlement is reached but also on how the lawsuit is finished, so whether on the basis of the settlement the claimant drops the claim, the defendant admits the claim, the parties mutually require the court to terminate the procedure or the procedure ceases after three months of intermission.

The parties are only required to turn to a mediator and attend the first information meeting.

As far as judicial settlement efforts are concerned,[66] the court can at any stage of the procedure encourage the parties to settle their case. As there is no separate preparatory stage, the first occasion to encourage the parties to settle their dispute is the first hearing, after the parties presented their pleadings. If the parties settle the case, the court approves the agreement unless it is contrary to the law.[67]

The methods of judicial settlement efforts are not set out in the HCCP., it depends very much on the judge's attitude. In case law there are some landmarks designating the framework of settlement. For example, a court may not approve a settlement submitted in writing by the parties unless the terms thereof are reinforced and repeated orally before the judge.[68] This limitation is not applicable where agreement was concluded as a result of mediation.

There is a special way for the parties to settle their dispute before a court without (or before) instituting litigation. This is a non-contentious civil procedure before the competent district court. This procedure is called summons to attempt to settle a case. One of the parties may require the court to cite the other party in order to reach a settlement before the court. If the parties settle their case, the court approves the settlement if it is in accordance with the law. The same applies if both parties appear before the court to settle their dispute. It may occur, for example, when the parties wish the court to approve the settlement arrived at in mediation. This procedure has the advantage of producing a settlement with the effect of *res iudicata*. Agreements resulting from mediation can be made enforceable without instituting a lawsuit in such procedures. Despite of the advantages of this procedure, it is not really used in practice.

8.7 Summary on the Current State of Preparatory Proceedings in Hungary and Future Prospects

I have found it fruitful to present and analyse in details the system introduced by the code of civil procedure of 1911 for two reasons. One of them is that several aspects of the solution adopted there serve as a model in present reforms. On the other hand, the divided hearing system realised a kind of 'preparation—main hearing' model where oral procedure played an outstanding role already in the preparatory stage, even though written preparations had also importance especially before the regional courts.

---

[66] As to settlements and also mediation see: Gyekiczky (2010), pp. 7–22.

[67] Only the *cogens* norms shall be taken into account, as parties can deviate from dispositive legal rules. It is also very important that the agreement must be enforceable and for this reason definite. (BH 1993.364).

[68] Supreme Court Pf.III.21 366/1992.

The HCCP. of 1952 repudiated this divided structure of civil actions in order to save time and concentrate the procedure; the single hearing system is still our present. The recent rules on preparation and hearing however do not necessarily result in a concentrated procedure.

The legislator made several attempts to induce the parties to exchange information early in the procedure and encourage them to settle the case. On the one hand it introduced rules empowering the judge to carry out (an optional) serious pre-hearing preparation, and, on the other, it intended to strengthened the preparation with a pre-action negotiation (but only in actions between undertakings). Mandatory negotiation, however, proved a miscarriage in practice both in the more active and in the moderate form.

Generally only disputes with simple legal and factual questions can be properly prepared under the present regime. These lawsuits are typically transformed order for payment procedures and proceeded under the special rules applicable to small claims proceedings. In complex cases written preparation would facilitate an efficient hearing, especially because the parties usually have legal representatives. In other cases, written procedure is not a proper means to complete successful preparation. There are situations where oral communication serves better the mutual understanding of the case. For such situations, it would be open for the judge to hear the parties in the presence of each other even before the hearing, but this solution is hardly ever used in practice. The reason for that is presumably that the role and the goal of such an *in camera* hearing is not clear and it cannot be distinguished in exact terms from public hearings. Instead, judges set a day for public hearing in order to clarify the main elements of the dispute.

One of the main objectives of the recent re-codification is to reform the structure of the first instance procedure.[69] The key of the solution is to divide the first instance procedure into two separate stages: a preparatory stages and a hearing on the merits (main hearing). This model stems from the code of civil procedure of 1911. The aim of the re-codification is not simply to restore the model of the previous century but to restore it in a way where the traditional solutions of long standing are saved and merged with the reactions to the challenges of the twenty-first century.

Under the concept of the new code approved by the government there will be a *caesura*[70] between the two stages. By the end of the preparatory stage, the claim, the counterclaim and the setoff shall be fixed, facts shall be presented and evidence shall be produced or moved for. The defendant will have to present a detailed statement of claim. The substance of the dispute therefore will be 'frozen', with certain precisely determined exceptions, and the main hearing shall be concentrated to take evidence and discuss the parties' arguments. The preparatory stage will be closed with a court order, but it will not sum up the parties pleadings. In clarifying the substance of the dispute the judge will have stronger powers than now and

[69] See the Concept of the new Code of Civil Procedure pp. 11–16.

[70] Ibid. p. 12.

shall carry out an active ‘substantive’ or ‘material’ case management mainly in the preparatory stage by asking questions and giving hints (e.g. on the proper interpretation of the legal provision referred to by the claimant) while not violating party autonomy. The aim of those questions and hints will be to help both parties to present consistent cases.

The judge will have the power to choose between written or oral preparation. In disputes before the regional courts presumably written preparation will be the rule, especially because legal representation will be mandatory. While before the district courts preparatory hearing probably will play greater role.

In the re-codification process there is a debate whether to use the *caesura* in order to freeze the claim only, or also the defence, including bringing forward any kind of new facts and new evidence. The first solution eliminates the difficulties deriving from the free modification of the claim and treats delaying tactics with a dynamic preclusion.[71] The latter—trying to solve the shortcomings of dynamic preclusion as it is in Hungary—is based on a general statutory preclusion that, however, might approximate to eventuality. Even though there will be exceptions when it will be possible to adduce new facts and evidence, make a new offset or modify the claim, the rigidity of the system will turn on how courts will interpret and apply the new rules.

Once the standpoints and statements of the parties are clear and it is identified which party shall prove which facts, so the parties might weigh more precisely their success and whether it is worth to take evidence, judicial settlement efforts might bring more positive results. Strengthening the role of mediation in avoiding civil lawsuits is among the objectives of the new code. In procedures before district courts where legal representation will not be mandatory, the court should give more information on mediation (the possibility and advantages thereof), while in procedures before regional courts where legal representation will be mandatory, advocates could perform similar duty. In order to enhance the significance of mediation, more advantageous cost rules could be introduced in the new HCCP. Amicable dispute settlements could be facilitated by empowering public notaries to summon the parties to attempt to settle the case and thereby approve agreements concluded via mediation.

References

1/2009 (VI.24.) PK vélemény a Polgári perrendtartás tájékoztatási kötelezettségre vonatkozó szabályainak alkalmazásával kapcsolatos egyes kérdésekről. http://www.lb.hu/hu/kollvel/12009-vi24-pk-velemeny-polgari-perrendtartas-tajekoztatasi-kotelezettsegre-vonatkozo. Accessed 25 November 2015

1/2014 (VI. 30) (2015) PK vélemény az ítélet hatályon kívül helyezésével kapcsolatos egyes kérdésekről. http://www.lb.hu/hu/kollvel/12014-vi-30-pk-velemeny-az-itelet-hatalyon-kivul-helyezesevel-kapcsolatos-egyes-kerdesekrol. Accessed 25 Nov 2015

[71] Éless (2013), pp. 25–26; Éless and Döme (2014), pp. 421–429.

A bizonyításra vonatkozó tájékoztatási kötelezettség a polgári perben (proposal discussed by the Civil Collegium of the Regional Court of Appeal of the Capital on 1 December 2008). http://fovarosiitelotabla.birosag.hu/sites/default/files/field_attachment/2008_-_a_bizonyitasra_vonatkozo_tajekoztatasi_kotelezettseg_a_polgari_perben.pdf. Accessed 13 August 2015

Az új polgári perrendtartás koncepciója - A Kormány 2015. január 14. Napján megtartott ülésén elfogadott Koncepció (Concept of the new Code of Civil Procedure approved by the government on 14 January 2015) http://www.kormany.hu/download/f/ca/30000/20150128%20Az%20%C3%BAj%20polg%C3%A1ri%20perrendtart%C3%A1s%20koncepci%C3%B3ja.pdf. Accessed 18 September 2015

Beck S, Névai L (eds) (1959) Magyar polgári eljárásjog. Tankönyvkiadó, Budapest

Éless T (2013) A kereset nyilvánvaló megalapozatlansága. In: Varga I (ed) Codificatio processualis civilis – Studia in Honorem Németh János II. ELTE Eötvös Kiadó, Budapest, pp 19–34

Éless T, Döme A (2014) A keresetváltoztatás kérdéséhez. In: Németh J, Varga I (eds) Egy új polgári perrendtartás alapjai. HVG-ORAC, Budapest, pp 417–429

Éless T, Ébner V (2014) A percezúra – az érdemi tárgyalás előkészítése. In: Németh J, Varga I (eds) Egy új polgári perrendtartás alapjai. HVG-ORAC, Budapest, pp 377–392

Fodor Á (1916) Polgári peres eljárásunk története az utolsó ötven esztendőben. In: Jogi Dolgozatok. A Jogtudományi Közlöny ötven éves fennállásának emlékére. Franklin Társulat, Budapest, pp 1865–1915

Gyekiczky T (2010) A mediációról. Gondolat Kiadó, Budapest, pp 7–22

Imregh G (2008) Gondolatok az előkészítésről. Magyar Jog 2008(11):785–794

Kengyel M (2014) Magyar polgári eljárásjog. Osiris, Budapest

Kiss D (2014) A polgári per titkai. HVG-ORAC, Budapest

Magyary G (1939) Magyar polgári perjog, 3rd edn. Franklin Társulat, Budapest

Nagy A (2008) Eljárás az elsőfokú bíróság előtt. In: Zs W (ed) Polgári perjog – Általános rész. Complex, Budapest, pp 287–363

Összefoglaló vélemény – A perorvoslati bíróságok hatályon kívül helyezési gyakorlata. (A másodfokú és felülvizsgálati bíróság kasszációs jogköre) http://www.lb.hu/sites/default/files/joggyak/osszefoglvelemeny.pdf. Accessed 17 August 2015

Oszovits A (2013) Keresetindítás és a tárgyalás előkészítése. In: Osztovits A (ed) Polgári eljárásjog I. – A polgári per általános szabályai. HVG-ORAC, Budapest, pp 175–235

Rechberger W (2012) Az osztrák polgári perrendtartás – mintául szolgált-e az 1911. évi magyar perrendtartás számára? In: Harsági V (ed) Közép-európai polgári perjogi reformok és kodifikációk az elmúlt negyedszázadban – Tradíció és megújulás. HVG-ORAC, Budapest, pp 19–40

'Rebooting' the Mediation Directive: Assessing the Limited Impact of its Implementation and Proposing Measures to Increase the Number of Mediations in the EU, pp 90–93. http://www.europarl.europa.eu/RegData/etudes/etudes/join/2014/493042/IPOL-JURI_ET(2014)493042_EN.pdf. Accessed 13 August 2015

Szabó I (2013) Tárgyalás és határozatok. In: Osztovits A (ed) Polgári ejárásjog I. – A polgári per általános szabályai. HVG-ORAC, Budapest, pp 236–337

Szalai P (2010) Kritikai észrevételek a polgári perrendtartás legújabb módosításához. In: Csöndes M, Nemessányi Z (eds) Merre tart a magyar civilisztikai jogalkotás a XXI. század elején? Pécs, pp 235–245

Varga I (2008) Foreign influences on Hungarian civil procedure. In: Deguchi M, Storme M (eds) The reception and transmission of civil procedural law in the global society. Legislative and legal educational assistance to other countries in procedural law. Maklu, Antwerpen-Apeldoorn-Kyoto, pp 275–289

Part III
Comparative Outlooks

Chapter 9
The Role of Court-Connected Mediation and Judicial Settlement Efforts in the Preparatory Stage

Lin Adrian

Abstract This chapter examines the role of court-connected mediation and judicial settlement efforts in the preparatory proceedings of civil court cases across four Scandinavian and eight former socialist countries. The two processes are defined and compared demonstrating fundamental differences between them. Most importantly, judicial settlement efforts are part of litigation and rules of procedure apply, whereas court-connected mediation takes place outside litigation within a different conceptual framework. The use of judicial settlement efforts varies across the countries and seems to be underused by some. The national rules regarding civil procedure usually contain provisions stating a duty to try and settle by way of judicial settlement efforts but are silent regarding to how this should be done. Mediation is a recent addition to civil justice and seven of the countries have implemented this service as court-connected mediation schemes. Studies suggest that court-connected mediation often saves money and time and many users find mediation processes and outcomes satisfactory. On the other hand, there are anti-competition concerns as well as concern regarding the negative effects of the privatisation of justice. Court-connected mediation is used significantly more in some of the countries than in others but only little in most, pointing to a potential for increase in the use of this alternative to litigation. The chapter concludes by asking whether court-connected mediation is a sign of a new legal culture and by highlighting a need for expanding our understanding of what promotes and inhibits settlement efforts in contemporary justice.

L. Adrian (✉)
Law Faculty, University of Copenhagen, Studiestraede 6, 1455 Copenhagen K, Denmark
e-mail: lin.adrian@jur.ku.dk

L. Ervo, A. Nylund (eds.), *Current Trends in Preparatory Proceedings*,
DOI 10.1007/978-3-319-29325-7_9

9.1 Introduction

Settling cases early in the course of civil litigation has many advantages. It saves time and money for the courts and the parties, the settlement is final and it gives the parties more direct influence on the outcome. Early settlement can also relieve the parties of stressful court proceedings and may be less damaging for personal and professional relationships. Hence, it is no wonder that attempts to settle court cases is built into court proceedings in many jurisdictions. Traditionally, settlement has been promoted by the judge (judicial settlement efforts), but recently mediation has been added as an alternative to litigation. Each of the contributions in this volume includes a section on these settlement activities in the preparatory stage. This gives us insight into the countries on an individual level. The aim of this chapter is to examine trends in settlement activities across the countries in order to identify patterns and discuss issues that are relevant on a general level. Hence, the chapter is not a detailed comparative analysis of judicial settlement efforts and court-connected mediation in all countries, but rather an analysis of settlement practices across the countries on a more general level illustrated by a number of examples from the countries at hand.

By way of introduction, the definitions of judicial settlement efforts and court-connected mediation are addressed and the processes compared. The chapter goes on to explore the two processes in turn. First, judicial settlement efforts are addressed and second, court-connected mediation is dealt with. Since court-connected mediation is a rather new settlement activity and draws much attention these years, the major part of the article is concerned with this newcomer to the judicial family. A few concluding remarks end this chapter.

9.2 Judicial Settlement Efforts and Court-Connected Mediation Defined

Judicial settlement efforts are fairly easily defined. As stated in Chap. 1, this type of settlement activity refers to any effort by a judge (or another employee of the court) to make the parties settle the case prior to a ruling. This embraces a wide range of activities such as asking whether the parties have considered settling the case, discussing the evidence, making proposals for settlement etc. Judicial settlement is part of the regular, adjudicative process. It can take place at all stages of the court case, but most likely the bulk of judicial settlement efforts take place in the course of the preparatory proceedings. A trial is typically geared towards a ruling but even so in, for instance, Denmark it is not uncommon that the judge tries to make the parties settle at the end of the trial after the presentation of the case has ended and only the formal ruling remains.

Judicial settlement efforts is one way of trying to end court-cases in the preparatory proceedings, mediation is another. In recent years, mediation has gained momentum not only as a tool to settle disputes prior to going to court but also as a tool to settle cases that have been filed. This volume is primarily concerned with the preparatory stage in civil procedure. Hence, only mediation that takes place in the course of preparatory proceedings is included in this chapter whereas pre-action mediation is not. Mediation that takes place after a case has been filed with no connection to the court or court proceedings, for example, where initiated by the attorneys using a private mediator, is excluded, too. When mediation takes place in connection with courts, it has different labels such as court-referred mediation, court-annexed mediation and court-connected mediation. Court-connected mediation seems to be the most commonly used expression in the literature and the one that we have chosen for this volume. It highlights the connection to court and leaves this connection open to having various forms. Independent of the name, the definition of court-connected mediation remains unclear. What type of involvement by the courts does it take to qualify as court-connected mediation? Is it sufficient that the judge suggests or recommends that the parties mediate? Does the court have to provide or at least oversee the mediation services? Must the mediators be judges?

Lithuania and Latvia are the two only countries in this volume where court-connected mediation is defined in the legislation. In all other countries, the understanding of this term is taken for granted. The Lithuanian definition in the Judicial Mediation Rules section 3 briefly states as follows: "Court-connected mediation is a procedure where a court-mediator or court-mediators help parties settle the dispute."

This definition is not very explanatory with its focus on the person and not the activity. It simply tells us that if a court-mediator helps settle a dispute it automatically qualifies as court-connected mediation but the section does not contain any requirements as to the process used to pursue settlement. Section 17(1) in the Latvian Mediation Law introduces two additional criteria, as it defines court-connected mediation as a mediation conducted by a mediator when the parties have expressed a willingness to use mediation upon recommendation of a court or a judge before adjudication has been completed. The decisive criteria in this definition are that the court has recommended mediation and that the case is pending. This section contains neither requirements of the mediation process nor the level of court involvement.

The American National Standards for Court-Connected Mediation Program uses an equally broad definition: "(...) any program or service, including a service provided by an individual, to which a court refers cases on a voluntary or mandatory basis, including any program or service operated by the court." [1]

The key in this definition is also referral by the court. The referral can be made by anyone in the court system (an intake officer, clerk, judge etc.) and it does not matter whether the mediation is provided by an outside agency or an in-house program. Nor does this definition require the court to oversee the program.

---

[1] Center for Dispute Settlement and Institute of Judicial Administration (1992).

In a questionnaire distributed by the European Council in 2014 court-connected mediation is explained in this way:

> This is a particular kind of mediation, based on the American model of mediation and which takes place in a court-annexed place. The mediation may be conducted by private mediators or by judges and court employees specially trained and accredited.[2]

This definition is clear on who can mediate, but otherwise more confusing than informative. What is the American model of mediation? Such model hardly exists and what if the mediation is conducted based on a locally developed mediation model—is it then not court-connected mediation? And what is a court-annexed place? This attempt to define mediation seems to be flawed by linguistic as well as conceptual confusion and is useless as a guideline for participants in a survey.

A last example comes from *Mediation—Principles and Regulation in Comparative Perspective* where three types of relationships between mediation and litigation are presented. The first is private mediation that takes place independent of court proceedings. The two others are:

> (2) *court-annexed mediation*, characterised by institutional coordination with court proceedings but separation on the procedural level from the court as an institution, and (3) *judicial mediation* characterised by a connection with the court and court proceedings in terms of venue and personnel but without the mediator possession adjudicatory powers in the specific case.[3]

Court-connected mediation in this understanding is quite narrow. It encompasses only mediation that takes place in a court-case and is coordinated with the proceedings in court but otherwise independent of the judiciary. If the court is more heavily involved by providing venue and mediators it is named 'judicial mediation.' Based on the use of 'judicial' and the wording that the mediator does not possess 'adjudicatory powers in the specific case', 'personnel' in this definition must be judges or others with adjudicatory powers and not administrative personnel or other in-house mediators.

In light of this lack of clarity as to what constitutes court-connected mediation, it was necessary to lay out a definition for use in this volume which is done in the introduction to this book. The affiliation with the court is central. For mediation to become court-connected, the court has to be involved. A mere referral to outside providers is not sufficient, as it is nothing more than a form of private mediation. The initiative comes from the court, but the court is not otherwise involved. In order for an activity to qualify as court-connected, the court has to have some responsibility whether it is for the mediators or for the process and this responsibility can take on different forms with varying levels of intensity. At the lowest level, the court provides an approved list of mediators for the parties to use, regulates the competencies of mediators or the like. At the highest level of intensity, the mediation is in-house with the court responsible for all aspects of the mediation.

[2] The European Commission for the Efficiency of Justice (2014), p. 542.

[3] Hopt and Steffek (2013), p. 20.

Whether the mediator is a judge or some other legal personnel from the court is not decisive in this understanding of court-connected mediation—the responsibility of the court is.

In addition to the responsibility of the court, a definition of court-connected mediation has to be based on an understanding of mediation as a distinct process with certain central features. An unsuccessful attempt to do so is seen in the referral to the "American model of mediation" in the European Council questionnaire mentioned above. In the mediation literature and in professional circles, the question of what is and what is not mediation is subject to intense discussion, primarily in terms of how much a mediator can engage in the content of the case before the activity should no longer be labelled mediation.[4] Without engaging in that discussion, mediation in this volume is understood as a dispute resolution activity with the parties' self-determination[5] as the defining feature and with a mediator who is concerned with the *process* leaving the *content* of the dispute and the resolution to the parties. In other words, this utilises a facilitative approach to mediation.[6]

In order to include the responsibility of the court and the demands on the process, the following definition of court-connected mediation is developed for this volume, see Chap. 1, too:

> Court-connected mediation is a voluntary settlement activity conducted by one or more neutral third parties who assists the parties in reaching their own solution in a pending court case. The court is engaged in the mediation – an engagement that can range from minimally providing a controlled list of mediators to which the parties can be referred to a full in-house service. The service is to some extend regulated by law, decrees, ethical guidelines, court rules or similar instruments. Mediation can take place at any point in time after the case is filed and before the final ruling.

9.3 Differences Between Judicial Settlement Efforts and Court-Connected Mediation

Although judicial settlement efforts and court-connected mediation both can take place at the preparatory stage of a court case and are aimed at ending litigation, they are distinct processes as appears from the definitions laid out in Sect. 9.2. The difference often remains blurred to many outside as well as inside the court system and in this section the differences will be spelled out in more detail. Most importantly, judicial settlement efforts take place as part of the adjudicative process. It is performed by judges 'in-robe'[7] and rules of procedure apply. In contrast, the court

[4] See for example Kovach and Love (1998), Riskin (2003–2004) and Vindeløv (2012), p. 213 ff.

[5] See for example Adrian (2012), 106 ff. and Welsh (2001), Kovach (2004) and Nolan-Haley (2005).

[6] For the term facilitative (as opposed to evaluative), see Riskin (1996). Also, see more on this in Sect. 9.5.

[7] Coined this way by Nylund in Sect. 1.5.

Table 9.1 Differences between judicial settlement effort and court-connected mediation

	Judicial settlement efforts	Court-connected mediation
Relation to litigation	**Inside** Is part of litigation and procedural rules for litigation apply	**Outside** Is outside litigation (paused) and rules of procedure for litigation do not apply
The third party and its role	**Facilitator and decisionmaker** Third party is typically a judge or another court employed legal person who acts 'in-robe' Facilitates process and participates in discussions of the legal content. Most often rules in the case if the parties do not agree	**Facilitator** Third party can be a judge who acts 'out of robe,' other court personnel or someone from outside the court Facilitates the process and makes no decision in the case
Role of the parties	**Secondary** Can take place without the parties' active participation and with only legal counsel present	**Principal** The parties must be present and participate
Role of attorneys (if present)	**Principal** Speak on behalf of the parties and can make procedural decisions on their behalf. Give legal advice	**Secondary** Parties speak for themselves. Attorneys support them in doing so and give legal as well as general advice
Role of law	**Central** Discussion and outcome typically within the boundaries of the law and the legal claims in the case	**Flexible** Discussion and outcome can be within or outside the legal claims and the parties determine the role of law
Private meetings (caucus)	**Not allowed** The judge cannot meet with the parties individually	**Allowed** The mediator can meet with the parties individually
Outcome	**Within claims** Typically settlement within the claims of the court case by meeting the legal claim of one party or a compromise	**Open** Can include whatever items the parties want and relate to the claims in the case or not

case is paused when a case is referred to court-connected mediation and rules of civil procedure do not apply. The mediators do not act as judicial decision makers but act 'out-of-robe'.[8] Table 9.1 outlines the differences on this as well as on a number of other parameters.[9]

The role of the third party is very different in the two processes. In mediation, the third party merely facilitates a process that enables the parties to discuss the aspects of their dispute that they wish to address and make decisions about how it can be resolved. If the matter is not resolved in mediation, the mediator as a main rule

[8] Ibid.

[9] For a similar distinction between mediation and case settlement, see Mironi (2014). Another way of understanding the differences is seeing judicial settlement efforts and court-connected mediation as belonging to different paradigms of dispute resolution, see Vindeløv (2012).

cannot rule the case. In judicial settlement efforts, the third party is a judge who discusses the legal matters with the parties and assists them in reaching a settlement. In doing so, the judge can evaluate the legal merit, discuss evidence, make recommendations etc. If the matter is not resolved, the judge typically continues to be the judge in the case.

The roles of the parties and the role of attorneys are reversed in the two processes. In mediation the parties are central. Their presence is typically required as well as their active participation. They speak for themselves and their concerns are central whether these are legal or not. The attorneys play a more withdrawn role by supporting the parties in their dispute resolution and giving advice—legal as well as other types of advice—when required. This is contrary to judicial settlement efforts where the attorneys play the central role. They speak on behalf of the parties, can make procedural decisions, give legal advice, and advise the parties on whether to settle or not. Judicial settlement efforts do not require the presence of the parties, and if they are present they are not required to participate actively.

In judicial settlement efforts it is up to the judge how to conduct the process as long as it happens within the boundaries of the rules of procedure. In court-connected mediation the details of the process are also up to the mediator but in collaboration with the parties. Consequently, the mediation process and the judicial settlement process can differ to a smaller or larger degree depending on the judge and mediator. However, private meetings (caucuses) can take place in mediation only. The mediator can choose to conduct the mediation in joint sessions or meet with the parties individually during the mediation. This is not allowed in judicial settlement efforts as the rules of procedure in court do not permit judges meeting with parties individually.

In court-connected mediation the role of law is flexible. The parties decide themselves the extent to which law applies to their framing of the problem, their discussion and the outcome. If they wish, they can focus on concerns that are not legal in nature. Contrary in judicial settlement efforts where the framing of the problem, the discussion and the outcome is centered around the claim and related to the law. The situation is similar with regard to the outcome. As appears in Table 9.1, in judicial settlement efforts the claims of the court case usually frame the outcome in that the parties settle either by agreeing to one of the claims, or—probably more likely—find a compromise. It is not impossible for the parties to include other items in the settlement. However, court-connected mediation is much more open to that. The parties can settle along the claims of the case if they wish but one of the purposes of mediation is to address concerns and issues underlying the legal demands and customize their agreement to the parties' needs.[10] The mediation process is designed to support this effort.

[10] See e.g. Kovach (2004) and Vindeløv (2012).

9.4 Judicial Settlement Efforts[11]

9.4.1 Judicial Settlement Efforts in Preparatory Proceedings

Judicial settlement efforts are part of civil procedure in all 12 countries in this volume. In most of the countries the judge not only has settlement efforts as an option but rather as a duty at the preparatory stage, see e.g. section 149(2) in the Latvian Code of Civil Procedure which declares that that the judge must strive to reconcile parties and section 268 in the Danish Administration of Justice Act declaring that the court must try to make the parties settle the case in all civil cases in the first instance. In some codes of procedure consensual resolution of disputes is even explicitly described as the primary goal of judges in litigation like the Czech Civil Procedure Act section 100. The revised Norwegian Dispute Act from 2008 has stressed this focus on settlement by including conflict resolution as one of the objectives of the act (section 1-1) as well as by letting the word 'mediation' be placed first in its revised title.[12]

9.4.2 A Brief Historical Account of Judicial Settlement Efforts

Even though judicial settlement efforts are common in all the countries in this volume, this has not always been the case. In the former socialist countries judicial settlement efforts were regarded with suspicion. As pointed out in Chaps. 5 and 6, personal interests, party autonomy and pragmatism were not a priority during socialist rule. Rather, conformity to rules and procedures established by those in power and material truth were central values in the administration of justice. This has changed in recent years, and judicial settlement efforts are now a regular feature in the preparatory proceedings in all the former socialist countries covered by this volume.

The Scandinavian countries, in contrast, have an uninterrupted history of judicial settlement efforts. In the Swedish Code of Judicial Procedure from 1734 which also covered Finland at the time there were rules of judicial settlement efforts. With the reform of the Swedish Code of Judicial Procedure in 1948, judicial settlement efforts were subject to reservations as pointed out in Chap. 2. The legislator was

---

[11] In the following sections, I draw on information from the other chapters in this book and from mail correspondence with the all of the other contributors (on file with the author). To ease reading, I have chosen not to reference from each source throughout Sects. 9.4, 9.5 and 9.6, but detailed reference to specific information is gladly provided by mail upon request.

[12] Lov om mekling og rettergang i civile tvister (Dispute Act). The 1915 Act was called Lov om rettergangsmåten for tvistemål (Civil Procedure Act).

concerned that settlements proposed by the court would harm the parties' trust in the judiciary. This attitude towards settlement has since changed and it is now an accepted and encouraged practice. In Finland, the reform of the Code of Judicial Procedure in 1993 introduced much more emphasis on judicial settlement efforts than had previously been the case and new rules to support this were introduced accordingly.

Denmark and Norway have had a preference for settlement efforts in conjunction with civil procedure for a long time. In 1795, while Norway was under Danish rule, out of court conciliation boards were instituted by the King. Parties were required to attempt settling their case in front of a board as a prerequisite to filing the case in court. The purpose of the conciliation boards was according to the King to "prevent unnecessary and costly litigation between subjects."[13] In Denmark, the conciliation boards were abolished in 1952 and instead courts were required to conduct judicial settlement efforts in all civil cases in the first instance as part of litigation, see section 268 in the Danish Administration of Justice Act.[14] In Norway, the conciliation boards exist to this day. In addition, in-court judicial settlement efforts have been in place since 1915 and other settlement activities have been added since then.[15]

9.4.3 *Judicial Settlement Efforts*

Most of the countries in this volume are silent as to *how* the judge should conduct settlement efforts at the preparatory stage, but a few exceptions exist. The Slovenian, the Czech and the Slovakian Civil Procedures Acts all include provisions with some instruction to the judge. For example, the Czech Civil Procedure Act section 99 requires that the judge informs about case law from the Supreme Court and makes legal evaluation of the case and the Slovenian Civil Procedure Act section 305a states that:

> At the settlement hearing, the court shall openly discuss the factual and legal aspects of the dispute with the parties in order to ... study the possibilities for court settlement and endeavour to reach its conclusion. *(An unofficial translation of the act)*

In Norway, the Dispute Act is limited to specifying what the judge is not supposed to do, see section 8-2:

> The court cannot make proposals, give advice or express points of view that may undermine the confidence in the impartiality of the court. *(An unofficial translation of the act)*

---

[13] See the introduction to the 10. juli 1795 Fr. om Forligelses-Commissioners Stiftelse overalt i Danmark, samt i Købstæderne i Norge.

[14] For a more detailed account on the history of the conciliation boards in English, see Adrian (2014), p. 158 ff. and in Danish see Vindeløv (1997).

[15] For the history of judicial settlement efforts in Norway and the current many forms of settlement activities, see Bernt (2011) and Nylund (2014).

With no or only limited instruction as to how the judge is expected to pursue settlement like we see in the examples above, the practice is left to judges individually. A recent study among judges and attorneys in Denmark (where there is no regulation of settlement practices) shows that there is no consensus as to what constitutes judicial settlement efforts and that in practice settlement efforts range from minimal activity such as simply encouraging the parties to settle the case to much more involvement in the case by assessing its merits or making predictions about the ruling.[16] Denmark is hardly unique in this respect.

The lack of direction leaves plenty of room for diversity and flexibility in the settlement efforts but also for hardly trying to settle at all and for potentially problematic practices. This suggests that it would be helpful with more formal instructions to judges as to different ways settlement efforts could be conducted and clear guidelines as to when the requirement for settlement efforts is fulfilled. Also, standards for appropriate practice are in place. Without such standards judges are free to adopt troublesome practices such as for example putting inappropriate pressure on the parties to settle or make judicial evaluations on an imperfect basis. General guidelines regarding practice ought to be included in legislation to give it weight and in order to make the duties of the judges transparent. The guidelines could be elaborated on in other types of regulation such as for example standards of professional practice or ethical guidelines for settlement efforts.

9.4.4 *The Role of Judicial Settlement Efforts*

What role does judicial settlement activities play in judicial practice during the preparatory stage and how many settlements are reached as a result? An answer to these questions is relevant in understanding the role of judicial settlement activities on a general level across the countries as well as understanding patterns for each country individually. Also, such overview could indicate what countries it would be interesting to study more closely. This seemingly simple task has however proven impossible. In preparation for this volume, it became clear that only very inadequate statistical information—if any—is available about settlement efforts and most aspects of civil procedure in general, and when information is available it does not compare very well. However, a very guarded estimate from the six countries with available information indicates that on the average 5–21 % of civil cases settle in the course of the preparatory proceedings.[17] The numbers do not distinguish between settlements achieved by judicial settlement efforts and by the

[16] Adrian et al. (2015).

[17] This estimate is based on information from the contributors of this volume supplemented with statistics and is on file with the author. Sweden seems to have a much higher rate of first instance settlement, see Lindell (2012), p. 303, but since the information is from 1986 and may have changed considerably since then, it is not included her.

parties' own efforts after filing the cases. However, it seems safe to assume that the majority of registered settlements are a result of activities on the part of the court as the parties and their attorneys have probably either exhausted their own settlement efforts prior to filing the case or believe that such efforts are in vain. This guarded estimate of settlement rates in the preparatory proceedings gives us little more than a very rough idea of the current use of judicial settlement efforts. Much better statistical information is needed to accurately assess its use and to be able to draw reliable conclusions. However, it does give us an indication that there is potential for using judicial settlement efforts more actively than is apparently the case today.

9.5 Court-Connected Mediation: Differences and Similarities

9.5.1 A Brief Historical Account of Court-Connected Mediation

Twenty-five years ago, mediation was virtually unknown in European civil justice whereas today, it is a recognized form of dispute resolution which has entered the Halls of Justice in various forms in all the countries covered by this volume. Seven of the countries (Denmark, Finland, Hungary, Lithuania, Norway, Poland, Slovenia) have introduced court-connected mediation, as per the definition in Sect. 9.2 above where the court has some level of responsibility for the mediation service. In the five other countries (the Czech Republic, Estonia, Latvia, Slovakia and Sweden), the courts encourage mediation, too. For example, the Czech Republic and Slovakia have optional information meetings about mediation conducted outside the court and in Sweden, the court can appoint and arrange a meeting with a special mediator with the parties' consent.[18] However, none of these countries have a formalized system of court-connected mediation, nor do the courts hold responsibility for court-connected mediation activities.

Norway was early in experimenting with court-connected mediation in Scandinavia. In 1997, the first pilot project with participation of five first instance courts and one appeals court was initiated and in the following years the pilot project was expanded to more courts. With the major reform of the procedural rules, that took effect in 2008, court-connected mediation was included in the Dispute Act as a possible dispute resolution form in all first instance and appeals courts.[19] Under strong Norwegian influence, court-connected mediation was brought to Finland through the Act on Court-Connected Mediation in 2006 and to Denmark by an

[18] In connection with the implementation of the EU-directive the government rejected a proposal tying mediation more closely to the court, see Sippel (2014), p. 187 f.

[19] Theoretically, mediation can take place in the Supreme Court, too, but this option is hardly relevant as the Supreme Court hears cases of general public importance.

addition to the Danish Administration of Justice Act in 2008 after five year pilot period. Legislation based on a pilot-project is known from Slovenia and Lithuania, too. In Slovenia, that pioneered court-connected mediation in central Europe, legislation regarding court-connected mediation took effect in 2010 based on pilot projects from the late 1990s and in Lithuania legislation took effect in 2008 based on pilot projects starting in 2005. In these two countries legislation on court-connected mediation was also spurred by the EU mediation directive regarding civil and commercial matters from 2008.[20] Even though this directive was aimed at certain aspects of *cross-border* mediation only, it became the catalyst for national mediation activities and regulation regarding mediation beyond what was required by the directive not only in Slovenia and Lithuania but in other countries as well.[21] In Poland, court-connected mediation was added to the Civil Procedure Code in 2005. The aim of the legislator was to provide a different and quicker process for the resolution of disputes that could improve the administration of justice by being more efficient and saving money. Hungary was the first of the countries included in this book to enact a mediation law. It happened in 2002 but it was not until 2012 Hungary brought in court-connected mediation making Hungary the latest of the seven countries with court-connected mediation to provide this service as an alternative to litigation.

Court-connected mediation in the countries studied has much in common despite the different national and legal contexts that they occur in. This is hardly surprising as court-connected mediation is a legal transplant[22] in all of the countries. Additionally, the countries studied have influenced each other and are in part influenced by EU regulation of mediation as well. Furthermore, most schemes are probably also informed in one way or another by American court-connected mediation that preceded European initiatives in time through the many individuals that have learned about court-connected mediation and other mediation efforts though cross-Atlantic professional and academic visits, trainings, articles and books.

9.5.2 Selected Aspects of Court-Connected Mediation

Court-connected mediation is voluntary in all the countries in this volume with court-connected mediation with the exception of Norway, where the court can order mediation against the parties' wish under special circumstances, see the Dispute

[20] Directive 2008/52/EC of the European Parliament and of the Council of 21 May 2008 on certain aspects of Mediation in civil and commercial matters.

[21] In, for instance, the Czech Republic, Estonia and Latvia the promotion of other forms of mediation than court-connected mediation were driven by implementation of the EU directive. For an overview of the implementation of the directive see De Palo and Trevor (2012).

[22] See Watson (1995) for more on legal transplants.

Act section 8-3 (2). However, this provision is seldom if ever used in practice.[23] This state of affairs reflects the fundamental idea in mediation of party self-determination. Voluntary mediation is particularly important in court settings as the legal protection built into litigation does not apply as the mediation takes place outside rules of civil procedure. Voluntary attendance in mediation as the main rule seems self-evident but over the past 30–40 years, American court-connected mediation has changed from voluntary attendance over voluntary participation to only voluntary settlement in many jurisdictions.[24] In Europe, Italy has recently introduced mandatory court-connected mediation.[25]

Parties are central in mediation and except for Lithuania and Poland, the parties are required to attend court-connected mediations. Even when the parties are not required to attend, they probably most often do. In Poland, mediators even suggest at times that the parties attend a first mediation session without their attorneys. Party attendance makes sense as parties can hardly exercise self-determination and be engaged in resolution of their own case if they are not present at the mediation meeting.

Some countries apply incentives for attending and settling cases in court-connected mediation. For example, in Hungary information meetings regarding mediation are provided. In Norway, a proposal in a mediation that does not end in settlement may be recorded by the mediator if requested by a party and the refusing party may be ordered to paying part of the other party's cost. And in Slovenia a party who refuses to participate may be ordered to pay the other party's cost in full or in part regardless of the 'loser pays rule' and participation in mediation may be a prerequisite for legal aid. Also, in many court-connected mediation systems the judge may actively recommend mediation during preparatory proceedings. These incentives are intended to increase the use of court-connected mediation probably from the point of view that mediation is beneficial for the courts and the parties. However, for some parties, these measures may be perceived as falling only little short of formal compulsion.

Court-connected mediation is typically provided free for charge. With the exception of Poland, the courts pay for the mediator. In Norway and Finland, the court only pays for a judge mediator. If the mediator is an attorney or another person with special expertise, as is possible in Norway, or if the judge mediator enlists an auxiliary mediator as it possible in Finland,[26] the parties have to cover the expenses. Even when the court pays for the mediators, court-connected mediation is not necessarily entirely free of charge. If the parties attend with attorneys, which is often the case, the court does not cover those expenses in any of the countries.

When it comes to the agreement that results from a successful mediation, it can be enforced in all of the countries. In Slovenia, though, it has to be approved by the

[23] E-mail from Camilla Bernt 15 january 2014, on file with the author.

[24] Adrian and Vindeløv (2014).

[25] Legge 9 agosto 2013, n. 98.

[26] Section 8-4 (1) of the Norwegian Dispute Act and Evarsti (2011), p. 126.

court before it is enforceable. By law, all mediated agreements must be approved by the court in Lithuania.

9.5.3 Mediator Role and Practice

Court-connected mediators have considerably freedom with regard to their mediation practice. The practice is regulated on a general level only such as in the Danish Administration of Justice Act section 272 stating that the mediator should assist the parties in reaching a solution themselves or the little more detailed Norwegian Dispute Act section 8-5 (3) stating that the mediator must be impartial and try and to establish the interests of the parties and that the mediator can propose solutions and discuss the strength and weaknesses in the arguments of the parties whether legal or factual. In Denmark, court-connected mediators are also bound by ethical guidelines that are more explicit regarding the mediation practice among others in supporting a practice that emphasises the parties' self-determination.[27]

As mentioned in Sect. 9.2 above, the question of how much a mediator can engage in the content of the case before the activity can no longer be classified mediation is quite discussed in the mediation literature. This is not a theoretical discussion only—it has important practical implications. The practice of mediation differs depending on whether the mediator uses a facilitative approach, where he or she guides the process but leaves the substance of the matter to the parties, or the mediator uses an evaluative or directive approach, where the mediator engages in commenting on the substance, makes suggestions, makes legal evaluation or predicts what a potential ruling in the case might be.[28] In Finland, Norway and Denmark, the legislation (and the *travaux preparatoires*) reflects ambivalence on this issue. On the one hand, court-connected mediation is supposed to be facilitative and, on the other hand, the mediator can apply evaluative measures at his or her discretion. An example is the Finnish Mediation Act section 7, which both states that "[t]he mediator shall assist the parties in their efforts to reach agreement and an amicable resolution" and that "the mediator may make proposals for an amicable resolution. The proposal may be based on what the mediator deems appropriate . . ." Hence, on the one hand, the mediator is supposed to facilitate the parties' own resolution and, on the other hand, the mediator can make proposals for resolution that are based on what the mediator (and not necessarily the parties) finds an appropriate solution.

Leaving the method of mediation largely at the discretion of the mediator ensures flexibility and supports the mediator in making sound, professional choices about what is an appropriate course of action in the case at hand. On the other hand, this lack of guidelines for practice opens up for very different types of practices and

[27] https://www.domstol.dk/saadangoerdu/retsmaegling/Pages/Etiskeretningslinjerforretsmaegling.aspx - accessed on the 17th of September 2015.

[28] For the terms facilitative and evaluative/directive, see Riskin (1996, 2003–2004).

lack of transparency as to what the parties and their attorneys can expect. It also makes it difficult to set standards for best practices and makes it impossible for court systems and politicians to oversee the practice and decide on the direction it should take. Additionally, the dominant legal practice of the hosting institution may spill over making mediation resemble judicial settlement efforts or arbitration. The longer American experience with court-connected mediation suggests that this is a danger to be taken seriously, as court-connected mediation in many jurisdictions seem to have turned into very legally oriented, evaluative and arbitration-like activity.[29]

9.5.4 Mediator Background and Training

When it comes to the background and training of court-connected mediators, the situation differs from country to country. In Finland, only judges are allowed to mediate (they can appoint an auxiliary mediator from outside the courts), in Poland, judges are not allowed to mediate, but others in and outside the courts are. In the remaining countries, judges can mediate and others as well. In, for example, Slovenia, court-connected mediation is administered by the court and mediators are assigned from a rooster. Many listed mediators have a legal background, but there are also psychologists, sociologists, economists and other type of professionals represented.[30] If the mediator is a judge, all countries except Norway prohibit the judge from ruling in the case. In Norway, the mediator judge can rule the case at the parties' request and if the mediator finds it appropriate, see section 8-7 in the Norwegian Dispute Act.

In terms of mediator training, there is no consistency either. In Norway and Finland, judges are allowed to mediate without any formal mediation training but many participate in trainings anyway. In the other countries, training is a prerequisite for being appointed court-connected mediator. The training can be provided by the court or by independent providers. In, for example, Denmark, the Courts of Denmark has its own internal mediation training for judges whereas in Slovenia, the mediators have to undergo general mediation training in order to be registered as mediators, which is a requirement for being appointed court-connected mediator.[31] It is encouraging that training is a requirement for court-connected mediation in most places. When mediation is conducted in a court setting alongside litigation and judicial settlement efforts and often with legally trained mediators, training is especially important. Otherwise there is a risk that mediators fall back into the practice they know as lawyer and judges resulting in an inconsistency between the service announced and the service performed.

---

[29] Kovach and Love (1998) and Adrian (2012), p. 413.

[30] De Palo and Trevor (2012), p. 322.

[31] Ibid.

9.6 Advantages and Disadvantages of Court-Connected Mediation

9.6.1 *Cost and Time*

Mediation is often promoted for its ability to save time and money compared to litigation. This makes intuitively sense when a case settles pre-action but also if it settles in the preparatory stage. In most jurisdictions, litigation takes a considerable amount of time. According to the OECD, the average trial length for first instance litigious cases in the countries covered in this volume was more than seven months (220 days) in 2012[32] and much longer if appeals are included. In comparison, mediation can be completed within weeks from the referral. Cost and time savings may be on the part of the court system, on the part of the parties or on both, and studies seem to confirm that time as well as money is saved for disputants and courts alike in many cases.[33]

Cost-savings are to a large extent dependent on whether the case settles or not. For example, a Dutch study has found that that on the average EUR 303 is saved for the court, when the parties settle in mediation, whereas expenses increase when the case only settles partially (by EUR 82) or not at all (by EUR 220).[34] A similar pattern is found for party cost. For example, a Norwegian study found that 97 % of the attorneys that participated in court-connected mediation reported that money was saved for the parties if they reached agreement.[35] When the parties did not reach agreement, only 14 % found that money was saved, whereas 63 % estimated that costs increased for the parties. Similarly, a report prepared for the Directorate-General for Internal Policies estimates that over EUR 7,500 can be saved by parties who successfully mediate since the average cost for litigation in the European

[32] OECD (2013), p. 211.

[33] In Europe, se for example Knoff (2001), Roepstorff and Kyvsgaard (2005), Pel and Combrink (2011), Directorate General for Internal Policies (2011) and the Danish Courts website http://www.domstol.dk/om/publikationer/HtmlPublikationer/Handlingsplaner/Danmarks%20Domstoles%20handlingsplan%202015/kap04.htm - accessed on the 17th of September 2015. For an account of a number of studies in primarily North America see Mediate BC Dispute Resolution and Design (2014) and Department of Justice, Canada (2007) (there is a slight overlap in the studies reported in the two studies). Cf. Wissler (2004) who in a review of a number of American and Canadian studies got inconclusive results with regard to cost of court-connected mediation for parties compared to litigation. Some studies found that money was saved compared to litigation and others not.

[34] Pel and Combrink (2011), pp. 51–52. A similar pattern is found in a Danish study, see Roepstorff and Kyvsgaard (2005), p. 85. The Dutch data does not include the cost of maintaining the referral service in the courts. When adding up all the cost and savings, the study shows that the referral service is almost cost-efficient and it is expected to be entirely cost-efficient with an expected increase in referrals, see p. 52.

[35] Knoff (2001), p. 80.

Union is EUR 10,449 for the parties whereas the average cost of a mediation is EUR 2,497.[36]

Settlement rates in mediation differ widely across the court-connected mediation schemes covered in this volume, from a high in Norway of 70–80 % over 48 % in Slovenia to a low of 10 % in Poland.[37] When the case does not settle in mediation, the cost of the mediation risks being added to parties' expenses in litigation and the time spent attempting settlement this way may increase the total time spent in litigation. However, even unsuccessful mediations may lead to later cases settlement or better preparation of trials. In countries with little emphasis on preparatory proceedings such as in, for example, Slovenia and Hungary, court-connected mediation in the preparatory phase can be a way of sharing information prior to trial avoiding too many surprises leading to postponement. Studies do indeed suggest that often cases go through litigation more efficiently after an unsuccessful mediation saving time and money even then.[38]

9.6.2 Party Satisfaction and Outcomes

Users of court-connected mediation usually give this type of conflict resolution very favourable ratings.[39] This is corresponds with studies of mediation in other settings.[40] A word of caution is place: many studies do not have a control group or a comparison group. Hence, we cannot always be sure whether the high rates of satisfaction are in mediation only or also apply to litigation. Satisfaction probably stems from a number of factors. First of all, as mentioned, disputants may experience savings in time and money when a case settles early leading to satisfaction. Also, disputants usually maintain a higher degree of control over the case and experience better implementation of an agreement when it is entered voluntarily in mediation rather than a result of a ruling.[41] In addition, mediation provides a process that many find fair and satisfactory independent of the outcome. Not that the outcomes do not matter—they do, but perceptions of the process are also important for the overall satisfaction of disputants.[42] Social psychology has identified four factors that seem to affect disputants' perception of the fairness in the process: Voice (the opportunity to present your side of the story), neutrality of the

[36] Directorate General for Internal Policies (2011), p. 4.

[37] This corresponds quite well with the findings in a number of American studies where the settlement rate in most instances was between 27–63 %, se Wissler (2004), p. 65. It is beyond the scope of this chapter to account for these differences.

[38] Knoff (2001), p. 80, and Mediate BC Dispute Resolution and Design (2014), p. 1.

[39] See, for example, Knoff (2001), Wissler (2004), Roepstorff and Kyvsgaard (2005) and Department of Justice, Canada (2007).

[40] See for example Wall and Dunne (2012).

[41] Department of Justice, Canada (2007).

[42] Hollander-Blumoff and Tyler (2011), p. 5.

third party, trustworthiness of the third party and being treated with courtesy and respect.[43] Court-connected mediation probably caters to all four factors. During mediation, parties usually decide what is important for them to talk about, speak for themselves and have the time and opportunity to tell their side of the story (voice). The mediator is a neutral and makes no decisions in the case and by being neutral and assisting the parties without making judgements, the mediator may be perceived as trustworthy. Additionally, since the parties play a central role in mediation, they probably feel that they on more equal footing with the professionals (the mediator and the attorneys) than in adjudicatory processes and consequently experience being treated with courtesy and respect.

Like mediation in other fields, court-connected mediation is often heralded for its ability to make tailor-made solutions based on the interests of the parties rather than on legal rights alone.[44] A recent study of settlements made in court-connected mediation in Denmark and Norway supports this claim but also points to a potential for more creativity.[45] By comparing the initial claims in litigation to the mediated agreements, the study found that 52 % of the agreements contained at least two elements that were not part of the legal claims in the case and about half of these contained five or more elements. The relative creativity in mediation may also contribute to party satisfaction.

9.6.3 *Justice in Private*

An often aired critique of mediation in general and court-connected mediation, in particular, is that it provides a private forum for dispute resolution undermining society's interest in rulings and lacking the procedural protection of litigation.[46] Courts and their rulings are fundamental in a democratic society. They provide dispute resolutions for the parties and have a normative function for society at large by setting norms and by regulating the behaviour of citizens through enforcement of the law. From the normative perspective, it is problematic if mediation (and other forms of alternative dispute resolution) replaces litigation.[47] We need an adequate number of trials or maybe rather an adequate number of the right trials. Many cases decided in court are routine cases that resolve a problem between two or more parties and these cases are not 'necessary' from the norm setting point of view.

---

[43] Hollander-Blumoff and Tyler (2011), pp. 5–6.

[44] Ury et al. (1988), Vindeløv (2012).

[45] Adrian and Mykland (2014). The article contains a review of other studies of creativity in mediation.

[46] See for example Farrow (2014). For an interesting account of the discussion among Swedish scholars with very different views on the place for mediation in the courts, see Dahlqvist (2014), p. 149 ff.

[47] Galanter (2004) has suggested this may be one explanation for the decline in the number of trials in the US.

However, rulings that on a more general level contribute to the understanding of the law, set precedent for others in the same situation or point out how specific issues should be dealt with are important for society at large and it is potentially problematic if many cases that address such issues are resolved in mediation. We do not know whether this is a theoretical concern only or it is a problem in practice due to lack of data regarding the types of issues resolved in mediation. What we do know is that mediation accounts for only a small portion of the total of cases resolved in all the countries with court-connected mediation in this volume. Numbers are hard to compare as the justice systems differ and statistical information is based on different types of information in each countries. With that uncertainty in mind, a cautious estimate based on data obtained for this article suggests that Norway and Finland top the list of litigious cases resolved in mediation with 14 % and 10–12 % respectively. In Slovenia, the percentage is 4 % and in Denmark, Lithuania and Poland it is 1 % or less.[48] These numbers show that at most one out of seven cases are resolved in court-connected mediation and in most countries, it is less than one out of 100 cases. Hence, at this point in time, the sheer number of mediations does not suggest that there is a problem of mediation taking over litigation in a way that is problematic. Rather, the problem may be reverse in that there is capacity to resolve more cases by mediation than currently happens in most jurisdictions.

9.6.4 Procedural Protection

The lack of procedural protection is another concern often raised and this issue has already been addressed in Sect. 9.5. If mediation becomes mandatory or if mediations become very evaluative, procedural protection poses a potential problem. The primary protection in mediation is voluntariness and self-determination of the parties which allow them to choose attendance, leave the mediation at any time, influence the agenda for the mediation and allow them to enter the types of agreements that *they* want. If, however, the parties are forced to mediate, the mediator decides the agenda, suggests solutions and makes recommendations for the final agreement, the lack of procedural protection in a legal setting becomes problematic. The answer to this problem is not to implement procedural protection imported from litigation, but rather set standards for good mediation practice. Such standards should include regulation of practice, education of mediators, safeguard voluntary participation etc. The optional European Code of Conduct for Mediators, which is directed at mediations in all settings, is an example of such standards, but it addresses only some of the important issues (voluntariness is not addressed for example) and mediators are not obliged to follow the guidelines. The Courts of Denmark has issued a set of compulsory ethical guidelines for court-connected

[48] There is no statistical information is available for Hungary – the last of the countries in this volume with court-connected mediation.

mediators. However, there is no complaint system in place if the guidelines are not followed and some of the sections are rather vague. Generally, there seem to be hesitancy in regulating court-connected mediation too closely. This makes sense from a flexibility point of view but may prove problematic from a point of view of protecting practice and participants as mentioned earlier in this chapter.

9.6.5 The Market

Another concern sometimes voiced against court-connected mediation is its anti-competitive impact. It is argued that by providing mediation free of charge, the courts take business from private providers. There is no available data to support or counter this claim. However, to the extent that parties would contract with a private provider, if mediation is not offered by the court, this concern holds true. This may occur in cases with low or no court fees and *pro-se* litigants, but hardly in cases where the filing-fee and the lawyers' fees exceed the cost of a mediator. Also, the relationship may be reverse. Implementing mediation in the court system may make it a more known and valued process increasing the private demand for such services.

9.7 Concluding Remarks

The purpose of this chapter was to examine the role of court-connected mediation and judicial settlement efforts in preparatory proceedings in civil litigation. As appears, settling cases in the preparatory phase is a well-known practice into all court systems covered by this volume although the type of settlement activities differs as well as the extent to which it is used.

Judicial settlement efforts exist in all the countries. However, regulation is usually limited to stating that the court has an obligation to try and settle the case but not how this could or should be done. This state of affairs points to a need for more attention to the practice of judicial settlement efforts in order to ensure the quality of this service as well as using it as an instrument to settle more cases than the 5–21 % of cases that are currently resolved this way.

Court-connected mediation is a recent addition to the justice systems and seems to be on the rise as a way to settle cases early in litigation. Mediation is part of the preparatory proceedings in all the countries in this volume but it is implemented quite differently and how much it is used differs, too. In five countries, the courts may initiate mediation but leave the service to outside providers whereas seven countries have court-connected mediation schemes. Apparently, the number of cases settled through mediation differs from under 1 % of civil court cases in some countries to more than 14 % in others suggesting that there is a potential for increasing the use of court-connected mediation in the preparatory proceeding in many jurisdictions.

Many users find the mediation process and outcome satisfactory and studies suggest that court-connected mediation often saves money and time for parties and courts alike. However, at times mediation adds to the cost of litigation. Even so, (an increased use of) mediation may be one of the answers to the problems faced by some countries in this volume, e.g. Finland and Slovenia, with time consuming and expensive litigation processes. When considering and implementing court-connected mediation, concerns regarding the potential problems of privatisation need to be taken into account as well as anti-competition concerns. Also, it is important to monitor and develop mediation practices to ensure that they live up to standards of good mediation.

Are we seeing the rise of a new legal culture across the Eastern and Northern parts of Europe with the emergence of court-connected mediation? It is hard to tell. On one hand, this development may indicate the rise of a qualitatively new way of resolving conflict where the parties are at the centre of attention and make decisions in their own cases with the help of a mediator. Also, it may be the sign of a nascent change in the perception of courts from adjudicative institutions to institution of dispute resolution. On the other hand, court-connected mediation may be little more than an instrument to save money at a time, where cost efficiency in the public sector is a mantra in many countries. Settling cases during preparatory proceedings by means of mediation may be perceived as a welcome answer to the challenges of identifying spending cuts. Either way, it is important to follow the development of court-connected mediation in the years to come in order to learn from best-practices of mediation in preparatory proceedings as well as critically assess the practice, regulation and use of this relatively new form of dispute resolution.

This chapter has shown great variation in the role that settlement activities play in the preparatory proceedings. In Norway, judicial settlement activities as well as court-connected mediation play an important role in the preparatory proceedings and many cases settle this way. In other countries, such as Estonia, only a low percentage of civil cases settle through judicial settlement activities and court-connected mediation is non-existent. There seems to be no consistent characteristics that account for these differences. There is great disparity between countries with similar judicial systems such as, for example, the Scandinavian countries and the Baltic countries. Various other factors must be at play. When it comes to court connected mediation these may be the amount of time the service has been offered, the legal culture, interest by the judges and attorneys, how closely mediation is tied to the court etc. Generally, it would be of interest to better understand the role of settlement activities in the different countries in order to enhance our understanding of what promotes and what inhibits the use of judicial settlement activities as well as court-connected mediation.

References

Adrian L (2012) Mellem retssag og rundbordssamtale: Retsmægling i teori og praksis. Jurist og Økononomforbundets Forlag, Copenhagen

Adrian L (2014) Court-Connected Mediation in Danish Civil Justice: A Happy Marriage or a Strained Relationship? In: Ervo L, Nylund A (eds) The Future of Civil Litigation. Springer, Cham, pp 157–184

Adrian L, Mykland S (2014) Creativity in Court-Connected Mediation: Myth or Reality? Negotiation Journal 30(4):421–439

Adrian L, Vindeløv V (2014) Angreb på mæglingens DNA : ansatser til en diskussion om tvungen mægling. In: Blume P, Henrichsen C (eds) Forvaltning og retssikkerhed – Festskrift til Steen Rønsholdt. Jurist- og Økonomforbundets Forlag, Copenhagen, pp 13–31

Adrian L, Bager S, Salung Petersen C (2015) Perspektiver på forligsmægling. Juristen 3:98–106

Bernt C (2011) Meklerrollen ved mekling i domstolene. Fakbokforlaget, Bergen

Center for Dispute Settlement and Institute of Judicial Administration (1992) National Standards for Court-Connected Mediation Programs. Washington, DC

Dahlqvist A (2014) Mediation in the Swedish Courts: Change by EU Directive? In: Ervo L, Nylund A (eds) The Future of Civil Litigation. Springer, Cham, pp 137–155

De Palo G, Trevor MB (eds) (2012) EU Mediation: Law and Practice. Oxford University Press, Oxford

Department of Justice, Canada (2007) The effectiveness of using mediation in selected civil law disputes: a meta-analysis. http://www.justice.gc.ca/eng/rp-pr/csj-sjc/jsp-sjp/rr07_3/index.html. Last accessed 12 Feb. 2016

Directorate General for Internal Policies (2011) Quantifiying the cost of not using mediation – a data analysis. European Parliament, Policy Department C: Citizens' Rights and Constitutional Affairs. http://www.europarl.europa.eu/studies. Last accessed 12 Feb 2016

Ervasti K (2011) Utveckningslinker för rättsmedling i Finland. JFT 3:267–289

Farrow TCV (2014) Civil Justice, Privatization, and Democracy. University of Toronto Press, Toronto

Galanter M (2004) The vanishing trial: An examination of trials and related matters in federal and state courts. J Empir Leg Stud 1(3):459–570

Hollander-Blumoff R, Tyler TR (2011) Procedural justice and the rule of law: fostering legitimacy in alternative dispute resolution. J Disp Resol 1:1–19

Hopt KJ, Steffek F (eds) (2013) Mediation: Principles and Regulation in Comparative Perspective. Oxford University Press, Oxford

Knoff RH (2001) Raskere? Billigere? Vennligere? – Evaluering av prøveordningen med rettsmekling., Rapport for Justitsdepatementet

Kovach KK (2004) Mediation – Principles and Practice. Thomson West, St. Paul

Kovach KK, Love LP (1998) Mapping Mediation: The Risk of Riskin's Grid. Harv Negot Law Rev 3:71–110

Lindell B (2012) Civilprocessen – rättegång samt skiljeförfarande och medling. Iustus Förlag AB, Uppsala

Mediate BC Dispute Resolution and Design (2014) A case for mediation: the cost-effectiveness of civil, family, and workplace mediation. www.mediatebc.com. Last accessed 12 Feb. 2016

Mironi MM (2014) Mediation v. Case Settlement: The Unsettling Relations Between Courts and Mediation –A Case Study. Harv Negot Law Rev 19:173–211

Nolan-Haley J (2005) Self-Determination in International Mediation: Some Preliminary Reflections. Cardozo J Confl Resolut 7(1):277–288

Nylund A (2014) The Many Ways of Civil Mediation in Norway. In: Ervo L, Nylund A (eds) The Future of Civil Litigation. Springer, Cham, pp 97–119

OECD (2013) What makes civil justice effective? OECD Economics Department Policy Notes., No. 18 June 2013

Pel M, Combrink L (2011) Referral to Mediation by the Netherlands Judiciary. Judiciary Q 25–52

Riskin LL (1996) Understanding mediators' orientations, strategies, and techniques: A grid for the perplexed. Harv Negot Law Rev 1:7–51

Riskin LL (2003–2004) Decisionmaking in Mediation: The new old Grid and the new new Grid System. Notre Dame Law Rev 79:1–53

Roepstorff J, Kyvsgaard B (2005) Forsøg med retsmægling – en evalueringsrapport. Justitsministeriets Forskningsenhed, Copenhagen

Sippel L (2014) Comparative Aspects Between the Nordic Countries and Austria: Court Mediation in or Out? In: Ervo L, Nylund A (eds) The Future of Civil Litigation. Springer, Cham, pp 185–209

The European Commission for the Efficiency of Justice (2014) European judicial systems – Edition 2014 (2012 data): efficiency and quality of justice

Ury WL, Brett JM, Goldberg SB (1988) Getting disputes resolved: Designing systems to cut the costs of conflict. Jossey-Bass, San Francisco

Vindeløv V (1997) Konflikt, tvist og mægling – konfliktløsning ved forhandling. Akademisk Forlag, Copenhagen

Vindeløv V (2012) Reflexive mediation – with a sustainable perspective. DJØF Publishing, Copenhagen

Wall JA, Dunne TC (2012) Mediation research: A current review. Negot J 28(2):217–244

Watson A (1995) From Legal Transplants to Legal Formants. Am J Comp Law 43(3):469–476

Welsh NA (2001) The Thinning Vision of Self-determination in Court-Connected Mediation: The Inevitable Price of Institutionalization? Harv Negot Law Rev 6:1–96

Wissler RL (2004) The effectiveness of court connected dispute resolution civil cases. Confl Resolut Q 22(1–2):55–88

Chapter 10
Conclusions

Laura Ervo

Abstract In this chapter the studies are summarised, research questions are answered and the fruits of the project are presented. In the Nordic countries, the preparatory proceedings play a significant role. One reason for this weight is that there are no actual pre-action procedures in Scandinavia with the exception of Norway. Because of the lack of actual pre-action procedure one of the main functions during the preparatory proceedings is to clarify the subject of the dispute, sort out the disputed and undisputed facts and investigate if there are provisions for an amicable settlement. Current trends in Scandinavia include court-connected mediation (excluding Sweden) and friendly settlements particularly through judicial settlement efforts (Sweden including). Party autonomy and flexibility is also typical of the current Scandinavian preparatory procedure. All of these efforts target the effectiveness of preparatory proceedings. The common feature to the former communist countries that were researched seems to be that all of them are struggling with the change from the Soviet-influenced civil proceedings towards western party autonomy and an efficient preparatory stage. The old habits with the powerful and active judge are still deeply in the legal culture at courts and, despite of legislative reforms, the new type of preparatory stage seems not to work. This study aimed at throwing light on two different but special streamlines of European development in this field: one of them was the Nordic trend and the other was the development in Baltic and other former East-European countries that received EU membership in 2004. Even though the original roots of all chosen countries were close to each other (i.e. adopting the continental system), after World War II, the development of these procedural regimes took different directions, while they now face similar problems again. The study unveiled similar ways of thinking, at least at the legislative stage. Still, the previous directions of developments in civil procedural laws have resulted in different practical situations. Surprisingly, we do share the main problems and goals in both study groups. We share even partly the solutions, but we still differ in daily-life and practices.

L. Ervo (✉)
Faculty of Law, University of Örebro, JPS, 701 82 Örebro, Sweden
e-mail: laura.ervo@oru.se

L. Ervo, A. Nylund (eds.), *Current Trends in Preparatory Proceedings*,
DOI 10.1007/978-3-319-29325-7_10

10.1 The Nordic Countries

10.1.1 East-Scandinavian Countries[1]

The entire *Finnish* court culture is undergoing a radical change. There is a growing emphasis on procedural justice, a client-centred approach, and communicative skills and interaction. Increasing focus is placed on conflict resolution and means are devised for alternative procedures alongside traditional adjudication. In essential ways, all these factors influence the traditional work of the courts and their personnel. Justice cannot be based merely on formal legal rules and procedures. Instead, the changing environment where courts operate requires a new kind of professionalism and proficiency involving ethical and moral dimensions.

In *Sweden*, there is very much discretion in procedural rules covering the preparatory stage. Especially the principle of orality has been modified rather radically in the name of reasonableness. Still, even the Swedish procedure as a whole is based on the orality, which has been seen as a very important and valuable principle even in post-modern proceedings, where the technical possibilities, that is phone and video conference, are increasing the possibilities refuse to organise the face-to-face sessions. In spite of these modern possibilities the oral hearing, where all the parties and the members of the court are at present at the same time, has been seen very important in order to maximise the communication in the proceedings. The best possible communication is important because it serves the effectiveness of the proceedings including time, costs and legal certainty.

10.1.2 West-Scandinavian Countries[2]

The idea of the *Norwegian* reform of civil proceedings has been that the civil disputes could be solved so far as possible outside the courts. When the dispute had not been solved by a friendly settlement, the procedure before the court should be effective and safe. The Norwegian proceedings differ from the usual Scandinavian proceedings with these very wide struggles for achieving the friendly settlement in the dispute. For that reason, there is even the pre-action procedure, which is very untypical for a Nordic Country. The negotiations are normally obligatory before the suit can be brought into the court. The Conciliation Board is one possibility for these negotiations. There has also been criticism against the existence of the Conciliation Board. During the preparation of the civil procedure reform it was suggested that the procedure before the Board should be voluntary. The criticism was based on poor grounds on the Board's earlier decisions and to other weaknesses

[1] See Chap. 2 (written by Ervo 2016).

[2] See Chaps. 3 (written by Nylund 2016) and 4 (written by Juul-Sandberg 2016).

on some decisions made by the Board. There was even a fear that the decisions could be against the European Convention on Human Rights. However, the Ministry of Justice disagreed and decided that the procedure before the Board were obligatory. The grounds for this were that the procedure before the board is cheaper than before the courts and the board system is even more decentralised than the court system is. Even if there is a possibility for wrong judgments is not problematic because the parties have a possibility to bring the case later before a court. The Norwegian preparatory proceedings, which follows the pre-action procedure, is quite similar to other Scandinavian countries. In the Norwegian Code of Civil Proceedings, it is underlined that the advocacy of the parties may not go at preparatory proceedings further than is necessary for the preparation of the case. The idea is to make a difference between the preparatory procedure and the main hearing. Especially in Finland, it has been a problem that the parties and their representatives will advocate too much during the preparation even if this task belongs to the main hearing. In Norway, the solution to this problem was that the injunction of the further argumentation has been taken into the Code. The results show that the Norwegian preparatory stage is working and the 2008 reform has been successful. The number of civil cases disposed of per judge had increased and the costs have been radically reduced. The court proceedings are an attractive alternative to arbitration. The amount of cases filed has namely increased, unlike in Finland, where the amount of civil cases has been lowering thanks to delays and high risk of legal costs mainly. Norway also spends little money on the courts as percentage of gross domestic product per capita and has fairly few judges. The Norwegian preparatory stage can, therefore, be described as well functioning and effective. However, behind this efficiency is the lack in preparatory hearings, which possibility could be used more often.

Additionally, in *Denmark*, there has been an ongoing effort to make procedures even more efficient. The reform of the provisions on preparatory proceedings in 2008 and 2014 has put more focus on getting civil cases prepared faster and more efficient by forcing the involved parties to consider how to approach the case. The judge has the tools to force the parties to initiate the preparation of the case and activate them. In 2014, the Danish Court Administration started focusing on digital procedures. The goal is that a civil case can be digitalised from filing the statement of claim and paying the court fee until the decision in the case is announced to the parties involved. The fully digitalised proceeding is possible since 2016.The Danish peculiarities are also so-called surveys, which mean external experts in the form of co-judges to give information on some specific topics. The survey can be conducted at the preparatory stage. The only threats that might exist in Denmark are in the judicial settlement efforts, which should not be used just to achieve other aims such as efficiency or other that type of unacceptable reasons to push parties to settle instead of giving them the possibility to get a judgment if they prefer that. The other critical point is spotted in court-connected mediation, which could have a higher amount of cases. In addition, the court-connected mediation should be realised according to the same standards in all courts.

10.1.3 Scandinavian Trends and Typical Elements

The preparatory proceedings play a significant role in the Nordic countries. One reason for this weight is that there are no actual pre-action procedures in Scandinavia except in Norway. The same aims are partly achieved instead during the preparation before the court. However, it must be remembered that there is already a suit brought before the court during this preparation. The Scandinavian system is based on the preparatory, not on pre-action procedures. Because of the lack of actual pre-action procedure, one of the main functions during the preparatory proceedings is to clarify the subject of the dispute, to sort out the disputed and undisputed facts and investigate if there are provisions for an amicable settlement.

Because of the failing disclosure, the parties may have difficulties in estimating their possibilities to win a case in the Scandinavian preparatory proceedings. The other problem can be that the parties will meet problems in collecting evidence and organising testimony. However, the current situation has not been seen as a problem and there has not been any wide discussion on the need to adapt disclosure. In spite of the very many and very wide procedural reforms in Scandinavian countries the rules on disclosure have not been amended. The obligation to produce a document or an object has been found enough and even this possibility is not used very often in practice.

Currents trends in Scandinavia include, most especially, court-connected mediation (excluding Sweden) and friendly settlements particularly through judicial settlement efforts (Sweden including). The reformed Codes of Judicial Procedure are based on the maximisation of decisions by a friendly settlement. In addition, the alternative dispute resolution even in its institutionalised forms is a current theme in Scandinavia (excluding Sweden). It has its traditional roots in Norway. It is also typical of the current Scandinavian preparatory procedure that the parties can choose and influence to some extent to the form of the preparation. In many situations, it is up to them if they prefer written or oral preparation. This trend seems to strengthen with the newest Scandinavian procedural reforms, which allow more flexibility in the name of appropriate and effective preparation based on the needs of the parties and characteristics of the single case.

The use of the preparatory system as a filter is typical for the Scandinavian countries. This has been very much stressed especially in the East-Scandinavian countries. As soon as the case matures for the decision, the proceedings should be finished and the case decided mainly to save resources for hard cases and to save the parties legal costs, as well which have been too high risking the access to court in many Scandinavian countries, at least in Finland and Denmark. This decision function of preparatory proceedings has perhaps been emphasised too much, especially in Finland, because one of the Scandinavian problems is that the preparatory stage, especially the oral hearing, gets a role as a mini-main hearing taking the weight from the main hearing and advocacy in that. The process has become too front-loaded. In Norway, this division has been fulfilled in a more successful way and the Norwegian preparation focuses on the preparation and clear making of the case, not on advocacy and arguing.

Orality has been the fundamental principle in the Scandinavian proceedings. First each reform was strongly built into the orality, for instance, the reforms 1948 Sweden and 1993 in Finland. Soon it was found out that the absolute value of orality was too much and the preparatory stage was not functioning effectively and appropriately, but it took too much time, resources and got expensive, whereas the main hearing almost dwindled away being just a formality before the decision making whereas advocacy had mostly happened already during the oral hearing during the preparatory stage. Re-reforms in both countries have reduced the strength of the orality quite a lot and nowadays forms for the preparation can vary in a flexible way between oral and written preparation up to the single case and the will of parties. Still, one reason behind all that might even be in the State economy. The preparatory stage has to be as effective as possible to save resources and costs. The tendency is also to decide more and more cases without a main hearing. Therefore, it is possible to decide the case even based on the material merits in a written preparation in some situations if there is no need to oral advocacy and when the pieces of evidence are only documentary.

The party autonomy and the active participation of parties during the preparatory stage are also typical in the Scandinavian countries. Judges 'have a proper arsenal of tools—like preclusion and the judgment by default—to activate them. This trend to put more emphasis on the co-operation and activation of parties has been strengthened especially in Sweden and Denmark recently.

Summa summarum the common Scandinavian legislative trend is to reach the efficiency in the preparatory proceedings. This common goal of legislators is working better in the West-Scandinavian countries (Norway and Denmark) compared with the East-Scandinavian countries (Sweden and especially Finland). The Swedish problem is in lacking court-connected mediation, whereas the Finnish problem is delays and costs, which can even risk the access to courts. The heavy preparatory stage has been one factor that has caused the named drawbacks.

10.2 Former Communist Countries

10.2.1 The Northern Trends: The Baltic[3] and Polish[4] Approach

After World War II, all three *Baltic countries* were annexed by the Soviet Union and the new codes of civil procedure were adopted according to the model law for civil procedure for Soviet Union States where the court had absolute power. These

[3] See Chap. 6 (written by Vėbraitė 2016).

[4] See Chap. 7 (written by Piszcz 2016).

codes with huge amendments were applied after the restoration of independence in all three Baltic countries. Until the new codes of civil procedure, preparatory proceedings in Lithuania, Latvia and Estonia were quite similar and understandably influenced by the tradition of Soviet-style civil procedure. The main idea of such preparatory proceedings was that only the judge was responsible for the preparation. The parties were not obliged to be active. The preparatory proceedings were not an important part of civil proceedings but the main idea of preparatory proceedings was to inform the defendant about the claim and upcoming main hearing. In the new codes of civil procedure, it can be seen that legal regulation of the preparatory stage has seen many changes. It is obvious that to change legal regulation is much easier than to change mentality and culture of actors of civil proceedings. For instance, even if possibility of preclusions is set in the laws, there are civil cases where this rule is not applied and principles of concentration and co-operation in civil proceedings are breached. Another example is still very seldom used judicial settlement efforts.

The *Polish* system is not uniform, transparent, technologically advanced or conciliatory. It is also said to be inefficient and long-lasting. The Polish Code for Civil Proceedings has been amended quite slowly and in parts so far. The Code of 1964 fully reflected the principles of socialism. Neither party autonomy nor procedural formalism existed. After the communist collapse in 1989, the principle of equality of arms between the parties was brought back. The rule of preclusion was also articulated. The discretionary power of judges has been discussed and according to some scholars that type of flexibility may lead to unequal treatment of the parties or judges' arbitrariness. Judges still see preparatory proceedings as a mini-main hearing, which gets expensive and is time-consuming. Therefore, they limit this stage to few activities in writing. They also think that collaboration with the parties may be detrimental for the impartiality of the judge. Judges should place a stronger focus on managing cases and collaborate with the parties. The change in manners and mentalities is needed, which is mainly the question of the education and training of judges.

10.2.2 The Southern Trends: From the Czech Republic to Slovenia[5]

There are several things that the three Slavic nations of Central Europe—*Slovenia, the Czech Republic and Slovakia*—have in common. First of all, they were all part of the Austrian-Hungarian Empire until the end of World War I. After the end of World War II, communist governments were installed in all of the discussed countries and finally, in 2004, they entered the European Union. However, the era of communist regimes was not identical in the named countries. Slovenia (as a part

[5] See Chaps. 5 Slovakia (written by Galič 2016) and 8 (written by Köblös 2016).

of Yugoslavia) stayed quite close to the West, whereas Czechoslovakia belonged clearly to the Soviet Bloc countries and had communist ideological principles and political slogans even in the law. In Slovenia, for instance, party autonomy was recognised in the law even during the communist era. Still, in practice, the socialist paternalism was daily-life also in Slovenia. After the downfall of communist regimes in the late 1980s and early 1990s, the three countries met again. The transition of legal systems and civil justice is still on-going. In all three countries, there exists a great public dissatisfaction with the functioning of civil justice, for instance, thanks to delays and other inefficiency in proceedings despite of the fact that the importance of a proper preparation has been recognised. Both the Slovenian reform of 2008 and the new Slovak Civil Procedure Act are in line with the worldwide trend of putting more emphasis on the preparatory stage of proceedings, as well as giving the judge more discretion in determining the manner of unfolding of proceedings even if the results have clearly not been satisfactory. The reasons for this are partly in insufficient legislative reforms but also in the old-fashioned court culture where the proper preparation has not been seen in spotlights of efficiency.

The *Hungarian* rules of civil procedure developed in the streamline of the German and Austrian models at the beginning of the twentieth century and were later influenced by the Soviet solutions in the second half of the century. Since the change to the regime in 1989 the legislator has made several attempts to concentrate the procedure and satisfy the requirement of hearing cases within a reasonable time but reforms have been only partly successful. It is typical to the Hungarian civil procedure that it is not divided into an efficient preparatory stage and a concentrated main hearing, which is still the inheritance from the Soviet times. For instance, the need to a written preparation is up to the judge's attitude and the type of the case. Usually, there is no preclusion and, therefore, the success of a written preparation is very much dependent on the parties' willingness to active participation. The first hearing usually functions as a preparatory hearing, which leads to adjournments that were typical in the old style of Finnish proceedings. According to the law, the goal is to prepare the case for a main hearing in case amicable settlement fails. However, the practice is far away from this goal.

10.2.3 From Soviet Times Towards Western Party Autonomy

The common feature to the former communist countries that were researched seems to be that all of them are struggling with the change from the Soviet influenced civil proceedings towards western party autonomy and efficient preparatory stage including the rule of preclusion and with the aim of procedural truth instead of material truth. The old habits with the powerful and active judge are still deeply in the legal culture at courts and despite of legislative reforms the new type of preparatory stage seems not to work in any of the countries researched. The problem is that it is difficult to change mentalities by legislative changes, which happened even in Finland in the beginning of the 1990s. The Finnish legislator chose very absolute principles almost without any space for the exceptions to make the change in legal culture and manners of judges efficiently possible, but still, the reform was more or less failed. The Finnish legislator was obliged to change the rules towards more flexible direction in 2003.

In the former communist countries, the legislation seems to have space for old-style of interpretations or there might be other reasons why the reformed rules are not totally followed in practice. Still, the common point is that the non-binding old type of culture and manners are usually stronger than binding legislative novelties. It takes time to make this change in a functional way. It shows us that the legislative reforms have to go hand-in-hand with the societal development. As long as mentalities have not been changed, the new laws are not fully working or followed. As *Piszcz* wrote in Chap. 7, this is mainly the question of the education of judges. With the new generation, the new approach can be achieved quite easily. It is something that can be seen when adopting EU regulations and the European Convention on Human Rights. The current generation, which has studied law during EU membership, can use the European tools in their daily professional life like the elder generation used the domestic laws only and found it difficult to mix with European instruments. The same change of generations is probably needed in the former communist countries before they again can adopt the western civil proceedings with the active parties, full party autonomy and efficient preparatory stages. So far, it was reported from each and every country researched that the inefficiency of the preparatory stage is the main problem. Also the delays were reported in the most cases. *Summa summarum*, the common goal seems to exist but the second step towards the common interpretation has still to be taken. It will for sure happen with the next generation as soon as they are fully educated, active legal actors in the field.

10.3 Towards the Common Goal of Efficiency

Legislators tend to introduce new legal institutions and carry out overall reforms affecting even the structure and the role of the judiciary and the course of civil litigation. This seems to be a common feature in the Nordic countries and the studied former communist countries, which entered into the EU in 2004. The recent past 25 years have been characterised by comprehensive procedural reforms. The tendency to make proper changes in civil proceedings started in the beginning of 1990s. Still, Sweden launched this trend already earlier but the set of reforms have still been continuing also in Sweden since 2008. One of the main ways—despite their geographical location—how legal disputes have tried to be adjudicated within a reasonable time and soundly is to emphasise the role of the preparatory phase of the proceeding and make the parties more active in solving their dispute.

This study aimed at throwing light on two different but special streamlines of European development in this field: one of them was the Nordic trend and the other was the development in Baltic and other former East-European countries that received EU membership in 2004. Even though the original roots of all chosen countries were close to each other (i.e. adopting the continental system), after World War II the development of these procedural regimes took different directions, while they now face similar problems again. The study showed similar ways of thinking at least at the legislative stage. All legislators seem to share the similar aims when reforming civil proceedings and focusing on preparatory stage and the key word seems to be efficiency. In aiming to that goal, the main tool to reach it seems to be the preparatory procedure. Still, bearing in mind, nevertheless, the previous directions of development of civil procedural laws have resulted in different practical situations. In each studied country, the preparatory stage seems to be nationally in the main focus. In many countries, there are still special procedural problems that are connected with the preparation. Minor re-reforms are probably necessary in the near future to make the preparatory stage work efficiently also in practice. The problem where the reformed laws are not followed properly in practice is the highest in Hungary mainly thanks to too traditional mentalities among judges. The same problem covers also Poland and even the Slovenian, Slovakian and Czech procedures are not functioning in the practice in the way that would satisfy the parties and the general audience. Also, Finland shared this problem of deeply rooted old-fashioned attitudes, especially straight after the first fundamental reform in 1993. In Sweden, court-connected mediation is difficult to gain a foothold despite of implementing the EU mediation directive. As *Kaarlo Tuori* has written, there are several sediments in law and justice.[6] The valid rules and current case-law, as well as interpretations, are just the surface level whereas cultural sediment is below that and in the bottom there are fundamental principles and other that type of staff that constructs the deep level of law. It takes more time to change the cultural sediment, which is very true in the studied procedural reforms in several but different countries. It is difficult to punch through new values in the form of rules if mentalities still remain in the past. Often, to change not only the surface level but also the cultural level needs the second generation to be fully realised.

In the introduction, it was asked if preparatory proceedings, as they are defined in the main hearing model of civil proceedings, provide for swifter and less costly civil litigation, how is the preparatory stage regulated[7] and how does the regulation affect the course and results of the proceedings? The aim of the preparatory proceedings is everywhere to provide a swifter and less costly civil litigation. There should not to be any proceedings just due to proceedings but the aim in the civil procedural law should always be an appropriate civil litigation. Even if this goal is quite clear and common throughout both studied groups of countries, the reality is not always that roseate. The wide Finnish reform in 1993 shows us how the legislator can go out of the frying pan into the fire. The absolutism of

---

[6] Tuori (2002).

[7] See separate chapters covering different countries and further more general comments in the conclusions on the similarities and differences in regulations.

fundamental principles: Orality, immediacy and concentration made the proceedings too upfront and, therefore, more expensive than earlier. Even the preclusion rule was too strict for reasonable proceedings. Delays are still a problem for instance in Finland, Slovenia, Slovakia and the Czech Republic. To work as a tool to prepare the main hearing and not to act as a mini-main hearing making the main hearing secondary, the rules must include enough space and flexibility to tailored preparation based on the nature of the case and the needs of parties. Judges should be willing and educated to interpret and apply these types of rules in an appropriate and sometimes even a courageous way to guarantee the well-functioning preparatory stage, which really serves the main hearing. If the attitudes and skills of judges are not updated, the modern legislation will not work in practice as seen in many former communist countries still today. The earlier Finnish experiences proof exactly the same and before that also Sweden had to reduce the fundamentality of the tree civil procedural leading stars (oral, immediate and concentrated proceedings) in the later reform. Still, to make fundamental reforms work in practice takes time.

It was even asked if preparatory proceedings enhance the quality of justice, and if so, how and why? As its best the preparatory proceedings enhance the quality of justice, as a matter of fact, because it offers a better field for communication and interaction compared with a traditional main hearing. At least, when this type of fairness, which is based on doing, is appreciated—and according to many empirical studies it is usually highly appreciated at least among the parties and the general audience[8]—the communicative and interactive preparatory stage is essential in guaranteeing not only the experience of justice being done but also formal justice according to the article 6 in the European Convention on Human Rights.[9]

It was also wondered if the same problems arise in different countries in spite of different structures and principles of civil proceedings. The study has shown us that at least the current legislative goals seem to be common in all studied countries despite of their earlier societal differences. The only exception seems to be Hungary where the structure still is different. As described earlier, the current problems do vary and, especially in the former communist countries, the reformed legislation is not always working as planned in practice. In Poland and Hungary even more fundamental changes in legislation are needed before the preparatory stage starts to work in practice as it should. In Slovenia, the Czech Republic and Slovakia the practice should be changed to follow the reformed legislation and its aims. The research shows us that procedural structures and principles are surprisingly quite identical in both groups. The question should be reformulated: Do the same problems arise in different countries in spite of similar structures and principles? Yes, they do. The reason is in differences in history and societal situation and especially differences in habits. In Denmark and Norway, things seem to work best. The reason for that could be that all actors have learnt their lessons, know their

[8] Ervo (2013), Niskanen et al. (2000), Tyler (1990), Tala (2002), SOU 2008:106.

[9] Ervo (2005).

duties and play their roles in a co-operative and flexible way complementing each other like spouses do in a well-working marriage. But as long as it is the "big brother"—in the other words, in this context the legislator—who decides how to play this relationship, it is not working in practice. It can be a marriage according to the law but not a real relationship in daily life; at least it takes time to get used to new, given circumstances. This seems still to be the current situation in the many earlier communist countries, and it was rather long the situation in Finland as well, new rules but old tricks. Still, the similar situation is current in Sweden concerning court-connected mediation, which is something new in Sweden. It seems to be difficult to get used to the news possibilities and alternatives it offers.

The last question was if different solutions to the same problem lead to the same or different results. It is difficult to answer to this question because mainly the legislative aims and solutions to the same problems have been more or less similar. Still, in some countries they are working and, in some other countries, not that well or not at all. This is the situation at least on the macro-level. However, there are differences on the micro-level. The Norwegian example shows us that the normative recognition of actors' roles can be a helpful tool to make the role-play clear and therefore working. But still I would stress the willingness to follow and apply. It is something that has to become intrinsic before novelties are functioning properly. The only Norwegian problem mentioned in the chapter is that there is a lack in preparatory hearings, which leads to the question if the Norwegian efficiency at the preparatory stage has already gone too far and is at least partly risking the one of the main purposes of the preparatory proceedings, namely, the possibility to meet in person to discuss the case for further litigation or settlement efforts if there is space for that in the case and among the parties. In Denmark, the main worry according to the chapter is that the practices concerning judicial settlement efforts and court-connected mediation may vary and is up to the judges' attitudes, which can be risky. Otherwise, these two systems seem to work. In Sweden, the main problem is that the possibilities of the court-connected mediation have not been seen and used. There is still lot of space in Sweden to make court-connected mediation more useful as an alternative to more traditional dispute resolution forms. Otherwise, the preparatory stage is working quite well. In Finland, the problem has been costly and delayed proceedings mainly or at least partly thanks to up fronted preparatory proceedings, which has led to find alternatives to civil proceedings and can be one reason for the topicality of the court-connected mediation. In the Baltic countries, the main problem is that the legislative reforms are not fully followed in practice which causes non-functionality whereas in Poland and Hungary the reforms even at the legislative level have been found insufficient additionally to the attitude problems and non-working practices in the field. The latter covers Slovenia, Slovakia and The Czech Republic. Despite of the fact that the legislation has been updated and is based on the western trends the daily life in practice is something else. *Summa summarum*, after the communist collapse, the aims and, therefore, even the problems to be solved have been similar in the both studied groups of countries. At the macro-level even the solutions have been similar but at the micro-level and, especially in practice, the daily life still varies a lot between the named groups.

Therefore, the basic problems are similar, even the solutions at the legislative level have been similar, but they have led to different results due to differences in societal situation and historical background. It is natural that the development in former communist countries will take longer before they reach the same micro-problems in the preparatory proceedings that are current in some Scandinavian countries. However, the difference is that especially in Poland and Hungary not even the legislative level has reached the same level yet but there are still many leftovers from the Soviet style of proceedings where the judge was active and the party activism was not appreciated or allowed.

Surprisingly, we do share the main problems and goals in both studied groups of countries, we share even partly the solutions but we still differ in daily life and practices. To help each other to reach the best practices and avoid the same problems, these types of comparative studies and practical discussions between different actors would be mostly welcome even in the future. The Scandinavian legal family and the former communist legal family have lot to be shared.

References

Ervo L (2005) Oikeudenmukainen oikeudenkäynti. Helsinki, WSOY

Ervo L (2013) Liability and social control of Scandinavian judges. In: Liability of public officers: selected issues. Oficyna Wydawnicza Szkoły Wyższej im. Pawła Włodkowica, pp 117–132

Ervo L (2016) Swedish-Finnish preparatory proceedings: filtering and process techniques. In: Ervo L, Nylund A (eds) Current trends in preparatory proceedings. A comparative study of Nordic and former communist countries. Springer, Cham, p 19

Galič A (2016) The preparatory stage of civil proceedings in Slovenia, the Czech Republic and Slovakia: halfway there yet? In: Ervo L, Nylund A (eds) Current trends in preparatory proceedings. A comparative study of Nordic and former communist countries. Springer, Cham, p 111

Juul-Sandberg J (2016) Reform and development of preparatory proceedings in the Danish civil justice system: towards (even) more efficient courts. In: Ervo L, Nylund A (eds) Current trends in preparatory proceedings. A comparative study of Nordic and former communist countries. Springer, Cham, p 81

Köblös A (2016) Hungary: towards more efficient preparatory proceedings. In: Ervo L, Nylund A (eds) Current trends in preparatory proceedings. A comparative study of Nordic and former communist countries. Springer, Cham, p 185

Niskanen H, Ahonen T, Laitinen A (2000) Suomalaisten luottamus tuomioistuimiin. Turun yliopisto, Turku

Nylund A (2016) Preparatory proceedings in Norway: efficiency by flexibility and case management. In: Ervo L, Nylund A (eds) Current trends in preparatory proceedings. A comparative study of Nordic and former communist countries. Springer, Cham, p 57

Piszcz A (2016) Polish civil proceedings: expanding the floor for preparatory stage. In: Ervo L, Nylund A (eds) Current trends in preparatory proceedings. A comparative study of Nordic and former communist countries. Springer, Cham, p 161

SOU (2008:106) Ökat förtroende för domstolarna – strategier och förslag – Statens offentliga utredningar. Betänkande av Förtroendeutredningen, 2008:106

Tala J (2002) Luottamus tuomioistuimiin – mitä se on ja tarvitaanko sitä lisää? Lakimies 2002:3–33

Tuori K (2002) Critical legal positivism. Ashgate, Darthmouth

Tyler TR (1990) Why people obey the law? Yale University Press, New Haven and London
Vėbraitė V (2016) Preparatory stega in the Baltic states: similarities and differences. In: Ervo L, Nylund A (eds) Current trends in preparatory proceedings. A comparative study of Nordic and former communist countries. Springer, Cham, p 414

Index

L. Ervo, A. Nylund (eds.), *Current Trends in Preparatory Proceedings*,
DOI 10.1007/978-3-319-29325-7

The manufacturer's authorised representative in the EU is Springer Nature Customer Service Centre GmbH, Europaplatz 3, 69115 Heidelberg, Germany. If you have any concerns regarding our products, please contact ProductSafety@springernature.com

Printed and bound by CPI Group (UK) Ltd, Croydon, CR0 4YY
25/09/2026
02222854-0019